The Battle of Fenny Bridges
1549
Prelude and Aftermath

The Prayer Book Rebellion

The Battle of Fenny Bridges 1549
Prelude and Aftermath
Also known as
The Western Rising
The Prayer Book Rebellion

Westcountry Heritage Publications

ISBN 978-1-5272-8999-4

Front Cover

Four of the photographs on the front cover were taken during the filming of the Battle of Fenny Bridges for the TV docu-drama *The European Reformation* that was based on a first draft of this book. It took place in the grounds of Feniton Court, the Church of St Mary, Ottery St Mary, and Sampford Courtenay. The fifth and sixth photographs are of Feniton's Church of St Andrew (bottom row, left) and the banner of the Five Wounds of Christ (bottom row, centre), which is in Exeter's Church of the Sacred Heart.

Printed in Great Britain by Short Run Press

CONTENTS

PART ONE
Background

PART TWO

The Prayer Book Rebellion

Acknowledgements

With special thanks to my two friends Barbara Roberts and George Roulson. Barbara first piqued my interest in the field close to my home known as Bloody Mead, the site of the Battle of Fenny Bridges, by giving me a copy of Philip Caraman's book on the Western Rising in 2000. This motivated me to spend several years digging further into the history of the events that took place in my village of Feniton in 1549. George, meanwhile, has provided me with invaluable technical help with producing this account over the years by salvaging my laptops whenever they surrendered under the strain. Also, thanks to my friend Ruth Yendell who wrote one of the articles in the Appendix.

I am also grateful to the following contributors (note: I have used Pixaby contributors' online avatars where given.)

Artist Donald Macleod for his kindness in permitting the use of his painting The Cornish Army Crosses the Tamar 1497, p.4.
Film director Stefano Mazzeo for granting permission for using the stills from his docu-drama series 'The European Reformation'.
The Westcountry Studies Centre, Exeter, for their help over the years.
Photographers: Veronica Szypillo for the photograph of the banner of The Five Wounds of Christ which hangs in The Church of the Sacred Heart, Exeter; Logga Wiggler for the photograph on page 2; Greg Montane for the metal sculpture of King Arthur on page 3; Madelaine Caudron for the photograph of Bodmin Moor on page 7; Dr Horst-Dieter Donat for the photograph on St Michael's Mount on page 8; Volker Lekus for the photograph of Glastonbury Abbey on page 20; Joaknt from Pixaby for the image of St Michael's Mount on

page 69; Tobias Albers-Heinemann for the image of the statue of Jan Hus on page 224; Peter H. of Pixaby for the image of the statue of Martin Luther at Dresden on page 191; Monikap of Pixaby for the photograph of the statue of King Arthur on page 68; Lucy Prior for the photograph of Dartmoor on page 136; Frank Meitzke for the image of castle ruins on page 73; Portia Jones for the photograph of Exeter Cathedral on page 57; Michael Schwinge for the photograph of the interior of Exeter Cathedral on page 58; Skeeze from Pixaby for the photograph of the night sky on page 73; Jurgen Krause for his illustration of the Carew coat of arms on page 51; Viv Payne for the photograph taken during the filming of the Battle of Fenny Bridges on page 78; George Roulson for photographs on pages 85 & 86; the Getty Museum, USA, for the illustration of the Landsknecht on page 110; The Battlefields' Trust for the battle plan of the Battle of Fenny Bridges on page 114; Ana Gic for the photograph of the Tower of London page 139; William Churcher for the photographs on pages 121 &126; Graham Smith for the photograph on page 116; Nigel Scarr for the photograph on page 116.

The remaining photographs were either taken by myself while a few, in addition to a small number of illustrations, have been in my possession for twenty years or more. Every effort has been made to contact those who gave them to me, and I wish to thank them for their contribution, even if they are no longer contactable. No infringement of copyright is intended, and I trust none has occurred.

Preface

The account which follows started as a series of posters that formed an exhibit called *The Battle of Fenny Bridges, 1549 ~ Prelude and Aftermath* - that was part of our village of Feniton's 'History Weekend' in 2008. It was a hugely successful venture, and, from it, our popular local history group was formed, which is still going strong ten years later.

Little was known locally about the Battle of Fenny Bridges and its important role in the Prayer Book Rebellion of 1549, even though it took place in the field that is known as Bloody Meadow, a short distance from Feniton's parish church. Some thought it was part of the English Civil Wars while others - for reasons I have not been able to fathom - thought it was associated with the Battle of Waterloo. Interest grew in its history as a result of the exhibition and local groups, including the University of the Third Age, requested talks on the subject. Over the next several years, I continued to research the history[1] but could find little on this important and neglected subject in local bookshops in either Devon or Cornwall. With so little printed

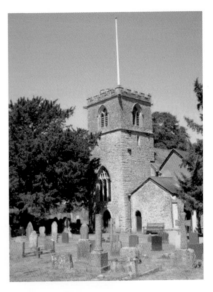

St Andrew's Church, Feniton

---

[1] The author gained a degree in History with Medieval Constitutional Law and Psychology, awarded with distinction from Oxford University, and is a qualified teacher of History.

material available, I decided to record this significant episode of history in which our village played an important role in a form that includes occasionally narrating the historical facts in conversational form between known characters where necessary, which I hope will make the account of this tragic chapter of Westcountry history easily approachable and readable.

Addershole, an early Feniton seventeenth-century cottage

The year 2018 witnessed an increased curiosity in the story as it was an exciting year for the village. A U.S.TV company acquired a draft of this book and used the account to create a number of scenes for their series *The European Reformation*. The docu-drama became a community project with local volunteers making forty Tudor costumes, banners and pennants, and playing the role of 'extras' in the film. I hope this and the written account of the story will serve to further interest in our Westcountry's fascinating past.

The Village Setting with the Church in the Centre

Above
The church interior, showing the fifteenth-century rood
screen, Feniton Cottages, and the site of the battlefield at
Fenny Bridges.

The Battle of Fenny Bridges
Prelude and Aftermath
1549

Also known as

The Prayer Book Rebellion
The Western Rising
The Anglo-Cornish War
The Great Commotion Time

Overview

The Battle of Fenny Bridges determined the outcome of the bloodiest rebellion of Tudor England. This first major engagement between the Westcountry men and the royalist army during the Prayer Book Rebellion took place close to Feniton's parish church on the water meadow below the bridges in late July 1549. The victors of the battle, the turning point of the Rising, dictated whether England's first Brexit and the rollout of Protestantism were to be overturned or enforced on an unwilling population.

Two years before, the tyrannical Henry VIII, whose ruthlessness and brutality ensured that every Tudor rebellion was doomed to failure, had been replaced with a child-king, Edward VI, and his divided Council, under the leadership of his uncle Edward Seymour, Lord Protector Somerset. The country that nine-year-old Edward inherited in 1547 was poverty-stricken: Henry VIII had squandered England's wealth on foreign wars and the continued military action against the Scots further depleted the country's meagre resources. Food was scarce, the coinage had been debased, and, by 1549, social unrest, fuelled by the threat of enclosures, exploded into open rebellions across the land, undermining the precarious stability of the country. A turbulent Edwardian England was in no state to face the challenge of a serious revolt by the men of Devon and Cornwall.

Under Henry VIII, the ripples of change that trickled down to disturb the traditions and way of life that the people of Feniton and their fellow-countrymen held sacred turned into a flood when Lord Protector Somerset, in the name of Edward VI, determined to frogmarch a devout Catholic people down the Protestant route. There had been major religious administrative changes over the previous decade. Papal influence had been evicted from England, the monasteries destroyed, the Roman taxes diverted to the royal coffers, and the King had replaced the Pope as head of the church in England. The impact of the revolution in church and state on the Westcountry had, however, been mitigated by the region's remoteness from London; the conservative people of Devon and Cornwall yet remained firmly devoted to the old religion in which they had been cradled for centuries. The South West was not ripe for Protestantism in 1549; but, within the space of a few months, the old world as they knew it fell apart.

From June 9th, 1549, the use of Cranmer's new Protestant Prayer Book was made mandatory by Edward VI and his Council, forcing the Catholic population of the South West to become effectively Protestant overnight. On Saturday, June 8th, 1549, the people of Feniton, along with their countrymen, went to bed Catholic; on Sunday morning, with the implementation of the *Act of Uniformity*, they woke up Protestant, whether they liked it or not. There was to be no gentle introduction to such a profound change. Tudor governments did not have the convenience of mass media to manipulate the minds of the people: they had to rely on the rack, block, faggot, and brute force for their methods of persuasion. The revolution in church and state ushered in by the Act of Uniformity changed the face of England forever and its ramifications left the Westcountry parishioners impoverished in every aspect of their lives. This last act of Tudor England's Brexit was, indeed, devastating and revolutionary. What else could the people do but risk what they had left, their lives, to fight to regain what was most precious to them? Such an avalanche of change swept the two counties of Devon and Cornwall into open resistance against the men they viewed as wrongly influencing the young King in their determination to promote their own Protestant agenda.

For the first time in history, an English king hired foreign mercenaries to slaughter his own people. These men, stationed in Honiton, had a terrible reputation for extreme brutality and terrified the civilian population. They boasted, according to the Venetian diplomat Sebastian Guistinain, of *'irrigating and inundating the ground with human gore'* and even the devil, it was said, was so fearful of their brutality that he banned them from hell.

When the Westcountry men encountered these well-armed foreigners on the battlefields of East Devon, they attacked their opponents with suicidal bravery, refusing to surrender until they were either dead or captured. Lacking both a cavalry and effective weapons, apart from the Cornish longbow, they were no match for the Royal army and were slaughtered in their thousands. The deaths in battle, the murders and the executions during the three months of the Rising were so numerous that the Cornish today refer to the bloody campaign as a case of ethnic cleansing. They accuse the English of an act of genocide and refer to the flag of St George as 'The Butcher's Apron'.

In less than three months, following the enforced introduction of Cranmer's Protestant Prayer Book, about one-tenth of Devonshire men and perhaps as many as one-fifth[2] of the Cornish were slaughtered in battles which, according to the seasoned professional soldiers of the King's troop, were the fiercest that they had experienced in all of their campaigns. Lord Grey de Wilton, a veteran of the wars with the French and Scots, informed us that the attempt to bounce a reluctant people into Protestantism unleashed not only one of the greatest atrocities in English military history on the Westcountry men, but the bloodiest conflict he had experienced under Tudor kings.

✑

---

[2] Some sources claim that 50% of all Cornish men of fighting age had been killed by the end of the three-month Rising. Tyron's Ten-Year War in Ireland (1593-1603), resulting in 100 000 dead, was the most brutal rebellion of the second half of the century.

Setting the Scene
Tudor Feniton

By 1549, like all people of late medieval England, the families of the East Devon village of Feniton had been nurtured for centuries in the life, faith, and colourful symbolism of the Roman Catholic faith. It undergirded every aspect of their existence, religious, social, and economic, and created a sense of purpose, meaning, and direction to their lives. It not only provided them with the liturgy and sacramental celebrations that marked the passing of each year from the Incarnation, with its elaborate festivities and processions, to the Resurrection and the promise of Redemption at Easter but also generated the structures upon which their community and pecuniary lives were supported. In this uncertain age, it connected the people to the saints that had passed before while providing them with the hope of heaven and the power to alleviate the suffering of their departed loved ones in purgatory. Their daily and weekly pattern of worship, rich with symbolism, colour, and tradition completed their liturgical life. The processions and hierarchical organisations created visible evidence of the security and certainty of authority and order. Their church building, dedicated to St Andrew, with both its fifteenth-century rood screen rescued, it is believed, from the destruction of Dunkeswell Abbey during the Dissolution of the Monasteries, and the rare transi-tomb, a symbol of extravagant wealth by its inhabitant[3], was the heart of the community. Its comforting, timeless presence enhanced the impoverished lives of the villagers when life was so precarious. It provided them with a communal place of beauty around which their lives revolved and generated a corporate sense of identity, a cohesive community, a sense of belonging. They willingly parted with their meagre resources to support the statues, jewels, decorations, and the sacred vestments which endowed their

---

[3] Believed to be either William Malherbe d.1493 or one of the Fry family. His left shoulder is blown away….by a cannonball? The tomb is believed to have cost £500, an enormous amount for the time.

priest with dignity and elevated him to a position above his fellow man, giving evidence of the dedicated lay piety that typified Tudor parishioners. The fairs and church ales interspersed between the celebrations and festivities that marked the saints' days, and their weekly services in Latin and daily devotions added variety, colour, companionship, camaraderie, and entertainment, all contributing to their psychological well-being. The guilds and the monastic welfare system, meanwhile, offered structure and some sense of security in this brutal age when life was cheap.

Feniton's Principal Inhabitants in 1549

Their priest, John Pring, who succeeded Thomas Hoy on Oct 25th, 1524, when presented to the living by Sir John Kirkham, Lord of the Manor, was destined to experience the most challenging, fundamental, and oscillating changes of circumstances of any priest who ever had the cure of Feniton souls, either in times past or in the future. Only his seventeenth-century successor, the Rev. Churchill, during the period of the English Civil Wars and its aftermath faced similar upheavals, but on a lesser scale. Between the time John Pring took up his post until his death, he was responsible for leading Feniton through most of the reversals and advances of fortune that marked the Reformation: the eviction of the Pope from England under Henry VIII, while most Catholic doctrine was yet retained; the establishment of Protestantism under Edward VI, resulting in the most savage and brutal rebellion in Tudor England that was first played out on Feniton's meadows; and Protestantism's bloody overthrow by Queen Mary I, whose reign brought England back under Roman jurisdiction once again. Then, surviving until 1559, John Pring lived to witness the pendulum swing once more back in the favour of Protestantism under the Elizabethan Settlement.

Sir John Kirkham, who had presented the priest to his living, inherited Feniton manor through his fourth wife, Joan Ferrers, the widow of Richard Ferrers. She was the daughter of William Malherbe, whose ancestors had become Lords of the Manor of Feniton during the reign of Henry II, from which time twelve generations of the family ruled the Manor. During this period, the village became known as Ffenyton Malherbe, and their coat of arms may be seen on the church pillars today.

The male line of Malherbe had been extinguished with the death of Joan's father, William Malherbe, in c1493, and the role of Lord of the Manor passed to Sir John Kirkham, the High Sheriff of Devon, William's son-in-law, who died in 1529. Following the death of Sir John's widow, Lady Joan Kirkham, in 1555, the Manor passed to George, son of Thomas and Margaret Kirkham and the grandson of Sir John Kirkham.

By the time of the battle, Thomas, son of Sir John Kirkham by an earlier marriage had married his second wife, Cecilia. She was the sister of Sir George Carew, Vice-Admiral of the Fleet, who drowned during the sinking of the ship, the Marie Rose, in 1545. Significantly, her other brother was Sir Peter Carew of Muhuns Ottery, the future local leader of the Royalist troops hired to suppress the Rising that included, following the battle, punishing his sister's family for giving aid to injured rebels.

Feniton's church, of which John Pring had charge, was built in the thirteenth century; however, its earliest rectors were recorded in the Norman period, giving evidence to an earlier building, possibly Saxon, which may have stood on the rise of the hill to the west of the present building. An examination of its external walls reveals some fascinating historical graffiti, including an example from the seventeenth century, carved with an educated hand, which gives substance to the village legend that a Prince James took refuge in Feniton when fleeing for his life from a charge of treason.

Set in a slight hollow, its westerly aspect bordered today by a blend of cottages and modern properties against a canvas of sloping small meadows and gardens, the scene exudes an atmosphere of stillness and gentle tranquillity that belies its bloody past. It is now encircled by a churchyard where generations of Fenitonians are commemorated by weather-worn chest tombs and headstones, some leaning at an alarming angle. One, of a seventeenth-century resident, another John Pring, who died in 1620, reminds the visitor as they enter through the gate of their mortality and commands them to: *Prepare for Death!*

The inscription gives evidence of the calamity that befell the Feniton Pring family who suffered the loss of four of their children within a few days in 1551, followed by the death of their mother a few weeks later. This tragedy was repeated in 1591 when Thomas Pring of Thorne lost his wife and four children, the likely result of the return of another pestilence, which, like its predecessor of forty years before, nearly exterminated the entire family of Prings. It is no wonder that the tomb of John Pring, in the probable event of his being a relative, provides such an urgent warning to all visitors to the church as they enter through the lych gate. Just two years before the first catastrophe experienced by the Pring family, they had witnessed and survived the burnings and executions suffered by the village during the aftermath of the Western Rising.

'Veniton'

'....a very picturesque scene of cots and ivy mantled bridges.'

We catch a glimpse of the village in earlier centuries through the words of the Rev. Shaw, in 1768, when he described the '*decayed*' village of 'Veniton' as a '*very picturesque scene of cots and ivy mantled bridges.*'

The 'ivy-mantled' bridges, originally built by the Romans, maintained by the Saxons, and repaired in 1326 when Bishop Stapledon bequeathed eleven shillings and sixpence to their upkeep, arched over the river Otter that runs through the water meadow, the site of the battle. The antiquarian John Leland (1503-1552), who visited in 1543, writes that the River Otter was divided into four channels at 'Veniton Bridge', three of which were crossed by bridges to feed grist and tucking mills. He describes the Great Bridge as having two arches and of being built of quarry stone, while the middle and most westerly bridges had one arch each. There is debate about the siting of the original Great Bridge as there is evidence that the river has changed its course over the centuries, and this does determine the site of the initial stage of the Battle of Fenny Bridges. An Order Book of 1711 held in the Devon Record Office helpfully states that two bridges and half of one were in the parish of Feniton and the other half in Gittisham. Thus, in 1543, the most western watercourse had no bridge, the next two were traversed by smaller bridges, and the eastern by a larger one. The fourth bridge over the Vine Water, from which Feniton derived its name, was not erected until the 1780s. St Anne's thatched chapel, thought to be a medieval chantry, stood close to the bridges until it was swept away by one of the great floods in 1752.

Leland, like the Cornish poet and historian Richard Polwhele in 1793, also informs us that the site was cursed by the Feniton blacksmith after his son dropped dead in Ottery churchyard, giving rise, according to local legend, to the notorious number of drownings that have occurred at this spot.

Following the battle, one of the two smaller bridges, St Agnes Bridge, fell into decay after being damaged during the fighting and Lady Joan Kirkham left provision in her will for its repair and upkeep, perhaps in memory of the local men who died there defending Fenny Bridges from the assault by the Royalist army.

A note on the different motivations of the Devonshire and Cornish men

For the Devonshire men, the Rising was indisputably essentially religious in nature, but for their neighbours, the Cornish, we find that it was more complex. While both counties resented the interference into their affairs by far-away London, the Cornish resistance to the Act of Uniformity was born not only from devotion to the Roman Catholic faith but from a defiant defence of their Celtic heritage that was forever in opposition to the Anglo-Saxon attempts to complete the final absorption of Cornwall into England. As history was to reveal in future generations, Cornwall's resistance to the institution of the Protestant prayer book was not so much motivated by a desire to cling to the comforting familiarity of the old religion as by defending her semi-autonomy from England: forever destined to be out of step with her neighbour over the Tamar, a century later the once-fervently Catholic Cornish would be fiercely defending religious non-conformity and swearing allegiance to the Protestant Duke of Monmouth.

Aftermath and Injustice

The Westcountry men's defence of their culture, faith, and, in the case of the Cornish, their native language, during the Great Commotion Time, left Devon and Cornwall completely crushed and many of the people destitute and starving. The properties of the bereaved families whose men had supported the rebels were transferred to loyal Protestant landlords. Others, like the Kirkhams, Lords of the Manor of Feniton, had their estates burnt to the ground during the reprisals. For Cornwall, there was one further punishment: England erased all evidence of her semi-autonomy from the map.

For nearly five hundred years, most historians have followed in the footsteps of the main contemporary chronicler, John Hooker, who, writing in the reign of Queen Elizabeth, gave free rein to his Protestant views and dismissed the Westcountry men as mere rebels and 'scum'. The reliance on Hooker's biased account has resulted in the Westcountry men, especially the Cornish, being effectively evicted from their own story, their reputations tarnished by centuries of historians. Instead of being hailed as heroes, these courageous men, who sacrificed their lives to defend their culture, language, and faith have been relegated to obscurity, and the obliteration of a whole generation is recorded as no more than a mere footnote in the history of the establishment of the Church of England.

It is time to repatriate these brave men back into their own history by relating a more balanced interpretation of the events, stripped of historical bias, that arose from their determination to protect their faith, culture, and, in the case of the Cornish, their language and semi-autonomy from annihilation by the English Government.

~ *This is their story* ~

Notes and comments on the primary sources upon which the following narrative is constructed

The account which follows incorporates the new evidence gleaned from contemporary letters written by those who participated in the Rising that casts fresh light on the accepted order of events.

The battles of the Prayer Book Rebellion are documented in five main contemporary accounts and some individual letters of those who participated in the Rising written from a government perspective. No graphics of the battlefields exist.

The narrative of John Vowell alias Hooker (1527-1601), uncle of Richard Hooker (1554-1600), theologian, who was present at the siege of Exeter, is the principal source for the account of the Rising. A close associate and friend of the Carew family, the local Royalist leaders, he wrote during the reign of Elizabeth when he could give free expression to the Protestant and governmental viewpoint. While he referred to the rebels as 'scum', he does, nevertheless, credit them with bravery and was clearly impressed with their dedication to their cause. His evidence is mainly restricted to the events in Exeter and the lifting of the siege while his limited descriptions of events elsewhere are supplemented by the reports from John Russell, the King's General, Haywood, and the letters from the Privy Council.

Haywood's contemporary evidence is more detailed, but his geographical accounts suggests that he had little knowledge or comprehension of the terrain. His descriptions of events seem confused and often at variance with Hooker's, particularly in the explanation for the position of the opposing forces at Fenny Bridges, while his descriptions of Bishop's Clyst are not realistic. Hooker's account of the events at Fenny Bridges is the more believable. Haywood's stated size of the rebel army is certainly over-inflated while he appears to be more prejudiced than Hooker against the rebels. He fails to give them the credit they deserve while underplaying the occasions of indiscipline in the Royalist army. His account does, however, suggest that he had access to secondary sources that were not available to Hooker.

The Spanish Chronicle considerably exaggerates the number of rebels and conflates events, making it a challenge to relate any situation to an individual or place. The author's record does, however, supplement Hooker's limited description of the battle at Carey's Windmill.

Given the reservations listed above, any examination of the available primary sources in order to compile a coherent and rational narrative and to identify topographical detail by which events might be located must be done with considerable caution. The account which follows draws on the most believable aspects of the available contemporary sources while the traditional chronology of events has been changed in the light of new evidence. Only future archaeological discoveries will clarify some of the uncertainties that yet remain.

The Potential of Future Archaeological Exploration

Future archaeological explorations of the battle sites would be valuable and would potentially confirm the actual precise locations of the engagements. It is uncertain how many artifacts have survived, and it is probable that their density will not be high, but, nevertheless, as recent discoveries at Clyst St Mary and Fenny Bridges indicate, there is likely to be sufficient remains to confirm, suggest or re-define the locations which witnessed the major actions and how events were enveloped within the landscape.

*

A Replica of the Rebels' Banner of The Five Wounds of Christ.
The Church of the Sacred Heart, Exeter.

The Battle of Fenny Bridges, 1549
Prelude and Aftermath

Chapter One

Cornwall: A Land Apart

Accccording to the words of a Cornish folk song, '*This is Cornwall: we are part of Britain and the UK, but this isn't England: that is up the other way!*'[4] Many Cornish believe that the visitors that flock to their beautiful county every year, or emmets, as they call them, are travelling to foreign parts when they cross the Tamar from England. Their claim is not without some legal justification as Cornwall was recognised as a country separate from England, especially by foreigners, for many centuries.

The insular ancient kingdom of Cornwall, with its haunting scenery of desolate moorlands and rugged coastlines, was always more than a mere county of England. As a Celtic nation, she shares a common heritage with the Bretons, Welsh, Scots, and Irish that stretches back beyond the Normans, the Saxons, and even the Romans to an age of far distant antiquity that still leaves remnants of memory on the Cornish consciousness today.[5]

Although the later Roman invaders made little impact south of Exeter, their successors, the Saxons, drove the Britons to the far corners of the island, creating the four main separate countries: Scotland, Ireland, Wales, and the forgotten country of West Wales, present-day Cornwall and much of Devon as far north as Exeter.

---

[4] By Jim Wearne, born 1950

[5] According to Prof. Peter Donnelly of Oxford University, a new study published in the journal *Nature*, March 2015, suggests that the people of the Celtic countries may be more culturally than genetically similar. Meanwhile, Professor Sykes of Oxford finds the Cornish, like many English, are descended from Spanish fishermen who visited the British Isles about 4000 years ago.

At about the time of the decline of the Romans, Christianity was introduced to the people of the South-West peninsular. The new religion did not, however, replace their rich cultural heritage, steeped in pagan practices with its myths and legends, but rather became entwined with their existing beliefs, creating a unique system of worship peopled with their own Cornish saints that were alien to both English and Catholic Europe.

It is probable that the final acts of the conquest of Devon as far as Exeter by Wessex came under King Æthelstan of the West Saxons (c895 A.D. - 939 A.D.) and King of the English (925 A.D. – 939 A.D.). This is confirmed by the twelfth-century historian William of Malmesbury who wrote that the Britons and Saxons inhabited Exeter *aequo jure* – in other words, '*as equals*', until King Æthelstan expelled most of '*that filthy race*' from Exeter in 927 A.D. and fixed the new border of the Cornish people at the Tamar.

A Cornish mine

After King Æthelstan[6] subjugated the people of West Wales, the Cornish developed their cherished and sincere belief that they would one day be rescued by their saviour King Arthur, the legendary Cornish warrior king, who was claimed to have led British resistance against the invading Saxons. Enshrined in tales of myth and magic, the Cornish waited for his release from enchantment when he would lead an attack on Cornwall's oppressors and free the

---

[6] There were two Æthelstans during this period: one whose name had previously been Guthrum, King of the invading Danes, who was defeated by King Alfred and baptised a Christian at Authelney, Somerset, with King Alfred as his Godfather, following Guthram's further defeat at the Battle of Ethandun in 878; the other was Alfred's grandson who, as king, determined to unite England.

ancient country from further encroachments by her enemy. This cherished belief was so strongly held that when a group of French clerics visited Cornwall in 1113 and provocatively suggested that King Arthur was not merely sleeping but, in fact, dead, they were attacked by angry Cornish men[7]. The Arthurian legend endured through the Middle Ages, encapsulating the deep Cornish resentment and desire for revenge against their English neighbours.

The geographical divide created by the Tamar and the Cornish determination to remain separate from their distrusted neighbour fostered the evolution of Cornwall's unique language that flourished until the rule of the Stuart kings, and was still spoken in parts of Devon until the 1300s. Even as late as the seventeenth century, an English traveller who strayed over the Tamar would be greeted with a defiant *Meea Navidria Cowzasawzneck![8]*.........I *will* speak no Saxonage. The Pope, aware of the rebellious spirit of this insular, feisty Celtic people with their unique cultural heritage and novel system of worship, granted them permission to use Cornish instead of Latin for their services - a privilege they would ultimately fight to the death to maintain in 1549.

Statue of King Arthur at Tintagel

---

[7] O.J.Padell: The Nature of Arthur, Cambrian Medieval Studies
[8] Richard Carew: *Survey of Cornwall*, p.56.

The Cornish Army Crosses the Tamar 1497
Artist: Donald Macleod (with permission)

During the second millennium, English kings, wary of their potentially troublesome neighbours of the South West, sought to placate their disaffected 'countrymen' by conferring considerable powers to the tin miners of Cornwall and Devon with the establishment of the legislative and legal institutions known as the Stannaries. These separate and powerful government institutions available to the tin miners reflected the enormous importance of the tin industry to the English economy during the Middle Ages.

Statue to Michael Joseph 'An Gof' and Thomas Flamank at St Kererne

In 1337, the first English dukedom was bestowed on Cornwall, allegedly expressing the English Crown's special concern for her disaffected neighbour. When Edward, the Black Prince, the first to hold the title, predeceased the King, Edward III, the duchy was bestowed on his eldest son, Richard. In 1421, a new charter decreed that the dukedom passed to the monarch's heir.

Further serious conflict with the English arose in 1497 when Henry VII attempted to overrule the Cornish Stannary Parliament. When Perkin Warbeck stirred up the people of the borders, the king demanded that the Cornish pay the huge sum of one thousand pounds with the levy of taxes known as tenths and fifteenths for his wars against the Scots. This breach of King Edward I's decree that exempted the Cornish from the payment of such taxes created great resentment. They flatly refused to pay and marched upon London to reason with Henry VII but were denied any opportunity to parley, and were thoroughly defeated and slaughtered by the King's men on Blackheath. Their ringleaders, including the blacksmith Michael Joseph, known as An Gof, who became the figurehead for festering resentments created by past and future grave injustices inflicted by the English government, were hanged, drawn, and quartered.

Warbeck, upon hearing of the Cornish troubles, in an attempt to seize the advantage, headed south, declared himself Richard IV at Bodmin and, with the aid of the Westcountry men, laid siege to Exeter; however, the enterprise ended in ignominy for the Cornish when, following defeat, Warbeck's men deserted, leaving the now desperate Westcountry force leaderless. Their hearts, said the historian A. L. Rowse[9], upon learning of Warbeck's flight, were *so increased and inflamed by deadly desperation that they earnestly determined and were steadfastly bent either to win the victory and overcome their enemies or else not one of them all to live any day or hour longer*. By early October, tasting defeat for the second time that year, the Cornish men were once more before the King in Exeter with halters around their necks, pleading for mercy. Henry spared many of their lives, but inflicted a crippling financial punishment on the region that beggared the Cornish into silence for the next half-century. The festering wounds of the double humiliation of 1497 increased their

---

[9] A.L. Rowse: *Tudor Cornwall*, p.133, where he quotes from Hall's Chronicle, *The Reign of Henry VII*.

bitter hostility towards their English neighbours. England would certainly pay.

Forty-one years before the Rising of 1549, the Cornish political position was strengthened. In 1508, the dying Henry VII temporally placated England's troublesome Westcountry men by granting them the *Charter of Pardon* that re-affirmed Cornwall's Stannary's right to reject English laws, a prerogative that has never been repealed. Even though Cornwall's Stannary Parliament last assembled in 1752-3, the principle of desuetude (a law being made obsolete by disuse) not being favoured in English common law, technically the Act remains legal and theoretically enforceable.

Throughout the sixteenth century, there is some contemporary evidence that Cornwall was still regarded as a country separate to England and the recorded comments of foreign travellers to the country provide additional support for the words of the Cornish ballad, *'This isn't England: that is up the other way!'*

The Venetian ambassador to Castile observed that when he and King Philip I were held up in Falmouth by bad weather, in 1506, *'We are in a very wild place which no human being ever visits in the midst of a most barbarous race, so different in language and custom from the Londoners and the rest of England that they are as unintelligible to those last as to the Venetians.'* In 1531, Lodovico Falier, an Italian diplomat to the court of Henry VIII, made a very unflattering observation when he compared the different characteristics of the island's separate peoples: *'The Welshman,'* he said, *'is sturdy, poor, adapted to war, and sociable,'* while *'the Cornishman is poor, rough, and boorish,* but *'the Englishman,'* whom he clearly preferred, is *'mercantile, rich, affable, and generous.'* A few years later, in 1535, Polydore Vergil, in his *Anglia Historia*, again confirmed that Cornwall was not regarded as part of England. He explained that four peoples speaking four different languages inhabited Britain, *'The whole Countrie of Britain ...is divided into iiii partes; whereof the one is inhabited of Englishmen, the other of Scottes, the third of Wallshemen,* [and] the *fowerthe of Cornishe people, which all differ emonge themselves, either in tongue, ...in manners, or ells in lawes and ordinaunces.'* Gaspard de Coligny Chatillon, the French ambassador in London, meanwhile, made reference to the differences when he wrote that the kingdom of England was ethnically by no means a united whole for it *'contains Wales and Cornwall, natural enemies of the rest of England, and speaking a* [different] *language'.*

Perceptions remained very much the same throughout the rest of the sixteenth century. Even in the seventeenth century, fifty years after the Western Rising when Cornwall's semi-autonomy had been effectively wiped off the map in retaliation for her resistance to the

Bodmin Moor

Reformation, the Venetian ambassador wrote, following the Queen's death, that Elizabeth had ruled over five different 'peoples': *'English, Welsh, Cornish, Scottish, and Irish.'* Even more than ten years later, Cornwall's separate identity and language was still not completely extinguished by her English neighbour. As late as 1616, the English ambassador to Madrid, Sir Arthur Hopton (1588 – 1650), observed, *'England is ...divided into 3 great Provinces, or Countries ...every of them speaking a several and different language, as English, Welsh and Cornish.'*

The Cornish retained their separate identity, despite England's repeated attempts over the centuries to completely subjugate the region, geographically, psychologically, and culturally, to the control of the English government. Even as recent as 1820, G.S. Gilbert, in his Historical Survey of Cornwall, observed, *'The Britons (Cornish) were a hard and obstinate nation, inflexibly fond of liberty and implacable against all conquerors. They knew not how to acknowledge themselves subdued and after a defeat only waited until the victor had disappeared in order to reinstate their efforts and rob him of the fruit of victory.'*

It would be half a century after their two ignoble defeats at Blackheath and Exeter before the Cornish indomitable, feisty spirit would endeavour to break free from English domination and, once again, attempt to pluck the fruit of victory from the hand of their hated conqueror. The events of 1549 gave them that opportunity.

St Michael's Mount

Chapter Two

Murder
Reformations
Treason
Paranoia
And
Executions

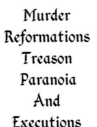

The Henrician years were a critical time in church history: the need for the Great Divorce was the dominant theme of the day; Lutheranism was launched onto the European stage; and the Reformation Parliament that seized the Church in England from papal control assembled.

The story of the Henrician Reformation, however, was not in the main a religious one; it was to be about spheres of influence. The battle that was fought under Henry was not essentially about doctrine but about who held the sovereignty of England. In other words, which system of law was to prevail in England: canon or civil? It was this struggle for supremacy between two legal systems that had dominated so much of medieval polemic since the murder of Thomas Beckett in 1170. In practice, medieval kings had maintained a balance of power between the two opposing camps of church and state that fluctuated along with the exigencies of the realm and papacy. The events of the early sixteenth century were about to seriously disturb that equilibrium.

How could a country as thoroughly papist as England be bounced, unwillingly, into Protestantism within a few short years? The story is a complex one and, arguably, involves a series of reformations[10], rather than one Reformation, as Henry led England out of her medieval past to lay the foundations of the modern state. There was no linear progression towards the new religion, while, importantly, especially for the South West, every disparate region experienced its own independent form of Reformation when it came.

Furthermore, the word Reformation itself also enshrined two separate concepts: for some, the educated minority, it incorporated both doctrine and organisational structure, while for others, it referred just to the eviction of the jurisdictional dominance of Rome while retaining Catholic doctrine.

On a national level, Henry's policy of the day had oscillated according to the exigency of the political situation: ever an equal-opportunities executioner, one day he would hang a few Catholics, and, the next, burn some Protestants. Henry's track record certainly proved him to be the worst and most inconsistent theologian in the country as he bounced between the two main factions: he both proscribed the works of Luther, allowing Sir Thomas More and the bishops to burn his supporters, while informing the Imperial Ambassador that there was much in the writings of the reformer with which he agreed. While promoting the views of William Tyndale, he facilitated his execution for holding them. It is not surprising that so many of his people chose to hide their religious allegiance when devotion to either cause could end in execution, depending on the

---

[10] See for example: *The English Reformations: Religion, Politics and Society under the Tudors: Christopher Haigh* (Clarendon Press, 1993)

ever-changing whim of their king. His policy was certainly shot through with inconsistencies, yet, as he vacillated between the opposing parties, there were unmistakable signs that the accepted order of things that had sculptured the medieval mind could not survive the challenge of a laity in London and elsewhere that was becoming increasingly literate. This was the advent of a new age when much of the medieval Catholic universe, with its claim to power based on forged documents, and its beliefs, an amalgamation of paganism and Christianity coloured by gruesome stories, could not convincingly respond to the challenge presented by an educated laity. Tyndale's[11] English translation of the New Testament, written in 1526, meanwhile, led a growing number to discard the twin Catholic doctrines of transubstantiation and purgatory. These two canons of faith were the foundation upon which much of the Church's power was based, while they also served to elevate the ordinary priest above his fellow man. Thus, as the reformers stripped the Catholic church of her claim to be the Maker of Christ in the Mass and no longer able to hold the educated hostage to her teaching on purgatory, the church became vulnerable to her critics. Increasingly, the old order was deemed unfit for purpose.

The refusal of both the Pope and Emperor to grant Henry his divorce brought increased urgency to the situation. Thomas Cromwell, Henry's cunning and wily minister, skilfully devised a corker of a suggestion to solve the problem. In practice, his plan incorporated confusing policies: eject the Pope; pit Catholic against Protestant; encourage Protestantism; uphold Catholic doctrine; then, at the same time, solve the problem of the empty royal coffers by plundering all the wealth in the country's numerous abbeys and parish churches. The Reformation Parliament enthusiastically put the plan into action - and swiftly tore the Roman church in England to pieces.

---

[11] Tyndale, a gifted scholar who spoke eight languages, was executed in 1536. Henry VIII placed a price on his head when the Bible translator criticised the King for contravening Scripture by seeking a divorce in order to remarry, but he was executed in the Netherlands after being betrayed by Henry Phillips.

Parliament had a powerful weapon in the store cupboard that had regularly been used in medieval times to prevent the popes from encroaching on royal authority: *The Statute of Praemunire.* It proved an ideal tool for Henry's current purposes as it empowered parliament to erode the legal power of the Church. In only a few short years, Parliament, under the direction of the King, by exploiting the Statute, made laws that impacted every aspect of national life, including religious practice and doctrine, that had previously been under the sole authority of the Roman Church. With the revolutionary statutes of the 1530s, Parliament became omnicompetent, leaving no area of the government of the realm outside its authority.

Ultimately, with the way cleared by the rushing through of the *Act of the Restraint of Appeals,* in 1533, the Archbishop of Canterbury, Thomas Cranmer, completed the grand plan by dealing the killer blow: solemnly, he declared that Henry's divorce was granted and Catherine of Aragon no longer queen, regardless of the wishes of the Pope and Emperor. By so doing, he ushered in an era that would witness Protestants and Catholics burn, torture, hang, disembowel, and hack each other to death in their hundreds. England's first Brexit, whereby she cast off the papal yoke, was indeed destined to be a hard and bloody one.

Entrance to Dunkeswell Abbey destroyed during the Dissolution of the Monasteries

Within days of the passing of the Act, Sister Elizabeth Barton, a Benedictine nun, became the first victim of Henry's bloodbath that targeted both Protestants and Catholics. Elizabeth, known as the Mad Maid of Kent, claimed, unwisely, that she had a vision of Henry dying within eight weeks, and damned to hell, if he continued his pursuit of Anne Boleyn. Henry took strong exception to the words of the Mad Maid of Kent and she was soon brought to the scaffold. After her execution, she was granted the questionable privilege of being the first and only woman to have her head

spiked on a pole over London Bridge. To Henry's credit, he managed to survive for thirteen more years after his divorce and re-marriage, proving that Sister Elizabeth was a false prophetess; or, maybe, she really was just a little mad.

It was the *Act of Succession*, in 1534, that legally declared Henry VIII and Catherine of Aragon's marriage invalid, and the Princess Mary, illegitimate. The Act, to which the whole country had to swear allegiance, affirmed the children of Henry and Anne Boleyn as heirs to the throne, while the *Treasons' Act* of 1534 made it high treason, punishable by death, to deny the Royal Supremacy. The first *Act of Supremacy* also imposed the

survey *Valor Ecclesiasticus* that began the process by which the Dissolution of the Monasteries was undertaken, clearing the way for future moves towards Protestantism.

Above: the crumbling walls of Dunkeswell Abbey, near Feniton, and left: the rood screen at Feniton Church believed to have been rescued from Dunkeswell Abbey when it was demolished by Henry VIII

The Revolt of the North 1536-37: The Forerunner and Prototype of The Western Rising

As the ripples of change caused by the King's break with Rome permeated the provinces, during the years that the Reformation Parliament[12] sat men did not meekly accept and ride the wave of adjustment that was generated by the Great Matter of the King's divorce. With the belief that the north was unfairly bearing the burden of rising taxes in a climate of growing economic insecurity, the religious changes were the last straw. Adding to the discontented voices of the laity was the great number of dispossessed religious who had been evicted from their monasteries and convents. As Chapuys, the Papal Envoy, wrote in 1536, '*It is a lamentable thing to see a legion of monks and nuns who have been chased from their monasteries wandering miserably hither and thither, seeking means to live, and several honest men have told me that what with monks, nuns, and persons dependant on the monasteries, there are over twenty thousand who know how not to live.*'[13]. Dispossessed clerics naturally found fertile ground for their discontent in the agitation of the ordinary people. A little over ten years later, it was these men and the priests who would provide leadership to the men of the West and convince them that they were in God's service by refusing to obey the new Protestant laws foisted on them by London.

In the minds of the ordinary population, the wealthy landlords who had benefited from the landgrab of monastery lands were also behind the changes in religion. They feared that the new development increased the power of the landed gentry over the poorer classes, creating greater tensions between the gentry and their tenants. The selling of the monastic properties, of course, firmly anchored the Reformation in the interests of the middle classes when the time came to roll out Protestantism across the country in 1549.

---

[12] The Parliament that severed England from Rome sat from 1529-1536
[13] Letters & Patents XI, page 42

THE BATTLE OF FENNY BRIDGES 1549
PRELUDE AND AFTERMATH

In 1536, the explosive mix of discontent that was generated by economic factors and ecclesiastical changes finally erupted into three rebellions[14], commonly referred to as the Pilgrimage of Grace. In the early summer of the year, rumours of unrest in the North in response to the unfolding events in London instituted by the Reformation Parliament were rife. Alarming stories spread from village to town like wildfire; their precious sacred vessels were to be seized by the royal commissioners, leaving them with only a tin chalice for their use; a fee was to be implemented for every christening, marriage, and burial; only one church would be permitted for every seven or so miles; taxes on staple foods were to be imposed; all their gold was to be seized and removed to the Tower to be 'touched'; and, to their dismay, their respected and popular Queen Catherine and her daughter, Princess Mary, had been discarded by the King. Moreover, the unpopular Anne Boleyn had not only become queen in 1533 but had been unceremoniously separated from her head by May 1536: a sordid and undignified episode that besmirched Henry's reputation and lost him the respect of many of his subjects. The men of the North were not prepared to tolerate such interference and desecration of their precious possessions and incursion into their meagre incomes by a king whom they increasingly distrusted and disrespected.

Just as in Cornwall, twelve years later, the rebellion in the north was triggered by the arrival of three sets of Commissioners in 1536. Their mission was to collect the subsidies, suppress the abbeys, and examine the efficacy of the clergy who, if found wanting, were to be stripped of their office. Determined to prevent any sacrilege, an angry crowd formed a welcoming committee for the Royal Commissioners, who harangued the King's men as they pushed their way through the restless crowds in their attempt to fulfil their duties. Insulting remarks about Henry VIII's low-born ministers, especially Chancellor Cromwell and his bishops, were hurled at the King's representatives, who became increasingly alarmed about their safety. At Louth, one

---

[14] The three separate risings in the north over the six-month period were: the Lincolnshire Rising; the Pilgrimage of Grace in Yorkshire; and Bigod's Rebellion in Westmoreland. They are usually considered as one whole, however.

just escaped with his life by swearing allegiance, to God, the King, and the Commonalty. The Bishop's Registrar, meanwhile, was forced to take the same oath before being dragged to the marketplace, and forced to witness his precious books being tossed on a bonfire. A monk dashed forward and tried to rescue the burning manuscripts from destruction, an action he was forced to regret. The crowd dragged him away from the flames and made him read the charred papers he had rescued to the people. Despite their actions, every time the monk read the name of the King aloud, they reverently bared their heads in respect. When he completed his assigned task, the rescued books were gathered up once more and again thrown into the fire along with all the English Service Books and Testaments that had been in possession of the royal messenger. The Bishop's Registrar was indeed fortunate to survive his unpleasant encounter with the northern men.

Still eager to spill blood, the crowd hurried to Leybourne Abbey that had just been suppressed by the Commissioner. Here, they captured the caretakers and placed them in the stocks, and, according to rumour, the mob covered one of their victims with a bull's hide and baited him to death. An angry throng, including a number of priests, made their way to the home of Dr Raynes, the Bishop of Lincoln's Chancellor, at Bolingbrook. He was sick in bed, but the crowd smashed their way into his home, dragged him out of the house, hoisted the frail man onto a horse and hauled him against his will to Horncastle. As he was escorted into the town, an excited mob greeted Dr Raynes, yelling, '*Kill him! Kill him!*' The furious crowd then lunged forward and pulled the cowering man to the ground. Terrified, Dr Raynes threw himself at their feet, pleading for his life, but to no avail: a gang of angry men thrashed him to death with their staves, stripped him of his clothes, and distributed his possessions to the poor of the town.

The day before Raynes was attacked, the rebels had ordered all the priests to assemble their congregations in Caistor to meet with the Commissioners to present their case. Any reluctance on behalf of the gentry to support the uprising was overcome with an ultimatum: either join us or be hanged from your own doorpost. However, when the news of the unfortunate fate of the Bishop's Chancellor reached the Commissioners and Justices who were heading to Caistor, they thought better of it and, wisely, moved off in another direction.

Meanwhile, some of the gentry joined the ranks of the rebels in order to mould the rabble into a more disciplined force. They thrashed out their grievances and prepared them in the form of six Articles to present to the King. Their complaints included the impact of the Dissolution of the Monasteries and the destitution of *'the pooralty of the realm'*, the transfer of the tenths and first-fruits of spiritual benefices to the King, the payment of the subsidy, the transfer of property by the *statute of uses*, and the presence of such commoners as Cromwell and Rich in the King's Council, and the promotion of the Archbishop and others who had corrupted the old faith. In addition, a large banner was created that bore the Five Wounds of Christ to remind them that they were fighting in Christ's cause. Along with the Five Wounds was a painting of a plough to encourage the husbandmen and a chalice to represent the church jewels that they were to lose. Subsequent events would ensure that this emblem in future years would alarm Edward VI's Council when the men of the West gathered behind the same banner when they lay siege to Exeter in preparation for their march on London.

While the gentry were attempting to both cool tempers and encourage the commons to bide their time as they awaited the King's answer to their six Articles, news came that the people of Beverley had already risen. It has been debated whether the commons had sufficient grasp of the affairs of state to comprehend the reasons behind any revolt or whether they were merely being manipulated by a more powerful force such as the gentry, the aristocracy, or, as in the case of the Western Rising, the large body of priests. Certainly, the men of Beverley rebelled first and then, bewildered, asked the vital question of the rebel leaders: *'Why are we fighting?'* In the main, however, the evidence does suggest that the people were politically aware and comprehended the dangers of the new acts of parliament that threatened the destruction of their way of life and their limited security. Meanwhile, men from Halifax swamped to the banner, swelling the ranks of the rebels at Lincoln to forty thousand.

Soon, Henry's reply to their Articles of protest arrived in the hands of the Lancaster Herald. They were a mastery of diplomacy - spiced with concealed treachery. Naively, the rebels were lulled by the King's persuasive words into a sense of security, and, after much discussion, agreed to disperse, and the gentry, in the interests of self-preservation, joined the royal forces. So ended the Lincolnshire Rising, to be followed within days by the more serious Pilgrimage of Grace, and Bidgod's Rebellion, which are viewed as one movement.

Foreshadowing the brutality that was later displayed towards the men of the Westcountry, despite the King's reassuring words to the contrary, the men of the north were not, however, to escape his justice, and, typically, the tyrannical King broke his promises of leniency and reason. A hundred men were rounded up and taken to London, tried and condemned by jurors who were probably coerced by the King, although all but thirty were, ultimately, pardoned. Martial law was proclaimed, and the King ordered that the captains of Louth, Horncastle and Caistor be detained with instructions that, if the Duke of Norfolk had any evidence of a new movement brewing, he was to 'run upon them and with all extremity...destroy, burn and kill men, women, and child (sic) (to the) terrible example of the others,' and especially in the town of Louth. The Duke, alarmed at the brutality of the King's punishments, fearing that it would ignite further rebellion, advised Henry to respond with more caution. His plea was ignored, and the King, swiftly sweeping aside the Duke's warning, reprimanded him for his leniency. Norfolk smarted under the royal rebuke and proceeded to wreak his own brutal vengeance on the people. Maliciously, he selected the parents, siblings, close cousins, and friends of the accused to be jury members. They were forced to sit in judgement of their nearest kin in order to test their own loyalty to the Crown: only a guilty verdict could protect them from the risk of a charge of treason. The ploy worked, and sixty-four were found guilty by the family members and hanged from the castle walls. The same vindictiveness was to be characteristic of the savage and cruel punishments that would be inflicted on the Westcountry men during the next decade when they too rose in revolt and marched behind a replica banner in 1549.

THE BATTLE OF FENNY BRIDGES 1549
PRELUDE AND AFTERMATH

The emblem of the Northern Rising known as the Five Wounds of Christ that was adopted by the Westcountry men a decade later when they rose against the implementation of Protestantism in 1549

The Pilgrim's Oath

Ye shall not enter into this our Pilgrimage of Grace
For the commonwealth, but only for the love that ye do have
unto Almighty God, his faith, and to Holy Church militant
And the maintenance thereof:
To the preservation of the King's person and his issue,
To the purifying of the nobility,
And to expulse all villain blood and evil councillors
Against the commonwealth from his Grace and his Privy
Council of the same.
And that ye shall not enter into our said Pilgrimage for no
particular profit to yourself nor to do any displeasure to any
private person, but by counsel of the commonwealth, nor slay
nor murder for no envy, but in your hearts put away all fear
and dread, and take afore you the Cross of Christ, and in your
hearts His Faith, the restitution of the Church, the suppression
of these heretics and their opinions by all the Holy contents of
this book

Written by Robert Aske, lawyer and leader of the pilgrimage

Executions and Paranoia

Little Jack Horner sat in the corner

Eating his Christmas pie,

He put in his thumb and pulled out a plum

And said, 'What a good boy am I!'

In 1539, Jack Horner, steward to Richard Whiting, the last Abbot of Glastonbury, was despatched to London with an unusual gift for his majesty: a Christmas pie. Hidden under the crust with the fruit were twelve title deeds to various manorial estates.

Ever since Henry's brutal and treacherous suppression of the Pilgrimage of Grace, he and his unpopular Chancellor, Thomas Cromwell, had continued sacking the monasteries, plundering their valuables, and selling the lands to various court favourites. After a further three years, there remained one prized fruit that was ripe for the plucking: the Benedictine Abbey of Glastonbury, the largest and wealthiest abbey in England. Its bishop, however, was determined to preserve it and decided that bribery was his only hope of protecting his abbey from desecration. The inventive bishop, therefore, despatched his steward with the unusual Christmas present for the King: the pie stuffed with manorial deeds. The ploy failed. Henry VIII seized eleven of the twelve deeds, although the twelfth, the most valuable, the 'plum', was missing. On his way to the King, the bishop's

Glastonbury Abbey where Richard Whiting was abbot

20

faithless steward, Horner, had dipped in 'his thumb' and removed the title deed of the valuable manor of Mells for his own possession. Horner did not believe the bishop's ploy would work, and, according to the legend, decided to keep the 'plum' manor of Mells for himself by stealing the title deeds. The remaining eleven were presented to Henry, but Horner was right; the bribery failed to save the abbey, which was subsequently looted by the King.

Henry, already embarked on his bloodbath, determined to destroy the poor abbot as well as his abbey and charged him with treason for remaining loyal to the Pope. Whiting was summoned to appear before a court and was found guilty by the jurors - one of whom was Sir Jack Horner, his treacherous steward. The unfortunate abbot was sentenced to the cruellest form of execution devised in medieval

Glastonbury Abbey

England: hanging, drawing, and quartering that was carried out on Glastonbury Tor. Following his brutal death, Jack Horner moved into Mells Manor, which he was permitted to keep. No doubt, this was a reward for sentencing his employer to death; thereby, it is claimed, inspiring the children's nursery rhyme that has been relayed down the centuries.

Regardless of the accuracy of the details of the tale of Jack Horner, Richard Whiting was certainly only one of many who lost their lives following their opposition to the changes instituted by Henry's Reformation Parliament. Their defence of the status quo had led to the greatest threat to his rule that, so far, a Tudor king had experienced: the forerunner and blueprint of the Western Rising of thirteen years later.

Executions of the Family of the Marquess of Exeter

For traitors on the block should die.

I am no traitor, no, not I!

My faithfulness stands fast and so,

Towards the block I shall not go!

Nor make one step, as you shall see.

Christ in Thy Mercy, save Thou me

Carved into her cell wall
by Margaret Pole

Two years after Whiting's death and eight years before the Western Rising, on the morning of May 27th, 1541, sixty-seven-year-old Margaret Pole received terrible news: she was to be executed by beheading within the hour on the orders of the King.

Lady Margaret's life was plagued by tragedy: her mother and brother died when she was only three and, three years later, her father was executed on the orders of his brother Edward IV in a ceremony in the Tower. According to rumour, he avoided the executioner's axe by choosing to drown in a vat of Malmsey wine instead. Margaret's brother Edward also met a similar fate after being kept prisoner in the Tower by Henry VII from the age of ten until he was executed in

1499. In 1487, the King ordered her to marry Richard Pole by whom she bore five children. However, Richard died in 1502, leaving Margaret struggling to raise her family on limited means. To ease the situation, she gave her son Reginald to the Church, a decision which, allegedly, caused a sense of rejection in the mind of the young boy that plagued him for the rest of his life. Margaret's fortunes fluctuated over the years, and her devotion to the Princess Mary, after the King determined to replace her mother, Queen Catherine, with the young black-haired Anne Boleyn, created a strained relationship between the Countess and Henry VIII. Margaret, as Princess Mary's lady-in-waiting, personally witnessed her change of fortune as Henry sacrificed his queen in order to extricate the country from the clutches of Rome. Catherine, however, had powerful allies: she was the aunt of the Emperor Charles V, and Catholic Europe reacted with outrage at the news of the Queen's rejection by the King. European opposition to the divorce forced Henry to prevaricate between opposing parties as he sought to cast off his wife, the Pope, and the Holy Roman Emperor.

The policy of the day, as always, fluctuated according to the exigencies of the realm and, throughout the last two decades of the reign, Henry's policy continued to oscillate between the Catholic and Protestant parties. As a devout Catholic family, the fortunes of the Poles naturally vacillated precariously along with that of the Catholic Church in England. The Countess, however, managed her affairs with considerable success and, by 1538, was one of the wealthiest peers in the realm.

Nevertheless, her Plantagenet blood placed her in great peril as Henry's paranoia drove him to attempt to eradicate the White Rose on account of their potential claim to the throne. For Margaret, there was one other fatal development: the career of her son Reginald[15]. In 1536, he openly opposed the King's anti-papal policy and fled abroad from where he challenged Henry's divorce and re-marriage to Anne Boleyn. Worse was to follow: Chapuys, the imperial ambassador,

---

[15] He was Dean of Exeter (1527-37), and then Cardinal and Archbishop of Canterbury under Mary I.

sealed the fate of the Poles by suggesting to Emperor Charles V that Reginald marry Princess Mary and combine their dynastic claims. Pole's swift response was to encourage the princes of Europe to depose Henry with immediate effect - a course of action that was to generate unhealthy repercussions on Reginald's family. Thoroughly alarmed by the turn of events, the Countess wrote to her son and reprimanded him for his follies.

Within a year, the situation became very serious for Lady Margaret's family: the Pope not only created Pole a Cardinal but put him in charge of the Pilgrimage of Grace of 1536 with the intention of replacing Henry with a government that supported the Catholic Church. The English government retaliated with a plan to assassinate the Cardinal, but he escaped and threatened to implement an embargo against England. The aging Countess's fate was inevitably sealed by the treasonous activities of her son.

Meanwhile, Margaret's second cousin Henry Courtenay, the Marquess of Exeter, also fell victim to the King's paranoia, and excuses were sought to bring him to the block. Courtenay, a popular figure who held almost royal sway in Devon, was certainly in communication with the exiled Cardinal Pole, an act which could be construed as treasonous. During the investigation into Courtenay, the name of Sir Geoffrey Pole, son of Margaret, and brother to Reginald, was, perhaps, conveniently found amongst Courtenay's papers. In August 1538, Sir Geoffrey was arrested and imprisoned. Terrified of the threat of the rack and of betraying his family under torture, he attempted to commit suicide by plunging a knife into his chest. Despite serious injury, he survived to be subjected to seven sessions of torture, during which he provided evidence against his family. Alarmed by the threat of further tortures, Sir Geoffrey admitted that his eldest brother, Lord Montagu, and the Marquess had been parties to his correspondence with Reginald Pole, leading to the arrest of Montagu, Henry, and Lady Salisbury in November 1538. Further contrived evidence from the Marquess' employee Jasper Horsey, nephew of Dr William Horsey, Canon of Exeter, and alleged murderer of Richard Hunne, was provided to the King for which Jasper was paid handsomely. Henry Courtenay was despatched to the block on December 9th, 1538.

For the Westcountry men, who were already grieved by the failure of the Government to compensate them for the loss of their horses after they had been commandeered by the King in 1536 for the Royalist army, the execution of their popular Marquess sharpened their hostility to the Government. Henry Courtenay's eleven-year-old son was also imprisoned, as was his mother. The boy was not released for fifteen years. A few days after Courtenay's death, Henry Pole, Baron Montague, also lost his head while his family remained prisoners for years. His son died, possibly of starvation, still locked in a cell, in 1542.

Geoffrey, meanwhile, was condemned to death on his own plea of guilty but, while his brother and the other members of his family met their fate, his life was spared. There were fresh victims still to be caught, and Cromwell viewed the unhappy Geoffrey as a useful source of future information. During Christmas, tormented by his betrayal of his family, he again attempted suicide, this time by smothering himself with a cushion, but survived. By January 1539, Geoffrey was so ill and broken that his wife claimed that he was already as good as dead, and he was finally released to survive another miserable nineteen years, during which time he witnessed the execution of most of his close family.

On the morning of May 27th, 1541, Lady Salisbury, Geoffrey's mother, was escorted from her cell to where a low block was waiting for her within the precincts of the Tower of London. As an aristocrat, she was spared a public execution, although about one hundred and fifty people were present to witness the grim proceedings. Margaret was dragged to the block, but refusing to co-operate, was man-handled and forced down. As she struggled, the inexperienced executioner swung his axe but missed her neck and made a deep gash in her shoulder. According to contemporary accounts, the terrified woman struggled free, sprang to her feet, and ran around the scaffold with the executioner in pursuit, wielding his axe. It took him ten more blows to sever her head from her body. The gruesome proceedings are related in the Calendar of State Papers, where the executioner is described as a '*blundering youth*' who '*hacked her head and shoulders to pieces*'. Lady Margaret's remains were buried in the chapel of St. Peter within the Tower of London.

As the news of the extent of Henry's bloodbath crossed the Channel, even the French, England's natural foe, were appalled at the King's extreme brutality. By 1542, he had executed and murdered so many of his people that the French observed that there was no reason for them to fear the English as their own king was conveniently exterminating them with such enthusiastic gusto that they did not even need to offer him a helping hand.

Chapter Three

The Immediate Causes of the Rising

On January 27th, 1547, as the freezing winds of the night bit into his flesh, Archbishop Cranmer sped through the icy blackness from Guildford to the bedside of the bloated body of Henry VIII as he sank into unconsciousness. Delayed by the bitter grip of the January weather that seized northern Europe in its grasp, the King had lost all power of speech by the time of his arrival.

As he rushed into the bedchamber, an offensive odour assailed the nose of the Archbishop. Henry's leg, which had become increasingly ulcerated and gangrenous since his serious jousting accident in 1536, was constantly festering with boils and oozing with pus that defied the administrations of the Tudor medical men with their magical potions. Over the last few years, his personality had also been deteriorating, his tempers were vicious, and he had become increasingly paranoid. As the vast hulk of the man lay dying in his bed, a privilege he had denied so many, his waist measurement now exceeded his age of fifty-six.

While the Archbishop ministered to the King, all he could elicit was a sign from the dying man that he trusted in God to care for his soul. At 2 a.m., Henry was despatched to eternity and the rule of a turbulent England passed from a brutal tyrant to a vulnerable nine-year-old boy-king, Edward VI, and a committee of men with conflicting agendas. This new Edwardian England, impoverished by Henry's wars and the continuing military action against the Scots, and threatened by economic unrest, was in no state to face serious resistance to its policies.

The old king left a challenging legacy. Rather than appoint a strong regent he had nominated a group of executors who would also act as his son's Council while forbidding that any changes should be made to his policies until his son came of age at twenty-four in 1561. A troubled England, accustomed to rule by a brutal tyrant, was now led by a weak, indecisive committee of people who held opposing views while a sickly nine-year-old boy inherited the throne. The future of England was precarious and was in no position to withstand any serious threat to the stability of the country. The Council also inherited a collection of policies that were shot through with contradictions. Henry may have broken with Rome, reduced the Church to dependence on the Crown and destroyed the monasteries but, while using Protestants to further these aims, he yet forbade any weakening of Catholic doctrine and forms of worship by leaving the *Act of Six Articles* that preserved Catholic worship and beliefs on the statute book. This state of affairs satisfied no one.

The financial situation was also dire. Henry VIII, once a strong king who had led England out of her medieval past by laying the foundations of the modern state, had squandered the country's wealth on his foreign wars while the debasement of the coinage towards the end of his reign plunged the country into penury. The vast sums released by the Dissolution of the Monasteries had been siphoned off into the pockets of the new squirarchy whose self-interest and greed ultimately served as a safeguard against the re-establishment of papal domination in England. The common man, meanwhile, had gained little from the Dissolution of the Monasteries. On the contrary, many tenants found themselves paying even higher rents to their new landlords than they had to the monks, and they also received a good deal less consideration and understanding of their problems. The abolition of the great religious houses which had, in part, been intended to benefit the people, had only contributed to making the poor poorer whilst the very poor were now starving. Economic discontent was rife and within two years more than a dozen rebellions erupted throughout the country.

When Protestant-educated Edward VI inherited the throne, much of England, despite the ejection of the Pope, was still firmly attached to the old ways. England was not Protestant by 1547; she was not generally willing to surrender her past. Apart from an educated minority who caught the crosswinds of Lutheranism originating from the continent, there was no general hankering after religious reform, no inextricable thirst for spiritual truth amongst the ordinary people of Tudor England. Essentially, this was not a spiritually-minded age in the sense that men followed their faith rather than material ambitions and religious traditions as they were to do a century later.

King Edward VI

The people of the South West, where the conservatism born of immobility was especially strong, were particularly firmly wedded to their Catholic past and resistant to change. Their distance from London had largely granted them immunity from the immediate ramifications of the reforms that had resulted from Henry's determination to rid himself of an aging wife and the interference in English affairs of a foreign power that emanated from Rome. They were unaware at the time of Henry's death that all that gave their lives meaning, purpose, security, and continuity was about to be swept away forever. The South West, along with most of England, was not ripe for Protestantism. Yet, under the direction of the Protestant Lord Protector Somerset, within the space of a few months, the old world as they knew it was to fall apart.

When Edward VI ascended the throne, the ripples of change that had trickled down to disturb the traditions, the social structures, and the economy of the people of Westcountry under the old king turned into a flood and the devout Catholic people, who had been cradled in their traditions for centuries, found themselves forcibly frogmarched down the Protestant road, despite the Act of Six Articles remaining on the statute book. By this, Henry had ensured the continuation of Catholicism until his son reached his majority at twenty-four years of age, but the security of this piece of legislation was to be put aside.

A few weeks after Henry died, the priest of Morebath in Devon was to be one of the first victims. In the spring of 1547, Sir Christopher Trychay was ecstatic. After years, even decades, of careful skimping and saving of the parish finances and the generousity of his dying parishioners, the village had saved enough money to buy him his long-coveted heart's desire: a set of black velvet vestments. His joy, and the realisation of one of his life's ambitions, however, was to be short-lived. With the passing of the old king, the writing was on the wall. England was now to be inexorably marched down the Protestant route as the parishes were abruptly and forcibly migrated from Altar to Table. Black velvet vestments were certainly not on the new royal agenda. Within two weeks of the realisation of Sir Christopher's dream as encapsulated in his jubilant speech to his congregation on the topic of his blessed velvet vestments, and recorded in the parish minutes on July 31st, 1547, the Council published a set of injunctions for religious reform. Praying the rosary, the most basic form of Catholic lay piety, was banned along with all such superstition; the destruction of treasured statutes and shrines was ordered; all lights and candles, apart from the two on the altar, were abolished, and all funds designated for ornaments and vestments were to be placed in the new triple-locked poor box. No more were devout, wealthy, aging ladies to leave their money to robe their attentive priest in sumptuous vestments but to the poor of the parish instead. The religious practices represented by the prized, long-awaited black vestments were obliterated at one stroke, leaving Sir Christopher a very disappointed and worried man. While the parishes had survived and largely ignored previous Injunctions from far-away London, these were a solid charter for the largely unwelcome revolution that was to come.

As the Protector and the Council promptly moved to further the establishment of Protestantism, the people grumbled that evil men with Protestant convictions were unjustly influencing the King in order to impose their views on the people. This accusation was essentially false, however, as young Edward was, himself a devout Protestant, and it was his custom to read ten chapters of the Bible every day. The evidence suggests he was a sincere Christian by conviction, but there were others, as always, not so sincere, the wealthy, who, just as in his father's time, would feign Protestantism in order to seize any financial gain that supporting the new cause, would release into their coffers. The Westcountry would witness the actions of many such people, devoid of integrity, over the next few months. There are always those in any community, the unscrupulous, the materialistic and the greedy, who, hovering like vultures, will seek to exploit any disaster that cripples a society. There are still wealthy families today who, at least in part, built their wealth on the misfortunes of the ordinary people of 1549.

Chapter Four

Trouble at Helston 1548

In the spring of 1548, William Body, the Archdeacon of Cornwall, a *'stupid, unscrupulous, drunken, bragging brute'*[16], was sent in the name of the King to prepare the way for the new Protestant changes in Catholic Cornwall. He was not a good choice! He so offended the Cornish that they spat on the ground at the very mention of his name.

Body was ordered by the Council to do away with all *'superstitious practices and errors touching man's salvation'*, which had led to *'devising and fantasying vain opinions of purgatory and Masses ....'* The King was *'to have and enjoy the goods, chattels, jewels, plate, ornaments, and other movables, belonging to the chantry chapels and colleges, and all the stipends of the priests serving them'* - a situation similar to that which triggered the Pilgrimage of Grace.

The conscientious archdeacon carried out his instructions with enthusiasm. After leaving the people

Stone commemorating the loss of Glasney College.

---

[16] Frances Rose-Troup *The Western Rebellion of 1549*, page 54

of Penryn distraught at the loss of their beloved Glasney College, an important centre of Catholic teaching and worship, he travelled on to Helston on 5th April.

On his arrival, a furious crowd of a thousand fisherman, farm labourers, and tinners, led by Father Martin Geoffrey, greeted him, all determined to prevent further vandalism. Body fled for shelter, but the angry mob broke down the door of the house where he had taken refuge. Grabbing the unfortunate Archdeacon, the crowd roughly dragged him out into the road, and stabbed him. Two men, William Kylter and Pascoe Trevain, then rushed forward and finished him off. Following the murder, John Resseigh silenced the mob and announced that they would have none of the new Protestant laws and would kill any who would try to impose them.

Local JPs attempted to seize Resseigh, but the growing crowd of now three thousand threatened to attack the King's Justices if they arrested anyone for the murder. They would, Resseigh instructed them, have all laws as were made by the late Henry VIII and none other until Edward VI reached his majority at age twenty-four, thus ensuring that Catholic doctrine was upheld; anyone, he added, who would defend the Archdeacon would meet his same fate. Fleeing for their lives, the JPs escaped to relay the news to London.

William Welche was chosen by the Justices to make haste to the capital to relay the news of the rebellion and the murder of the King's official to the Privy Council. He arrived in the capital by April 8th, bearing letters written by Sir William Godolphin which gave details of the death of the Archdeacon and the riotous behaviour encountered by the JPs. After being rewarded with a pay of four pounds, he was immediately despatched westward again with the Council's reply.

When villagers along the road south heard the clatter of approaching hooves, they congregated in their market squares to hear the alarming news. Welche, breathless from his non-stop dash across the country, raised the alert that a rebellion had taken place in Cornwall and the King expected the support of the people to suppress the Cornish rebels. Amidst the general excitement, men seized their weapons, some donned their armour, mounted their ponies and plough horses and joined the fray while their wives and families looked on with growing alarm. Others who sympathised with the Cornish must have watched in dismay and quietly cursed under their breath as they watched the increasing force of men canter out of the village until they disappeared in a cloud of dust.

*

On May 19th, a lone, weary rider, his horse spent from the last stage of the journey from London, made his way up the steep road to Launceston Castle. The news that a messenger from the Council had arrived spread like wildfire, and people flocked to learn of their fate. A large crowd congregated on Castle Green amidst rumours that the King was prepared to offer a general pardon. A hush fell as a dignified official dressed in his ceremonial robes rose to read the royal proclamation that was dated May 17th. Many were to receive a general pardon, the crowd was told, but twenty-eight of them were selected for trial on charges of murder and high treason. Their names were nailed to the wall, and the anxious people pressed forward to learn which of them were excluded from the pardon. The crowd pushed those who were literate to the front, and all must have held their breath while the names of those who were exempted from the pardon were read aloud.

On May 28th, those chosen to face trial were led out of the filthy rodent-infested dungeons situated under Launceston Castle. Emerging from the cold blackness of their cells into the bright May morning, the exhausted prisoners blinked in the strong sunlight. Bone-weary from lack of sleep after nights spent on the bare stone floor, the men made their way through the sympathetic crowd congregating around the courtroom. With much pomp, designed to intimidate men in fear of their lives, the prisoners were summoned one by one to answer the charges.

William Kylter and Pascoe Trevain were the first to be arraigned. Neither could deny that they were guilty of high treason and murder, but all the others pleaded not guilty and threw themselves on God and the country for judgement. After formal questioning and the presentation of evidence the jury returned their verdict: Kelyan and

Ryse were not guilty; James Robert was guilty of murder only but had no possessions to confiscate. John and William Kylter, Martin Resse, Henry Tyrelever, Richard Rawe, John Trybo Senr and Thomas Tyrlan Vian were all found guilty of high treason[17].

A total of nine men were condemned to be drawn through Launceston to the town's gallows. There they were to be hanged and while yet living to be cast down to the ground, their *'entrails removed and burnt before their living eyes'*. Their heads were then to be cut off, their bodies quartered, and these to be carried and raised on poles in places appointed by the King. The executions, however, were delayed, and, on September 3rd, Rawe and a few others received a pardon, but the remainder almost certainly endured the traitor's death. Moreover, the Launceston prisoners were not the only men who suffered execution for the opposition to the injunctions: the Plymouth Municipal Records supply details of the execution of a 'Traytor of Cornwall'. This unknown individual was drawn to the Hoe and there hanged, drawn, and quartered in the presence of the Under-Sheriff of Cornwall. One-quarter of him was set upon two poles outside the Guildhall and a shilling was paid to haul another quarter to Tavistock for public display.

The executions in the Westcountry were not the end of the matter. Other suspected rebels, including the priest of St Kerverne, Martin Geoffrey, were arrested and sent to London for trial. Sir John Gage, Constable of the Tower, brought the men to Westminster Hall on June 11th, 1548, where they were arraigned before the Justices. The prisoners pleaded not guilty to the charges, but the verdict went against them.

On July 7th, we learn from Lord Wriothesley's records that Martin Geoffrey was drawn from the Tower to Smithfield and there hanged, drawn, and quartered, his bowels burnt, and his head set on London Bridge, while his four quarters were hoisted onto the gates of the city. With the execution of the priest, the reprisals for the death of the King's official ended. In total, about twenty-nine men were executed for the crime of murdering the Archdeacon. The executions and the

---

[17] Rose-Troup: *The Western Rebellion of 1549*, page 92

reprisals that followed scraped deep the festering sore of resentment that the men of the far South West harboured for the English. Within one year, shortly after the anniversary of the execution of Father Martin Geoffrey, the Cornish would seek to extract their revenge by overturning the Edwardian Protestant Reformation and marching on England.

Throughout the following twelve months, to add further insult to injury, and, reminiscent of the events that led to the Pilgrimage of Grace, the Westcountry men witnessed the royal commissioners ruining their religious buildings, riding away decked in spoils of desecrated chapels with copes for doublets or saddle-bags, and silver reliquaries hammered into sheaths for their daggers. The last straw came the following year.

*

Following the executions, the final act of the roll-out of Protestantism was abrupt. Disregarding both the peoples' addiction to the old religion and the precarious political position, the King's Council relentlessly continued with their determination to force the country down the Protestant route with the passing of the Act of Uniformity, in January 1549. This made England (and Cornwall) uniformly Protestant on Sunday, June 9th. On Saturday night, June 8th, Westcountry men went to bed devout Catholics, and, whether they liked it or not, woke up Protestants. Whereas the rest of the country had experienced moderate, vacillating, and gradual modifications over the years, they had not been enforced in the far South West. The new Act was to abruptly change all that.

The new 'Protestant' Westcountry men, from June 9th, 1549, were mandated to use Cranmer's new prayer book. The consequences of this were overwhelming, but, in this age, there could be no gentle introduction to such a profound change. Tudor governments did not have the convenience of mass media to manipulate the minds of the people: they had to rely on the rack, block, faggot, and brute force for their methods of persuasion. Thus, when the changes were implemented, the people were unprepared for the wide-ranging revolution that was forced upon them. The attempt to bounce a reluctant people into Protestantism was to unleash one of the greatest atrocities in English military history, and, according to Lord Grey de Wilton, the bloodiest conflict he had experienced under Tudor Kings.

The consequences of the institution of the Protestant Prayer Book on the Catholic population were, indeed, cataclysmic, and it had profound and far-reaching consequences, social, religious, and economic, on the people. It served to not only abruptly strip them of their corporate life, secular and spiritual, but also abolished and removed their church's cherished assets. In the mind of the Tudor, and especially in that of the very conservative Westcountry man, when Protestantism was rolled out at Whitsun, 1549, the abolition of prayers for the dead left his loved ones suffering the tortures of purgatory: the new Act stripped him of the means to alleviate their sufferings, just as his own would remain unalleviated when his turn came. This presented the Tudor man who sincerely held this belief with a fearful future: he could only anticipate a terrible afterlife with no one to relieve his relentless sufferings while the certainty of his loved ones' present anguish in purgatory, which he was now powerless to mitigate must have been hard to endure. The Act of Uniformity also divorced him from the communion of saints who had gone before, while the abolition of the Mass, the central part of their religion that the Catholic Church taught was necessary for salvation, tore from him the centrality of his belief system, and even perhaps his eventual hope of heaven. The destruction of the images that adorned their church, rich with symbolism and deeply rooted in their belief system, left the people bereft. The associated loss of the welfare and educational system, previously provided by the monasteries, and the destruction of their guilds all had a seriously impoverishing impact on the ordinary man who struggled for survival in this very precarious age. With their spiritual community destroyed, their hopes of salvation removed, the welfare system axed, and their parish church denuded of its sacred decorations for which they had given their scarce resources to maintain, all must have seemed lost. The revolution in church and state would change the face of England forever and left the Westcountry parishioner impoverished in every aspect of his life.

The last act of Tudor England's Brexit was, indeed, devastating and revolutionary. What else could the people do but risk what they had left, their lives, to fight to regain what was most precious to them? Such an avalanche of change swept the two counties of Devon and Cornwall into open resistance against the men they viewed as wrongly influencing the young King in their determination to promote their own Protestant agenda

For the Cornish, there was an additional insult. They were incensed that the new Act enforced the use of English instead of Cornish, a privilege that had been granted to them by the popes, in their religious services, which they refused to accept. To them, English was a foreign tongue spoken by their enemy over the Tamar. This act of parliament ultimately marked the demise of Cornish as, unlike the Welsh, the English government, after the Rising, refused to give them a Protestant prayer book in their own language as further punishment. Still enraged by the harsh reprisals inflicted on them following their resistance to the changes the previous year, it was more than Catholic Cornwall could tolerate. Following the implementation of the Prayer Book, the men of the two counties of Devon and Cornwall rose almost simultaneously in revolt. The most serious opposition to the Reformation in England, and the bloodiest rebellion in English Tudor history, began.

The Making of the Prayer Book
1549

The aim, clearly set out in the preface, was to create a service which the people could understand on the grounds that 'the service in the churche of England (these many years) hath been read in Latin to the people, which they understood not: which they have heard with theyr eares onely; and theyr hartes, spirit, mind, haue not been edified thereby'.

A major influence on the Prayer Book was the Great Bible of 1539, based on the work of Tyndale, Matthews, and Coverdale. Two sources were incorporated into the Prayer Book: the litany of 1544, influenced by Luther, and the English Order of Communion of 1548, also Lutheran. It was later revised in 1552 and then in 1559 with Calvinistic influences. King James I made alterations that eventually gave rise to the version of 1662 which was more Catholic in influence. This version remained in use until 1928 when it was revised again.

Chapter Five

Sampford Courtenay
Whitsunday 1549

Sampford Courtenay's Banner
of the Five Wounds of Christ

On Sunday, June 9th, 1549, the day the new prayer book was introduced, a large group of excited people made their way through the deep Devon lanes to the church of St Andrew's in the pretty village of Sampford Courtenay. Farm labourers and their families, donkeys pulling rickety carts, friars, hawkers out to make a quick profit, and a gaggle of excited residents from the tiny cob cottages that lined the picturesque village, surrounding the church set in its hollow, all sensing the whiff of trouble, congregated to witness the new Sunday service. Buzzing with speculation, the large

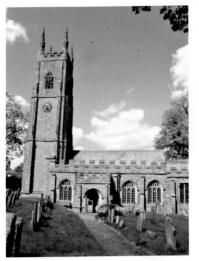

crowd entered the church and took their places, the gentry in the best and probably only seating, and the servants at the back. A respectful hush descended on the congregation as the priest, seventy-year-old William Harper, arrived.

The congregation was shocked at the sight of their priest: he had discarded his rich embroidered chasuble and was wearing drab garb and, even worse, dutifully proceeded to read in English from a copy of the new prayer book. Gone was the colourful procession inside the church accompanied by plainchant, gone were the lights on the altar and rood screen, and the centrepiece of the service, the

Sampford Courtenay Church, the site of the first outbreak of the resistance

elevation of the Host, was abolished. Their religion that had given colour to a harsh existence was replaced with shades of grey. The angry and disappointed congregation shuffled impatiently and looked around them to measure the reaction of their neighbours. Harper was known to be a devout proponent of the old order and was reputed to be a confidant and supporter of Mary Tudor. His flock expected him to hold fast to the old ways. They had relied on him to make a stand, to resist the new law yet, clearly, the old man had capitulated. The congregation did not like it. Following the service, the very disgruntled

The Protestant Prayer Book

parishioners streamed out into the church yard to exchange their views on the new order of service and what they might do about it

Dave Retter, Honiton's Town Crier, takes the role in the TV docu-drama of the first Catholic priest to read from the English Prayer Book and has exchanged his decorative vestments for simple Protestant garb.

when they returned for the festivities of Whit Monday.

The following day, an even larger crowd appeared outside the church. As the elderly priest made his way down the church path, William Segar, a wealthy labourer, and Thomas Underhill[18], a tailor, blocked his way and demanded to know of the old man whether he intended to offer the traditional service or read the new once again, as he had the day before. Harper, no doubt feeling the burden of his years, just wanted a peaceful existence and, although his allegiance was to the Catholic Church, he did not want to risk the wrath of the Council.

'*I must obey the new law!*' he told the two men.

'*You will not!*' Underhill commanded him fiercely. '*We will stand by the laws and ordinances touching the Christian religion as appointed by King Henry VIII until the King's Majesty attains his majority.*'

The crowd whistled, stamped their feet, and called out their approval to Underhill's order. In the words of the contemporary chronicler Hooker, '*Whether it were (sic) with his will or against his will he replied to their minds and yielded to their wills and forthwith*

---

[18] Underhill was frequently mentioned in the Privy Council's letters and he has been referred to as the 'fyrst captain' of the Rebellion. A few years after the Rising, it was called 'Underhill's Rebellion'.

ravessheth (clothed) *himself in his old Popish attire and sayeth mass and all such services as in times past accustomed.'* Flushed with the victory, the people flocked excitedly out of the church after the service to celebrate the rest of Whit Monday in high-holiday mood.

In every village, the people were gathering for their festivities that afternoon: ale and cake were shared around the village while sports were played, and men competed in archery competitions. People visited neighbouring villages, perhaps checking if anything better was on offer, and so word spread of the ruckus in Sampford Courtenay. As the day wore on, and people's behaviour and voices became increasingly well-lubricated with ale, heated speeches were made against the new religious changes to the delight of the crowd.

The Church House, Sampford Courtenay

The people were also still smarting from the loss of their chantry at Sticklepath, two years before, around which much of their lives had been structured. It had been sold to Sir Anthony Aucher, while additional nearby chantry lands had been purchased by other members of the gentry. With the disposal of the church lands and properties, of course, the Protestant Reformation was, inevitably, securely anchored in the pockets of the upper classes, a situation that became a source of conflict between the people and the landowners. This grievance would be reflected in a copy of the rebels' third set of demands that were sent up to London, during the rebellion.

A day or so later, the villagers heard the expected clatter of the approach of many horses: the magistrates had arrived to quell the resistance. Underhill and Segar refused to speak with the Justices unless they dispersed their armed retinue. Sir Hugh Pollard, one of the magistrates, who was probably shocked at the seriousness of the situation, finally agreed to their demands. Instructing his men to stay at a safe distance, he consented to meet with the village representatives to discuss the situation without an armed presence. Hooker, the contemporary chronicler, was later very critical of the magistrates' failure to use more forceful measures. Describing the conference between the gentry and the villagers, he records, '*There having had conference a pretty while together did in the end depart without anything done at all whereof as there redounded some weakness in the said Justices which were so white livered as they would not or durst not to repress the rages of the people, so thereof ensued such a scab as passed their cure and such a fire as they were not able to quench: for the commoners having now their wills were set up upon a pin that the game was theirs and they had won the garland before they had run the race.*'

Sampford Courtenay Cottages

After a day's discussion, the magistrates left empty handed. If Pollard had been less '*white livered*' and had used a show of force, maybe the revolt would have been strangled at birth, and the West spared the suffering of the coming months. Given the state of the country, this was certainly not the time for conciliation.

The magistrates' failure to take control of the situation at Sampford Courtenay was to have serious consequences on the two counties, and, ultimately, unleashed a virtual genocide that not only established Protestantism but marked the final absorption of Cornwall into England.

*

Within a day or so of Pollard's departure, a minor gentleman farmer called William Hellyons[19], a pugnacious and, judging from Hooker's account, a tactless, quarrelsome, and overconfident individual, decided that he could succeed where the magistrates had failed. His abrasive intervention only added fuel to the flames. First, Hellyons attempted to reason with Underhill and Segar. When that failed, he made an appeal to the villagers who had congregated in the street, but he clearly seriously misjudged the mood of his listeners. Berating his audience, he instructed them to accept the new order and become obedient subjects to the King. His pleas for restraint and obedience to the new law served, however, only to thoroughly exasperate his audience who completely lost their patience with him.

As tempers frayed, the crowd shouted their opposition as they surged forward threateningly. Hellyons, apparently oblivious to the very real danger he was facing, unwisely stood his ground and continued to lecture the angry crowd that menacingly moved closer to the target of their fury. Grabbing the unfortunate 'peacemaker', they dragged him roughly to the foot of the steps of the Church House, the headquarters of the resistance. While still quarrelling with the people, he was hauled up the stone staircase, hurled into the room, and

The Church House steps where William Hellyons was murdered

the door banged shut and locked. Still not deterred by his harsh treatment, the prisoner continued to loudly scold his captors until they

---

[19] See pages 168-170 for further discussion concerning the death of William Hellyons.

let him out. Hooker finishes the story for us: '....*where he so earnestly reproved them for their rebellion and so sharply threatened them of an evil success, that they fell in a rage with him: and not only with evil words reviled him, but also as he was going out of the Church House and going down the stairs one of them named Lethbridge with a bill struck him in the neck, and immediately notwithstanding his pitiful requests and lamentations, a number of the rest fell upon him and slew him and cut him in small pieces'* (Hooker) - the first blood of the Rising.

The crowd surrounded the chopped remains of their tormentor lying at the base of the steps, uncertain what action to take. Father Harper quickly took charge and pushed to the front. He called out an instruction to gather up the remains and put them in a grave facing north to south, instead of the traditional east to west, to indicate that Hellyons was a heretic. Perhaps, by this action, he was giving a sign that the murderers were granted absolution for killing a man who did not support the Catholic Church. Harper was, obviously, deliberately encouraging the villagers to continue their dangerous resistance. The priest's blessing on the murder of Hellyons could only strengthen their resolve.

On Whit Monday 1549
SAMPFORD COURTENAY
people killed a local farmer
WILLIAM HELLYONS
and then joined the Cornish in
the Prayer Book Rebellion which
ended in defeat by the King's army
outside this village

News of the unrest in Sampford Courtenay, the weak response of the magistrates, and the murder of the farmer spread rapidly to the neighbouring villages of Exbourne, Jacobstowe, Tawton, and elsewhere *'as a cloud carried by a violent wind and as a thunder clap sounding at one instant throughout the whole county is carried and noised abroad throughout the whole country: and the common people so well allowed and liked thereof that they clapped their hands for joy and agreed in one mind to have the same in every one of their several parishes'* (Hooker).

The situation for the Government was now very serious. The country was threatened by widespread revolts based largely on economic grievances, her reserves were fully stretched by war with the Scots and French, and now the events in Devon had reignited the fear of a resurgence of the Pilgrimage of Grace of a dozen years before. If that happened, the North and East could join forces with the men of the West and the Council would lose control. There was also the alarming possibility that the French would take advantage of the situation. London was aware that they could invade, amalgamate their army with that of the Westcountry peasants, and attempt to overthrow the English Government.

In the Northern Risings of 1536-7, forty thousand men or more had marched behind the banner of the Five Wounds of Christ. The Government had good cause to be concerned when the men of the West assembled behind the same emblem in 1549.

Chapter Six

Sir Peter Carew
Honiton Man (c1510-1575)

The Battle of the Barns

S ir William Carew was thoroughly exasperated! A messenger from Alderman Hunt, his 12-year-old son's landlord, had arrived at Mohuns Ottery, just outside Honiton, to say that Peter had absconded from Exeter grammar school again and, this time, had shinnied up the city walls and was threatening to throw himself to the ground should anyone attempt to fetch him down. Alderman Hunt had been forced to make a career out of chasing Sir William's young son around Exeter when the boy should have been listening to his tutor, Mr Freer. Sir William was furious at the news of Peter's latest antics and, taking a servant with him, stormed into Exeter to tackle the boy.

Peter was no match for his irate father, and, within minutes, found himself not only plucked from the walls but tethered to the end of a dog leash. Sir William was not prepared to tolerate his son's challenging behaviour anymore and ordered that the boy be dragged home to Upottery from Exeter on the end of an animal lead, a distance of over twenty miles. Neither did his punishment end there. For days, Peter was tethered to a dog that was suckling her new litter. His father further instructed his family and servants to deprive his son of food so that the child's only source of nourishment was the milk supplied by the lactating bitch.

After one more failed attempt to educate the unruly youth, his father washed his hands of his wayward son and packed him off to service in France. Here, Peter was demoted to the position of a mere muleteer until he was rescued by a passing relative on his way to the siege of Pavia. His good fortune was short-lived, however, and the relative died, leaving the boy to seek employment elsewhere. Fortunately, he found a new position with a marquis but his employer soon died in battle, casting Peter perilously adrift once more. His luck changed again when he later found service with Philibert, Prince of Orange. When the Prince died, his sister sent Peter to King Henry VIII with letters in despatch. Henry was impressed with Carew's horsemanship, and his proficiency in French, and took him into service. Having won royal favour, Peter dared to return to his family home where his promotion in life ensured that the young man was welcomed back into Mohuns Ottery from where he had been banished as a schoolboy. He soon established his authority in the area, and, in 1545, became Member of Parliament for Tavistock. Two years later, he was created M.P. for Dartmouth and High Sheriff of Devon.

Sir Peter Carew of Mohuns Ottery, near Honiton

In 1549, Peter was on his honeymoon with his bride, Audrey Gardiner of Buckinghamshire, when he received an urgent message from the young King, Edward VI, and his Council. His countrymen in Devon, where the Carew family held authority, were assembling in their thousands and marching behind their adopted emblem of the Five Wounds of Christ from the serious revolt of a dozen years before, the Pilgrimage of Grace, – a deliberately provocative choice that alarmed London. The King's Council ordered the Honiton man to leave his new wife and instructed him and his uncle Sir Gawen Carew to deal with the Rebellion with all haste.

Using eleven changes of horse, the two men galloped the two hundred miles from London to Exeter, where they met the local gentry at the Mermaid Inn. Their instructions from the Lord Protector were to speak with the *'poor, deluded, simple people'* and offer them a free pardon, if they quietly returned home. More accustomed to negotiating with the finest French military commanders, the Carews did not expect a bunch of village peasants to give them much of a problem. They were proved wrong.

Without resting for the night after their exhausting dash from the capital, the Carews set out immediately for Crediton but, when they and their entourage entered the town, they found their way blocked by hefty plough chains positioned between two barns. As they cautiously approached the barricade, a flight of arrows rained down upon them. Outraged and shocked by the ambush, the Carews beat a hasty retreat. Then one of the group of Royalists, a man named Foxe, a retainer of Sir Hugh Pollard, devised what seemed to him to be a brilliant plan. Taking advantage of the strong wind and piles of straw, he set fire to the barns where the rebels were hiding. It rapidly turned into an inferno, and, raging out of control, destroyed the livelihoods of some of the town's people. It was a disastrous move. All the rebels fled the town, leaving the Carews empty-handed, surrounded by ten corpses[20] and with the royal pardon, still unread, in their pocket.

It was a wonderful propaganda coup for the rebels. The news of how the gentry had destroyed the livelihoods of the common folk and had killed ten of the Westcountry men was seized by the priests who stirred up the people by broadcasting the story from the pulpits of Devon. The King's men, it was said, were '*altogether bent to overrun, spoil and destroy them*' for refusing the new religion. As the story grew in the telling, much of the county then rose in revolt, building barricades, entrenching themselves in, and mustering large numbers of troops. The flames of Crediton swiftly set the whole county ablaze.

As Hooker wrote in his own account of the event years later,
'The noise of this fire and burning was in post haste and as it were in a moment carried and blasted throughout the whole country and the Common people upon false report and, of a gnat making an elephant, noised and spread it abroad that the gentlemen were altogether bent to overrun, spoil and destroy them: and in this rage as it were a swarm

---

[20] According to Rose-Troup, who was probably quoting Hooker, the rebels killed about twenty of Carew's men; however, Sir John Frye, who was a witness, claims that the dead which numbered about ten, were all Westcountry men (see p. 52 for more details).

of wasps they cluster themselves in great troops and multitudes, some in one place and some in another, fortifying and entrenching themselves as though the enemy were ready to invade and assail them.'

The original gatehouse at Muhuns Ottery, home of the Carew family near Honiton

The Coat of Arms of Carew

There have been conflicting stories concerning the number of casualties at Crediton on June 21st. According to Rose-Troup and the contemporary writer Hooker, Carew lost about twenty comrades during the Battle of the Barns. However, Professor Stoyle points out that this is contradicted by Sir John Frye, one of Carew's men who rode with him into Crediton.

In a letter written to Sir John Thynne in August 1549, Frye observed that 'our fyrst fight with (the protestors) was at Kryton wheare were slayne of the rebels about tenne and of our men none.' Frye's account accords with the Council's later accusation against the Carews that they had instigated an unnecessary fight and thus 'provoked the escalation of the disorder'.

As Professor Stoyle states in his paper Fullye Bente to Fight Out the Matter (see page 251), the Council would hardly have regarded the Carews' attack as unjustified if hordes of Cornish men had already joined their Devonshire colleagues by this time.

So, while Pollard under-reacted at Sampford Courtenay, the Carews inflamed the situation further by their heavy-handed tactics at Crediton. Maybe the history of the Rebellion would have been rather different if the exhausted Sir Peter Carew had waited until he had rested a night in the Mermaid Inn before embarking on such an important mission.

Crediton Church

Chapter Seven

Trouble at Clyst St Mary

23rd June 1549

The morning after the burning of the barns, a Saturday, as the parishioners of Clyst St Mary gathered in the church, preparing to celebrate a holy day, the reprisals taken against the people in Crediton were a hot topic of conversation. Suddenly, with a loud clatter, an elderly woman burst through the door. Heads turned, and silence fell on the congregation. Highly agitated, the distressed woman blurted out her story to her now very attentive audience. She had been walking to church, she breathlessly told them, carrying her rosary beads, when a gentleman named Walter Raleigh[21] rode up and chastised her for carrying such a popish trinket. Clearly, the sight of the beads had deeply offended his Protestant faith. Raleigh reprimanded the elderly woman for her foolishness and instructed her to become a good Christian by obeying the new Act of Uniformity or face punishment. After delivering his lecture, he rode away, leaving a frightened and bewildered old woman behind him.

By the time she burst into the church, the story, according to Hooker, had grown in the telling. In the wake of the events at Crediton the day before, the tale was certainly a believable one to the anxious and agitated people who clustered around her, eager to hear every detail. Not only had a strange gentleman accosted her, ordered her and her fellow parishioners to throw away their rosary beads, and renounce holy bread and water, but had warned them, she excitably

---

[21] This was Sir Walter Raleigh's father.

continued, no doubt enjoying the attention and warming to her subject that, if they failed to obey his orders, he and his friends would return, burn down their village, and sell their possessions.

The story related by the breathless woman electrified the congregation into action. Thoroughly alarmed by this new revelation, the crowd hastened out of the church and, after sending messengers to surrounding hamlets to alert them to the threat, set to digging ditches and erecting ramparts across all the approaches to the village.

With the barricades partly constructed, someone suggested that a group of men should make haste to Topsham to seize some guns from the ships and haul them back to protect the village. On the way to fulfil their mission, they overtook the instigator of the trouble and were about to attack him, and, no doubt, kill him, when a group of sailors from Exmouth, probably the worse for wear with drink and looking for a fight, rescued Raleigh. He was not treated well by his rescuers; neither did he escape for long for, within a day or two, he was re-captured, and spent the following months locked up in the tower of St Sidwell's Church, Exeter, where he suffered considerable abuse until freed in August.

By late afternoon, the guns had been dragged back to the village. As men installed them at the end of the long bridge that joined Clyst to Exeter, their comrades hacked down trees to lay across all the entrances to Clyst St Mary. Thoroughly barricaded, the villagers settled to rest - and wait.

*

By the evening, Sir Peter, still seething from the Crediton debacle, received yet more bad news: the people of Clyst St Mary had attempted to murder Walter Raleigh, and the culprits had barricaded the village. A meeting of the justices was hastily summoned to deal with the deteriorating situation. After much-heated discussion, a decision was made: Sir Peter and his uncle, accompanied by Sir Hugh Pollard, Sir Thomas Denys of Bicton, and a few others, should set off to restore the King's peace - again. This time they wisely decided to snatch a night's sleep before tackling the Devonshire men. The next

day, Sunday, 23rd June, the company of gentlemen were in the saddle and making their way to the fortified bridge at Clyst St Mary. Despite the disaster of the previous Friday, Sir Peter remained confident of his ability to suppress the unruly yokels and, on approaching the barricaded bridge, dismounted his horse and strode determinedly towards the men blocking his way. Just as he had overestimated his ability to suppress the Crediton resistance, he now underestimated the contempt with which he was regarded following the burning of the barns.

Clyst St Mary: The oldest bridge in Devon, dating c1200

As he walked towards them, John Hammond, a blacksmith from Woodbury village, who manned one of the large ship's guns, decided to seize the opportunity. He lined up the weapon, aimed straight at Carew, and was just about to light the match when Hugh Osborne, a servant to Sergeant Prideaux, grabbed his arm and prevented him from firing the gun. Unaware that he had just been saved from being killed, Carew did at least sense that he had to act with more caution than he had two days before, and drew back to discuss the situation with the accompanying gentlemen. A decision was finally made: a messenger was despatched across the bridge to inform the villagers that the gentlemen wanted a peaceful resolution to their disagreement. To this end, they desired three of their number to meet and parley with a few representatives of Clyst St Mary.

After a quick discussion, the villagers flatly refused to negotiate with the King's men. They did not believe that their intentions were peaceful, and they certainly did not trust Carew. However, they had reached an impasse, and they could not stay holed up forever. The deadlock had to be broken. Reluctantly, the villagers agreed to discuss their issues with a few of the royalists and sent a message to the gentlemen. They would, they informed them, negotiate with Yarde, Denys, and Pollard - provided the rest of the King's men waited at the far end of the bridge and made no move against the village or attempted to cross the river while they held the discussions. The day dragged on until late evening when they finally broke down with considerable animosity. According to Hooker, the contemporary chronicler, it was a crestfallen retinue of men who rode back to the Mermaid Inn that night.

During dinner, Hooker informs us, the magistrates *'were in a dump'* at the news of the day's events, which made it plain to all that the attempt to quell the Rising had failed, and now it was every man for himself. The Mayor realised that a siege of the city was inevitable. As Exeter was short of supplies and could not withstand a prolonged attack, he advised the gentry to leave immediately for home. Nearly all but about half a dozen promptly fled, hoping to reach their homes and families before the situation deteriorated further. Informants who were watching and listening to the events at the Mermaid Inn, however, quickly relayed the news that the King's representatives were disbanding their mission and were preparing to desert the city. As Hooker reported, *'every man shifted for himself, some one way and some another'* as they made for their homes with all speed. They were too late, however. The people had taken swift action at the news, and many of the gentlemen found their way blocked by ramparts, ditches, and felled trees. A number were seized by the rebels, taken prisoner, and locked up in St Sidwell's tower for the duration of the rebellion. Others decided to surrender themselves to the Westcountry men, hoping that they would thereby receive lenient treatment. Some, finding their routes home blocked, hid in the woods to escape capture. Within just four days of Sir Peter's arrival with the instruction to pacify the people and send them home with the offer of a pardon, the whole county had fallen into anarchy.

Chapter Eight

The Situation in Exeter
and
Ottery St Mary

The clergy of Exeter Cathedral, under Bishop Veysey (c 1462-1554), had always been loyal supporters of the papacy. Reginald Pole, great-nephew of both Edward IV and Richard III, the future cardinal, and, ultimately, the last Catholic Archbishop of Canterbury during the reign of Mary I, was appointed

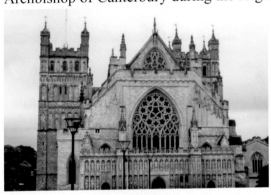

Exeter Cathedral

as one of the cathedral's deans, and this obviously attracted the dangerous attention of the King. Following the executions of Montague, and of Henry Courtenay, Marquess of Exeter, relative of Reginald, Henry VIII relieved Pole of his position. In 1537, the King sent Dr Simon Heynes[22] as his replacement with the remit to destroy the Bishop's and Canons' allegiance to Rome; however, following his arrival, he found himself mired in a web of devout popery. Despite Pole's fate

---

[22] Dr Heynes (also spelt Haynes), graduate of Queen's College Cambridge, attended Prince Edward's baptism and signed the decree that invalidated the marriage of Henry VIII and Anne of Cleves. He died in 1552, leaving a wife and two sons.

and subsequent exile, his colleagues, including Dr William Horsey, who allegedly murdered merchant Richard Hunne for refusing to hand over his dead baby's Christening gown as a mortuary fee, remained firm in their allegiance to Rome, ensuring that Dean Heynes and his Catholic staff were set on a clear collision course.

After assessing the situation, Heynes rapidly formed a very unfavourable impression of the calibre of the priests in the county, and wrote to the King to inform him that he found the Devonshire clergy to *'be of a strange kind with few of them persuaded of anything learned*[23]*'*. The cathedral clergy were similarly unimpressed with the antics of their new Dean as he set about wrecking the cathedral's prize possessions: the statues of saints, the brass, and iron memorials, and the choir books were all destroyed by Heynes. After he had caused considerable damage to the building's pillars and walls as he

Interior of Exeter Cathedral

embarked on his spree of destruction, the clergy were further scandalised when the King's emissary also removed the wax light that had burnt before the High Altar for two hundred years and extinguished its flame.

As Commissioner for the removal of images, Heynes did not confine himself to thoroughly upsetting the cathedral staff either. He was also *'marvellously hated and maligned at'* (Hooker) by parishioners for his wanton destruction of statues in local churches. Underestimating the people's devotion to the old ways and their cherished possessions, Heynes's mission, however, was doomed to fail spectacularly, and he was completely unsuccessful in his efforts to prise the clergy from their passionate devotion to the old order.

---

[23] Also see pages 62-63

Even when Elizabeth ascended the throne in 1558, many of them remained staunch supporters of the Roman church, and moved to Hereford where their Catholicism was tolerated. The population of Exeter were, in the main, as conservative and devoted to the old ways as were their clergy. On the one rare occasion that a local man called Dusgate[24] made public his support of anti-papist views in 1531 by unwisely nailing an article denouncing the Pope as the Anti-Christ on the cathedral door, he was quickly arrested after his servant was discovered fixing another poster in a public place, and hauled before the Bishop's court. Dusgate, however, defended himself so well that he surprisingly won the sympathy of many, and members of the court worked hard to convert him to their Catholic beliefs to save him from the flames. Despite their best efforts, however, he steadfastly refused to recant and, consequently, the clergy, defeated, applied for the fatal writ of *'de comburendo'* on 15th

St Nicholas Priory

January 1531. Dusgate was delivered into the hands of the sheriff, Sir Thomas Denys, who committed him to be burnt at Livery Dole, where he was subjected to particularly savage treatment by a very hostile audience who turned up for the entertainment.

Three years after Dusgate met his fate, the King sent reformer Bishop Hugh Latimer, destined to be one of the three famous Oxford martyrs burnt at the stake in 1555, to preach the Protestant faith to the ardent Catholic citizenry of Exeter; however, even the Bishop could gain only one convert. The city's allegiance to Rome remained so strong that any visiting preacher who delivered a sermon in Exeter favourable to the Protestant cause had to be accompanied by a

---

[24] He may have changed his name to Benet at about this time.

bodyguard, supplied by the Carew family, or face a lynching by the congregation.

In 1536, the attempt to suppress the smaller religious houses also met with fierce resistance in the city. As two Bretons were obeying the Commissioner's order to destroy the rood loft in St Nicholas Priory, a group of angry women broke down the door and attacked the workmen. They were so aggressive that one of the Bretons fled up to the tower to escape the onslaught. He was chased up the staircase by the women and was so frightened of the irate ladies of Exeter that he jumped from the window to avoid further attack, breaking his ribs on his descent to the ground. Alderman Blackaller, on hearing of the disturbance, hurried to the scene to pacify the enraged women but received a hefty beating for his efforts, which sent him packing to gather reinforcements. By the time they were finally overpowered and imprisoned, the furious women had delivered such powerful blows that Blackaller and his fellow officers initially assumed that they were men in disguise.

So, as the siege of Exeter loomed on the horizon, the majority of the citizens were, as described by the words of Hooker, '*of the old stamp and of the Romish religion*'. Few people in the city adhered to the New Learning by the time of King Henry's death and most of the citizens sympathised with the goals of the protestors. With both the clergy and the residents devoted to the Catholic faith, Carew and Russell, with their local knowledge,

The statue of Richard Hooker (1554-1601), theologian, Exeter Cathedral Green. His uncle John Hooker, who was present at the siege, was the main chronicler of the event.

unlike the Council, realised that there was a high risk that Exeter might agree to allow the rebels to seize the city. Expecting an easy victory, especially after the events in Clyst St Mary, the rebels sent a message to the city, instructing the Mayor and citizens to capitulate and join their cause, an invitation that was initially rejected. It was a very anxious wait for the two royalists: given the political and economic situation, the decision taken by the ardently Catholic citizens of Exeter had the power to clear the way for the overthrow of the Reformation and facilitate the return of England to Rome.

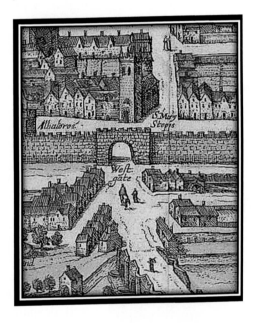

The Medieval Bridge leading to the
West Gate

The Disreputable State of the Clergy of the Church of St Mary's, Ottery St Mary, and The Ship of Fools

Dean Heynes was not the only ecclesiastical authority to lament the disreputable state of the clergy in Devon, and elsewhere: as far back as 1510 Dean Colet had publicly described the individuals who sought employment by the church as *'rude and nought men'*. These individuals were career criminals who sought employment by the church to take advantage of the privilege of the Benefit of Clergy. This gave them the right to escape the rigours of the kings' courts, and punishment for their crimes, by merely swearing on their own oath.

The Church of St Mary the Virgin, Ottery St Mary

It seems extraordinary today that an organisation that expected the secular officers, the sheriffs, to seize anyone condemned in the ecclesiastical courts and despatch them in the market square by burning should be so squeamish about permitting her own to face judgement in the temporal courts. Moreover, the type of men who had power of life and death

'The Ship of Fools' based on the nefarious behaviour of the clergy of Ottery St Mary

over their fellow man while being unanswerable to the common law for their own behaviour were, without doubt, reputed to be an unsavoury bunch. The general picture painted by reforming Catholic clerics and Protestant reformers of the period is of a priesthood composed of an ill-educated and uncouth collection of individuals who, in the words of Milton, were more renowned for their *'dicing, drinking, hunting, and wenching'* than for their Christ-like lifestyles. According to Alexander Barclay D.D. (Oxford), who was appointed priest at Ottery St Mary at the end of the fifteenth century, he found the church of St Mary's and its hangers-on in such disarray that he penned an adaption of the epic poem *The Ship of Fools* in 1508[25], inspired by his observations of the religious community of Ottery church. Here, monks and priests spent much of their time, and most of their energies, hunting, *'hawking at Honitoe[26]'*,

Rare Medieval clock showing the sun revolving around the earth in St Mary's Church, Ottery.

'wenching', indulging in drunkenness, and gambling. Bosch picks up the allegory in his famous painting of a ship populated by men and women who are deranged, frivolous and oblivious, passengers aboard the vessel without a pilot, and, apparently, ignorant of the direction in which they are heading. The phrase *'a ship of fools'* has been incorporated into the language ever since based on the nefarious behaviour of the clergy of Ottery St Mary.

---

[25] Based partly on a translation of Sebastian Brant's original German poem
[26] Honiton, which is six miles from Ottery St Mary and five miles from Feniton.

Chapter Nine

Lord John Russell (1485-1555)

Baron Russell, later Lord John Russell, first Earl of Bedford and Lord Privy Seal, had scarcely settled himself at Sir William Paulet's home at Hinton St George, Somerset, when a clatter of hooves was heard in the courtyard. After the rider's exhausted horse was led away to rest, a dishevelled and weary man was escorted into Russell's presence.

On about 25th June, Russell, the possessor of extensive estates in the area, a past president of the Council of the West and an executor of Henry VIII's will, had been despatched south with a paltry grant of three hundred pounds to oversee the suppressing of the threatened revolt and was eager to hear of the latest developments.

The unexpected visitor was anxious to speak with John Russell and share his serious concerns about the deterioration of the situation in the West.

After being ushered into the presence of the Lord Privy Seal, Sir Peter Carew described the troubling events at Sampford Courtenay, the disaster at Crediton, the lawlessness at Clyst St Mary, the failure of the local gentry to control the peasants, his suspicion that they were Catholic sympathisers, and the immediate threat to Exeter. Listening intently to Carew's assessment of the dire situation in Devon, Russell had no doubt that the Council had completely misjudged the seriousness of the uprising in the West. It was clear to the two men that Lord Russell must travel with all haste to Devon, and he gratefully accepted Sir Peter's offer of hospitality at Mohuns Ottery, at Upottery, just outside Honiton. His mission at Hinton St George accomplished, Sir Peter hastened to London to discuss the developments with the Council while Lord Russell headed for Mohuns Ottery.

*

As the saddle-weary Lord Privy Seal sank down into the comfort of the crimson silk-covered armchair with its gold lace edge, and surveyed his quarters with appreciation, sunlight streamed into the large room through the six windows that overlooked the beautiful countryside of Luppitt. The covers and curtains used for the splendid bed were made from the same fine red and white embroidered silk as the arm chairs. The windows were framed with drapes of green[27] that blended with the attractive scenery that surrounded Mohuns Ottery. His host, meanwhile, arrived in London and was experiencing a much more uncomfortable time as he faced the wrath of the King's Council.

*

Lord Somerset was appalled and shocked at the news that the whole of Devon was in revolt. The man standing before the Council had been despatched to Devon to placate the people and to offer them a pardon, if they quietly dispersed and agreed to obey the new law. Instead, this firebrand had inflamed the tempers of the peasants, failed to quell the disturbances, and driven the poor wretches to understandable fury by burning their properties to the ground, thereby destroying their livelihoods.

---

[27] From an inventory of Mohuns Ottery, written in 1554.

Facing the anger of the Privy Council, Sir Peter retaliated and agreed he had taken strong measures. However, he argued, he had had no choice as he and his retinue had been attacked. Besides, he retorted, he possessed the King's warrant to take offensive action if the circumstances demanded.

Furiously, one member interjected, contradicting his claim that he had acted lawfully.

Peter hastily pulled a document out of his pocket and threw it on the table before his angry inquisitors. *'Here is the King's own signet,'* said the beleaguered knight as he thrust the evidence in front of them. Members of the Council snatched the document, and, as it was passed from one to another, silence fell as they read, *'If any manner person after this our writing, pardon and commandment shall eftsoons attempt to repugne or resist our godly proceedings in the laws by us and our parliament made by gathering or assembling in companies or otherwise, to apprehend the same, and to see our laws and statutes, duly and severely executed against all such offenders as appertaineth………'.*

'You see!' exclaimed a triumphant Carew, *'I have acted according to the King's orders!'*

Somerset shifted uncomfortably in his chair, uncertain how to respond, and glanced anxiously at his colleagues and enemies around the table.

Lord Chancellor Rich, however, was not persuaded and, determined to attribute the blame for the disastrous debacle in Devon on Sir Peter, roughly commanded, *'Give me that paper!'*

Scanning the document, he glared at Carew and his colleagues. *'There is no authority given here for your actions,'* he snapped. *'For such actions as you have taken, you needed the authority to be granted under the Great Seal. By law, you should be arrested and hanged!'*

'Rubbish!' shouted Sir Peter, his temper rising. *'Look, it says here, "Given with our hand and under our signet,"'* his finger jabbing at the words.

Rich's lip curled with annoyance at the impudence of the man stood before him. *'No, you needed the authority of the whole Council and that you did not have!'*

'You are wrong!' snapped Carew. *'Look, here it says, "By the advice of our most entirely beloved uncle, the Lord Protector, and the rest of our Privy Council." So, if my King and the Lord Protector say they have the authority to speak on behalf of the whole Council, then that is enough for me - unless you claim that they do not possess that power,'* taunted Sir Peter, glaring at his accuser.

Silence fell once more in the room. The Council could not admit to the dissensions within their ranks, nor could they undermine the authority of the King and his Protector. Sir Peter had backed them into a corner.

When Sir Peter Carew made a speedy return to Mohuns Ottery, he ensured that he was armed with letters from the King's Council, stating that he had not acted *ultra viras,* an insurance policy that would protect him from further threats of the scaffold on a charge of exceeding his orders. He also brought a written promise to Lord Russell, which claimed that men, reinforcements, and money, were about to be despatched to Honiton.

After Russell ripped open the letter from the Council, both men must have felt a mixture of exasperation and amusement with its contents. Russell was ordered to hasten to Sampford Courtenay to placate the rebels and threaten the men with the terror of the rack in order to extract the names of other ringleaders. That particular horse had well bolted, of course, and revealed the degree to which the Council misunderstood the situation and events. The leader, Underhill, still remained in residence in the church tower and would have been a prize catch for the royalists; however, both Russell and Carew were, of necessity, far more concerned with the immediate threat to Exeter, whose cathedral staff and citizens remained staunchly Catholic.

Chapter Ten

The Rising begins in Cornwall
July 1549

E lizabeth gazed anxiously out of the mullioned window, searching eagerly for a sign of her husband's return from Bodmin, her face ashen and drawn with the effects of the advanced pregnancy of her third child. She felt a chill of fear as she strained to see through the gloom, longing for Humphrey's appearance, but the gardens that encircled Helland in the late evening remained eerily silent. Only yesterday, men from the town had pounded on the door and demanded that her husband, freshly released from his military command on St Michael's Mount, accompany them the two miles to the town to take charge of the thousands of men who had gathered there from all over the district.

Elizabeth hated the unattractive county town with its squalid open sewers, pouring human filth from the sloping hillsides, which formed the backdrop of the mile-long row of little cottages. She wrinkled her nose with a grimace as she imagined the impact that an influx of six thousand more would have on the stench of human waste as it ran in rivers through the main street.

St Michael's Mount

Unable to sleep in the late stages of pregnancy, Elizabeth, raising her kirtle, turned from the window and walked slowly and awkwardly

Bodmin Church

down the stone steps to the hallway. As she reached for the massive bolt of the heavy door to the garden, in her haste, she clumsily knocked into the old oak table, causing the pewter plates to rattle. She pulled back the thick tapestry curtain that hung from the heavy oak door which kept out the worst of the blast of cold winter winds that swept through Helland from across nearby Goen Bren, as the Cornish called Fowey Moor[28], and slipped out into the grounds. All around her the black velvet robe of night was softly draping the Cornish landscape in its folds, creating sinister shapes that exuded menace until dawn's early

---

[28] Now known as Bodmin Moor.

light once again retraced the familiar forms of day. The scent of rosemary and roses, a legacy of yesterday's summer day, still lingered on the warm night air as the flickering light of her lantern cast faint shards of mellow light before Elizabeth's feet. As she looked up, scanning the night sky, shadowy wisps of cloud drifted across the face of the moon. A sudden breeze that gusted from the moor made her shiver as it ruffled the petals of her favourite roses, scattering their sweet scent as their boughs swayed gently in the light wind. Standing in the cooling late evening air, unidentifiable shadows tugged at her imagination, and, with a shudder, she felt sudden fear clutch at her throat. These were troubled times, and she had never felt so alone and vulnerable in her young life.

It had been just a year since Martin Geoffrey had been brutally executed. Now, with the passing of the new Act of Uniformity, on Whitsunday, June 9th, the English had forced the Cornish and their Devonshire neighbours to become Protestant overnight. Even more intolerable was the fact that the new prayer book service replaced their beloved Cornish with English, a language which some of the people, especially those in the far West, did not understand. This was an unacceptable assault on their Celtic heritage and was a clear signal that England intended to further encroach on Cornwall's semi-autonomy. Elizabeth knew that neither her husband nor her neighbours would tolerate such an insult from their enemy over the Tamar. It would not be endured, particularly by those in the far West. Elizabeth understood well that the interference by the English into their affairs would, inevitably, create fierce resistance and lack of compliance. She was also aware of how serious the consequences would be for those who refused to accept the new law and, with good reason, she feared for her future and those of her children if the inevitable protest failed to move the King and Council. Parents had long grumbled that such had been the bloodshed over recent years that they felt that they were merely raising their children to provide garnish for the royal gallows' trees, and Elizabeth now feared for the future of her own children. However, even her troubled imagination could not have foreseen the extent of the devastation that would be visited upon her home, friends, neighbours and family, and how her life was about to be changed forever.

Only just turning twenty-one years of age, Elizabeth had married Humphrey a few years before, some say when she was merely ten. She had given him two sons: Humphrey, who was now three, nearly four; and two-year-old Richard. They were half-brothers to her husband's illegitimate son, Giles. Elizabeth was the daughter of Sir John Fulford, who had been High Sheriff of Devon, and his wife, Lady Dorothy Bourchier, the younger daughter of the first Earl of Bath. Elizabeth was descended from Edward I and was also a kinswoman of the Courtenay family, Earls of Devon. Her husband's ancestors had played important roles in the ecclesiastical and civic affairs of Cornwall since the thirteenth century: John Arundell had been Bishop of Exeter in 1502; and his kinsman Sir Thomas had fulfilled the role as commissioner for the suppression of the monasteries, while a younger member of the family, Sir John Arundell, had married Queen Catherine Howard's sister and was now serving the Government of Edward VI as a privy councillor. Ten years before, following Roger and Joan Arundell's death, Humphrey had inherited large estates in Devon and Cornwall. This had made him one of the wealthiest men in the peninsular and a suitable match for the daughter of Sir John Fulford.

Now heavily pregnant with two toddlers to care for, and sixty miles from her family home near Exeter, with her husband gone to take charge of the mass of men descending on Bodmin, Elizabeth had responsibility for the Arundell's home and heirs. Dismayed, she was forced to acknowledge that rebellion was in her husband's blood: his maternal grandfather had marched with Perkin Warbeck half a century before. Humphrey also possessed a quarrelsome and turbulent nature: he had deprived his siblings of their rightful inheritance, following the death of their parents, and showed a clear disrespect for the law if it contravened his own desires. His behaviour had earned him the reputation of being an 'unquiet' person who was not prepared to be trammelled by the inconvenient restrictions of legal niceties. Nor was he above dishonouring his debts. With his proven military prowess and his feisty nature, he was the peoples' natural choice of leader, if they chose to challenge the new laws inflicted on them from London. However, Elizabeth recalled, too, that Humphrey had been prepared to fight for the old King in 1544, so she fervently hoped his recent royalist past would ensure he would quieten the people, and disperse them to their homes, rather than seek to mould them into a fighting force that would march on London as had their ancestors more than fifty years ago.

Elizabeth retraced her steps to the house, anxious for the security of the comparative warmth and light of her home. There was, after all, no hope that Humphrey would return tonight. She reached for one of the candles that were casting their long flickering light across the flagged floor of the hallway, and, guarding its spluttering flame with her cupped hand made her way to the room where her boys were sleeping. As she pulled aside the curtain leading into the bedroom, pools of light momentarily scattered the darkness, and she drew comfort from the reassuring sight of the sleeping forms of her two young sons. Silently withdrawing, she disappeared into her own chamber, waiting for the first pains of labour. Like all Tudor women, she had arranged for a midwife to attend her and had made the usual plans which were to be put in place in the event she died in childbirth, a likely outcome at the time. She might have drawn some further comfort, had she known, that the daughter whose birth was imminent would survive not only the *Commotion Time* to come but outlive Charles I by nearly two years until she died at the age of 101 in 1650. Anna[29] lived to witness not only the future genocide of her countrymen, and the last attempted invasion of the Spanish in 1597, but the execution of Charles I in 1649, when Cornwall, forever destined to fight for the losing side in her struggle to preserve her Celtic Cornish heritage fatefully fought for the King a hundred years later.

---

[29] This information is to be found on Ancestry.co.uk

THE BATTLE OF FENNY BRIDGES 1549
PRELUDE AND AFTERMATH

When Elizabeth finally fell into a fitful sleep, two miles to the south and east of Helland, a star-studded sky scattered its ghostly midnight hues over the haunting, scenery of Fowey Moor; as the eerie

light turned tors into fearful forms, the mild summer breeze caught faint echoes of the sound of a thousand marching feet of old. Impregnated with foreboding, the moorland night softly whispered its ancient tales of fear and despair, the harbinger of the bloodshed, misery, and atrocities that were about to engulf the Westcountry.

The following day, as dawn broke over the ruined castle of Kynock, half a mile from Bodmin, the last swirls of moorland mist promised to give way to another bright July morning. Humphrey Arundell sat at a long rustic rough-hewn table in the makeshift camp

that had been erected in the long, dark shadows of the ruinous castle walls that loomed high overhead. He had received troubling news: the Devonshire men had already risen in rebellion, were barricading the routes into Exeter, and, worse, had already committed murder. Arundell realised that this had

inevitably changed the rules of engagement with the Crown and placed the Cornish petitioners in great peril if they amalgamated with the rebels over the Tamar.

'If we don't get this right, John, we will be dragged on hurdles to the Tyburn gallow-tree!' Arundell thumped the table with his fist to give extra emphasis to his remark.

'*It's surely good news about the events in Devon, though,*' interrupted one of the younger men eagerly before John could reply. '*They will provide us with reinforcements?*'

John Wynslade, to whom Arundell had addressed his remark, shook his head. '*I'm not so sure about that,*' he responded to the young man. '*They have already spilled blood but we are not rebels, as they appear to be, but petitioners. Our intentions are to seek counsel with the King and persuade him to respect his father's will,*' he explained to the confused young man. '*His Councillors have taken advantage of a mere child to push their own agenda on the country. We are not challenging the law, but acting within our rights to save our religion and constitutional status. We do not want to be associated with bloodshed. The murder at Sampford, if true, has changed their relationship with the Crown. They are now in danger of the executioner's axe. We must choose our friends carefully if we are not to share their fate,*' he instructed the youth.

'*The news is they are barricading the routes into Exeter,*' added Arundell. '*We may not have any choice but to join them if we are to clear the route to London. If we take control of Exeter, and, as most of the citizens there are good Catholics, we should meet with little resistance, so our way will be clear for the march, and thousands of others should join us as we cross the south. The whole country seems to be rebelling against this minority government, and, together, we will be a force to be reckoned with.*'

When he finished speaking, Humphrey glanced around the table, taking stock of his companions, and must have surveyed the men assembled before him with a twinge of dismay. John Wynslade, to whom his remark had been directed, was at least a member of the gentry class and his presence was crucial to grant some degree of legitimacy to the proceedings. Henry's purge of the White Rose ten years earlier that witnessed the demise of the Courtenay family, descendants of the Plantagenet kings, had ensured that the West lacked members of the aristocracy that could potentially grant guaranteed legal status to any resistance to the royal decrees.

Seated alongside John Wynslade was the Mayor of Bodmin, Henry Bray, who had granted them permission to set up camp at the castle;

Arundell's brother-in-law Robert Smyth from Blisland; his neighbour John Bury, later described as *'the chief captain saving one'* and a formidable soldier; Wynslade's son William; Thomas Holmes, a representative of the yeoman class; several priests, including John Thompson, Roger Barrett, and Simon Moreton; and the sour-faced William Kestrell, appointed as Arundell's secretary, whose future treachery as a royalist informant was to cost them dear, sat at Humphrey's side. Smyth's burly shoulders gave witness to his outstanding accomplishment with the Cornish longbow, but some of his companions had depressingly little military experience. Meanwhile, outside in the summer sunshine, an unpromising gathering of several thousand farmers, fishermen, and labourers lay idly in the shadows of the ruined walls of Kynock[30] Castle, waiting to be turned into an efficient, disciplined fighting force capable of marching successfully on London and overthrowing the rule of the King's Council by negotiation, and, if need be, by the threat of force.

John Wynslade and his son William from Tregarrick House were popular members of the gentry class, reputed for their hospitality and generosity while, crucially, John's imposing presence naturally generated a sense of confidence and respect in the men who served under him. The son of William Wynslade and his wife Joan Easton, daughter and heir of John Easton of Easton[31], had his main family residence in Buckland Brewer in Devon, so, like Arundell, his influence spread across both counties. John had first married Jane, daughter of Sir John Trelawney and his wife, Jane, daughter of Sir Robert Holland and half-sister to William Kendall, who was executed for the Exeter Conspiracy. John and Jane Wynslade's son, William, was to marry Jane Babington, a former nun of Ottery St Mary, relative of Sir Anthony Babington whose future plot to place Mary, Queen of Scots on the throne resulted in the execution of the Scottish Queen. On account of their considerable wealth, the Wynslades were elevated to the title of Esquires of the White Spurs, a rare hereditary honour that engendered much respect. With the lack of presence of

---

[30] Also spelt Cynack
[31] Also spelt Eston

aristocratic families in the South West, the Arundells and Wynslades were the two natural leaders of any local challenge or resistance to royal authority.

Abruptly, Humphrey's perusal of his colleagues was interrupted by a crash, and everyone's head turned. An elderly, breathless priest burst into the roofless room and hurled an object down on the table, causing a dust storm to rise in the light of the flickering lantern that cast a faint glow in the deep shadow of the castle walls.

Cranmer's 1549 Prayer Book

'ere's the piece of blasphemous foreign trash!' scowled the priest, in explanation of his explosive entrance.

All eyes fixed on the pristine leather-bound prayer book that the priest had thrust down on the table. Arundell seized the offensive object and roughly flicked through the pages still pungent with the odour of fresh ink, his contempt for the contents evident. Those who understand the language read short passages aloud to those who were illiterate, as it was passed around the table. To some, the language was as familiar and comprehensible as Venetian. Cornish, they understood and loved, Latin was familiar, but this was the tongue of those who for centuries had persistently encroached on Cornwall's status as a separate country, and had brutally abused and plundered her into beggary for generations. It was the tongue of their enemy.

'I can't imagine how that blasphemy of nonsense will sound echoing in the hallowed air of our churches,' grumbled one. *'Our neighbours further west don't even know the English tongue!'*

'We shall have our language back, won't we, Father?' asked an anxious youth to the priest by his side. *'They can't really take that from us, can they?'*

'They will, and they have unless we stop them!' exclaimed the elderly priest. *'It is all set out in the Act of Uniformity, it seems,'* he said with his lower lip curling in disgust. *'We are not only all Protestant now but English too,'* he added sarcastically. *'Now*

remember this!' he exclaimed to the young man, reverting to Cornish, and banging his fist on the table with a passion as he glared at everyone around the table, waiting until he had their attention: *'Bes den heb tavas e golhas e dir! We are not just fighting for our faith, but for our country and independence from the hated foreigner!'*

The new prayer book's arrival provided the camp with a focus for their anger and galvanised them into action. It was a concrete symbol of what they were about to lose if they did not overturn the new policy by appealing to the young King, who was being so misled by his wicked councillors. It added fresh urgency to the situation. This was no far away nebulous Act of Parliament which, as in the past, would likely fail to penetrate the far south. The Act was about to change their lives with immediate effect. They determined to save their faith, their culture, their language, and Cornwall.

*

After long discussions, the commanders decided that a set of demands should be sent to the King while those who, like Sir Richard Grenville, sympathised with the Protestant cause, must be taken prisoner. Crucially, before the army began its march to London, St Michael's Mount must be seized so that there would be no threat to its rear.

With the added impetus provided by the arrival of the proof of the Council's intention, makeshift tables were hastily erected, and long lines of men eagerly assembled to swear their allegiance to Cornwall and the Catholic faith. Arundell, a skilled tactician, divided his men in military fashion under colonels, majors, and captains while the priests were given special responsibilities. The clergy busily reassured the newly-formed peasant army that their cause was just and legal: they were not rebelling against the Crown but merely aiming to march to London, not to fight, but to present their grievances before the King, in a peaceful manner, as was their legal right.

By the time that the afternoon sun sank slowly in the west, the shadows of the ancient tors stark black against the purple haze of moorland, several thousand men surrounded by a collection of crosses, banners, candlesticks, holy bread, and water, so necessary to ward off the devils, and wearing full harness – a helmet, a gorge to protect the throat, and a coat of leather with small leather plates - were divided into military units, and sworn in to the new Catholic army.

From the high walls of the castle, a trumpet's lament pierced the moorland air, and a hush fell on the camp. Men swiftly removed their hats, reverently bowed their heads, and sank to their knees as the priests raised their hands to bless the army in preparation for the conflict ahead, whatever form it would take. After the priests fell silent, Arundell's loud voice rang powerfully around the castle walls, *'Rag Kernow ha'n kryjyans gwir!'* [32] he cried as he swore allegiance to God, the King, and the Catholic faith.

Sometime during the first half of July, a formidable sight left Bodmin: the large Catholic Cornish army crossed into England. At the head of the six thousand men and priests, who assembled under the canopy of the symbols of their faith, was carried the pyx that contained holy bread and water to protect them against the devil and his schemes. In front of the large army was the unfurled banner of the Five Wounds of Christ, the emblem of the Pilgrimage of Grace, which proudly guided the way across the Tamar

Westcountry men preparing for battle with Feniton's banner of the Five Wounds of Christ
Photograph by Viv Payne

---

[32] For Cornwall and the true religion.

into England. Three hundred years later, a local man, The Rev. Sabine Baring-Gould penned the words to the hymn 'Onward Christian Soldiers.'[33] Perhaps as he wrote the famous hymn, his imagination was influenced by the story of the ancient army that had marched close to his home generations before.

---

[33] The Rev. Sabine Baring-Gould (1834-1924) was one of the Church of England's more eccentric members of the clergy. Born to an ancient and privileged Devonshire family, he was obsessed with the subject of werewolves, and was noted for his penchant for teaching with his pet bat perched on his shoulder. His marriage to an uneducated mill girl scandalised Victorian society while his attempts to improve her intellectual accomplishments inspired his friend George Bernard Shaw to write Pygmalion. Meanwhile, Baring-Gould himself was allegedly the character upon whom Sherlock Holmes was based. He spent the last forty years of his life travelling to Westcountry farms where he bamboozled reluctant farm workers to serenade him with local ditties which resulted in the compilation of one of the most significant collections of English folk songs ever assembled.

> ## The rebels' demands sent to the King's Council
>
> ## Written on 8th June 1549
>
> N.B. There is no mention of Cornwall's specific demands, which were written from Exeter during the siege, so these were probably written by the Devonshire men.

1. That the mostly Catholic laws of Henry VIII remain in force until Edward VI attains the age of royal competence (twenty-four years).

2. That the Host be reserved in churches as had been the custom.

3. That priests should not marry.

4. That bishops carry out confirmation on request.

5. That worshippers have holy bread and water.

6. That Mass be celebrated as when transubstantiation was accepted.

7. That baptism be available on every day of the week.

8. That their church service continues in its familiar Catholic form, and not be set out like a 'Christmas play'.

New evidence: The Date of the Cornish Rising Was 6th July 1549, not 6th June 1549

For over a century, historians have accepted Rose-Troup's thesis that the Bodmin Rising was finalised on June 6th, three days before the events at Sampford Courtenay. However, there is much evidence to counteract this assumption.

Rose-Troup based her claim that contradicted earlier historians on the indictment for Humphrey Arundell, which stated that the Bodmin rising commenced on June 6th. However, new evidence discovered by Professor Stoyle now suggests that this was an error and that the date was actually July 6th.

Hooker's earliest writings, the Bodleian manuscript, fails to mention the supposed Cornish presence in Devon prior to July; indeed, his manuscript suggests that all the people involved in the Crediton protest were Devonians, and no Cornish presence is mentioned. Sir John Frye's report on the events at Crediton suggests that the royalists experienced an easy victory, and this would account for the Council's furious response when Carew took such strong measures to suppress the resistance in the town. If a strong Cornish contingent had been present, it is unlikely that Lord Somerset would have regarded Carew's decision to attack as unnecessary.

If the Cornish had assembled on Bodmin on 6th June, why did it take them so long to cross into Devon? According to Rose-Troup, they needed to ensure that both the Mount and Trematon were under their control, but the financial accounts for the month of June suggest that these two fortifications were entirely unaware of any threat from a Cornish rising during the month of June.

(cont'd overleaf)

According to the accounts submitted in 1551 for the summer of 1549 by the paymaster for fortifications, John Killigrew, on June 23rd, 1549 - the day of Sir Peter Carew's troubles in Clyst St Mary - had received a routine payment £100 at 'Trerowe' from the deputy receiver of the Duchy of Cornwall. Such a transaction suggests that there was as yet no knowledge of a threatened uprising. More importantly, Sir William Godolphin shipped one hundred soldiers to the Isles of Scilly from Penzance on June 26th. If the nearby Mount had been in danger of a rebel attack at this time, Godolphin would not have made such an arrangement when a strong military presence would have been required to protect St Michael's Mount.

We also know that King Edward made this written statement in response to the first set of articles forwarded to the Council following the receipt of the rebels' demands: WHY SHOULD DEVONSHIRE BE THE <u>FIRST</u> TO SLANDER OUR REALM? There is no mention of Cornwall when this response was penned towards the end of June to early July. Furthermore, the Arundell indictment following his capture on the 18th or 19th August states that he had been in rebellion for six weeks, suggesting that the date on the indictment was in error and that the Cornish had risen in early July, not June. Furthermore, Killigrew's accounts record that he summoned soldiers to defend Pendennis Castle on July 10th, four days after the Bodmin uprising. It was about this time that the defenders of the Mount were defeated and William Trewynard mortally wounded, giving evidence of the severity of the assault. His lands were seized and his possessions destroyed, suggesting that the local people had not forgotten that he had aided and abetted the defeat of the local people of West Cornwall the year before.

Several of the gentlemen were imprisoned in the Mount, suggesting that the whole of West Cornwall was partaking in the revolt.

(cont'd overleaf)

THE BATTLE OF FENNY BRIDGES 1549
PRELUDE AND AFTERMATH

In West Cornwall, Sir Richard Grenville, who led the resistance of Trematon Castle, found himself outnumbered and surrendered. It was then that Arundell mustered the troops at Bodmin, which would be approximately one month after the rising began in Sampford Courtenay.

Letters from the Council also reveal that the Mayor of Plymouth was still in charge of the town during the third week of July, which, again, suggests a much later date for the march from Bodmin than has been accepted for the last hundred years.

*

Trematon Castle

Chapter Eleven

The Siege of Exeter
July 2nd–August 6th, 1549

As dawn broke on July 2nd, the Mayor and his councillors, dressed in full regalia, hurried to Exeter's West Gate. There, beyond the River Exe and the tower of St Thomas's Church, they saw the glint of light reflecting from gold and silver ornaments. Approaching them was the protestors' banner of the Five Wounds of Christ, rippling in the summer breeze, with a company of priests following, robed and chanting solemnly, and, beneath a heavily embroidered canopy, was the pyx. From swinging censors, the scent of a cloud of incense wafted up to tweak the consciences of the Catholic defenders of the city while the sound of chanting choir boys, wearing cottas and cassocks, and carrying huge processional candles, served to stir the emotions of the listeners standing on the city walls. The unspoken message of the protestors to the Catholic citizens of Exeter was clear: was it better to rebel against the King or the holy Catholic Church? Should they risk the gibbet and the traitor's death or face eternal

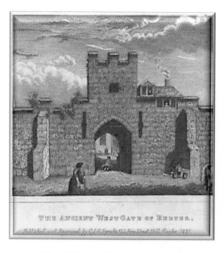

The West Gate of Exeter

damnation? It was a question set to cause dissension within the city during the long weeks of the siege ahead.

When the protestors reached the sandstone walls of the city, there was a flourish of trumpets to call attention to a herald who demanded that the people of Exeter reject the new Protestant laws. As the citizens gazed down anxiously on the several thousand strong army that was gathered below, their potential invaders shouted warnings that if they did not open the gates to them and join their cause, they would lay siege to their city, starve them until they declared defeat, and sack their homes and Exeter's valuables.

Exe Bridge completed 1238

The Westcountry men surrounding the walls, however, underestimated not only the Mayor's allegiance to the Crown but also his natural aversion to a charge of treason, and the peoples' determination to protect their possessions from the threat of strangers rampaging through their houses and streets.

Crucially for the future of the Reformation, the Mayor decided to pledge his allegiance to the King and the rule of law and rejected the city's religious preference. He shouted out a defiant response to the men pounding on the gates below the anxious spectators, gathered up his robes, and rushed back to the Guildhall to make plans for the defence of Exeter and her inhabitants.

The citizens hastened to obey Blackaller's orders to collect every piece of armour while all able-bodied men were mustered, and captains instructed to guard every ward and each section of the wall.

*The Guildhall, Exeter –
parts of which are dated
to 1160*

Before the five gates were slammed shut, a few of the men of the city, however, slipped out to join the rebels while others chose to remain in order to sabotage the Mayor's determination to keep the invaders out. With so many of the citizens and most, if not all, of the clergy still devoted to the Catholic Church, it was to be an anxious time as the people of Exeter did not know which of their households would remain loyal to the Mayor or choose to betray them to the rebels.

There was feverish activity by both sides as attackers and defenders prepared their positions. The thousand-strong citizen-army chosen by Blackaller to defend the city hastily placed cannons in tactical places; others loaded the vast, wide-mouthed port pieces[34], last used in the siege of 1497, which haphazardly discharged lethal quantities of missiles by the bucket load. The attackers, meanwhile, feverishly set to work chopping down trees with which to barricade the city, smashing the bridges, placing sentries at every strategic position to prevent the people from entering or leaving Exeter, stripping the markets of produce, and erecting their ordnance at every gate.

*An Exeter Tudor House that
stood at the time of the siege*

---

[34] One of them remained outside the old gas show room near Princesshay until recent times.

THE BATTLE OF FENNY BRIDGES 1549
PRELUDE AND AFTERMATH

By the following day, the rebels had spread out in a circle around the entire perimeter of the city: across the wastes of Southernhay, onto the South Gate, the West Gate, thousands of men had the city surrounded. The besiegers were hopelessly under-equipped for their task and their numbers were not adequate to take a city as large and well-defended as Exeter. They lacked the siege train necessary to breach the walls, and the guns that they had seized were too small to cause any significant damage. However, although they lacked the weaponry for an effective siege, they well understood the psychology of that type of warfare, and exploited it to the full to make the lives of the citizens as unbearable as possible until they wore down their resolve. They plagued the inhabitants with nightly feigned attacks, picked off individuals as they left their homes, slowly starved the trapped citizens, and relentlessly appealed to their allegiance to their faith to further weaken the city's resolve.

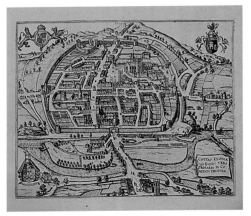

Medieval Map of Exeter

Night after night, they kept the terrified people awake as they staged false alarms with all the trappings of a full-scale assault, which played havoc with the nerves. During daylight hours, snipers situated on the higher ground outside the city walls shot the careless citizens as they walked down their streets searching for provisions or appeared at their bedroom windows. A man named Smith, we are informed by Hooker, was soaking up the July sunshine outside his door in Northgate Street when suddenly he was hit by a bullet from the area near St David's outside the city boundary. Hooker tells us he bled to death in the gutter.

Early in the siege[35], the exhausted citizens heard a huge cheer from outside the city walls. Urgent messages were sent to the Mayor. In the far distance, another large army loomed into view, and this one was considerably larger than the Devonshire army already camped around the perimeter: the Cornish reinforcements, under Arundell's leadership, had finally arrived from Bodmin.

According to Hooker, a large number of women with horses bearing empty baskets ready to receive the loot, including the velvets and silks, plate, money, and other great riches that they allegedly planned to plunder from the city, accompanied them. Although it was quite usual for wives to follow their husbands to battle, so their presence is not in question, the rebels viewed their Devonshire neighbours as friends and potential allies; it is unlikely that they intended to steal the valuables from the city. In 1497, when the Cornish had marched through Devon and had laid siege to Exeter, during their fateful trek to London, they had avoided damaging the possessions of their fellow Westcountry men and it is highly likely that Hooker's allegation was merely a piece of propaganda spread abroad to strengthen the citizen's determination to resist the army outside the gates.

The defenders who stood guard must have been dismayed and disheartened to witness the approach of thousands of fresh reinforcements wearing armour, marching under a panoply of crosses, banners, candlesticks, and brandishing weapons, including the famous deadly Cornish longbows. The eight thousand[36] besieged inhabitants must have felt near despair at the news that they were now surrounded by about ten thousand men. How could the city survive such an onslaught?[37]

---

[35] This version of events accords with the new contemporary evidence that supports the pre-Rose-Troup view that Cornwall rose on July 6th.

[36] Some authorities claim that Exeter had a population of 3 000, others, 8 000

[37] According to a Spanish chronicler at the time there were 30 000 rebels. In 1603, Hereford claimed there were 15 000 which included men from Somerset. Hooker in 1575, Hollingshead in 1578, Hayward in 1599 and Pocock in 1884 all maintained there were 10 000. Carew meanwhile records that 6 000 Cornish marched into Devon.

The Westcountry men swiftly organised their joint forces on a military footing. Arundell, Wynslade, and Holmes, representing Cornwall; Pomeroy, Bury, and Coffin, representing Devon; and Underhill, Sloeman and Segar, all three from Sampford Courtenay, were chosen as leaders. These men made the major decisions. Two priests, Thompson and Barrett, two civic leaders, Mayors Bray and Lee, of Bodmin and Torrington respectively, and, according to Hooker, Mawnder, a shoemaker, and Ashridge, a fish-driver, were all given responsibilities, some of them as governors of the various camps, that encircled the besieged city.

Old print titled: EXETER – A scene in the Rebellion of the West, 1549. Burning of the West Gate by the Rebels

The Cornish, although they too lacked weapons for siege warfare, soon made use of their skill as tinners, and began tunnelling under the wall by the West Gate. They did their best not to gain attention, but suspicious sounds of subterranean noises began to alarm the citizens. Fortunately for them, John Newcombe, a tinner from Teignmouth, was trapped in the city, and he offered to investigate. People gathered on the wall and watched in fascination as Newcombe carried a wide, shallow pan of water which he moved gently to and fro, tracing the line and extent of the mining by the tremors on the water's surface. There was no time to lose, and he ordered that a counter-mine be constructed with all speed from inside the wall. He was so accurate that when he finally broke through, he could see the rebels loading gun powder and pitch into a chamber at the end of their shaft. The planned explosion would inevitably bring down a large section of the structure between the West and East Gates, allowing the Westcountry men to swarm into the city.

Newcombe, taking advantage of the fact that Exeter was situated on a hill that sloped down to the West Gate, persuaded everyone living in the area to fill a large tub of water and place it outside their front door. At a given signal, they all emptied their tubs simultaneously: the water cascaded down towards the gate, gushed down Newcombe's shaft and into the mine, destroying the explosives and drowning the miners. At the same time, it is reported that a massive thunderstorm broke overhead, which added to the torrent of water. Never again did the Cornishmen attempt to dig another mine, although this was their most powerful and potentially successful weapon. Certainly, if Newcombe had not been visiting the city at the time, history might have been very different as Exeter could have fallen into rebel hands that day.

With the failure of the mine, the attackers were left with a choice: they could either burn the city down or starve the people into surrender. The latter would inevitably be a protracted affair, so they set out to burn the city's wooden gates. This involved piling a cart with old hay, and pushing it in front of the gate, and then igniting it. In theory, the hay protected the attacker on his approach, and the flames prevented a marksman from shooting him on his return. At the West and South Gates, however, would-be arsonists were spotted, and some killed with the port pieces. Where they were successful, the citizens foiled their ploy by adding dry fuel to the fire, which served to bar the entrance, keeping the potential invaders out. Those who entered were slain on the ramparts that the town's people had constructed behind the gates.

Meanwhile, the rebel army's leaders and camp governors drew up a fresh set of articles to send to London. The tone of these demands was very different to the previous set of eight articles, reflecting the confidence generated by the amalgamation of the two forces. They were more comprehensive than the original Articles and were insolent in tone, suggesting that they believed that the Government was about to surrender. The Cornish influence was now apparent as they refused to accept English as part of their service, while, in addition, their new-found confidence was reflected in their demand that all who did not adhere to the Catholic faith should be executed as heretics. They called for the exiled ex-Dean of Exeter cathedral, Cardinal Pole, to be pardoned and sent as the King's representative to the Vatican. They further demanded the part-restoration of the plundered religious houses, now in secular hands. Lastly, they insisted that their leaders be given a free pardon.

An Exeter Tudor House

The exact date of the set of demands is uncertain; however, replies from the Council suggest they were written by mid-July. A reply in response to a lost letter from Russell that he had written on 18th July indicates that the arrival of the Cornish insurgents on Devon soil was a new development[38]. It also severely criticises the treasonous actions of the Mayor of Plymouth in yielding to the rebels. The Council was harsh in their condemnation of the town's capitulation and their flight to St Nicholas Island, but Plymouth possessed no fortifications and, therefore, the decision taken to seek refuge on the island in Plymouth Sound was an understandable one. However, the fall of the town was a great shock to the King's Council and was the jolt they needed to take the Western men seriously. In a letter to Russell, dated 25th July, when the siege was entering its third week, the Council referred to Arundell's *'poison, sent abroad by his letters'*. No doubt they were referring to the new set of demands where Arundell identified himself as the chief leader of the

---

[38] Ever since Rose-Troup wrote her book on the Western Rebellion a hundred years ago, it has been accepted that the Bodmin men gathered on June 6th; however, new information discovered by Professor Stoyle contradicts this and it appears that the date was July 6th, and therefore after the beginning of the siege of Exeter. Thus, the Cornish joined the siege at a date later than July 2nd but probably before July 18th.

amalgamated forces of Devon and Cornwall. The Council was also particularly irritated and alarmed to read the new Articles that related to the Cornish alone, particularly the demand that *'certein Cornishmen be offended because they have not their service in Cornishe'* and that they thoroughly rejected the new English language.

While the Council was in an increasing state of alarm with the news that was coming from Devon, they received further disturbing information that threatened the safety of the realm: whispers of treason and of invitations to foreign invaders had trickled out from Cornwall's jostling ports. At the time that Russell's alarming news and the fresh demands from the rebels forced the Council to, finally, recognise the serious nature of the Western Rising, a letter from a Mr Hobbue (*sic*) warned them that the French were planning to exploit the situation by invading Cornwall. So, by the fourth week of July when the Council was still distracted containing a number of rebellions around the country and with its resources concentrated in the north where it was conducting a war with the Scots, Plymouth had fallen, ten thousand men were besieging the eight[39] thousand inhabitants of Exeter, and the French were planning to invade. Lord Somerset must have felt an overwhelming sense of desperation when he, at last, grasped the seriousness of the situation in the South West.

Model of Exeter's East Gate

Meanwhile, nerves were becoming increasingly frayed within the city, and, on one occasion, when the Mayor had summoned all the commoners to appear at the Guildhall in their armour, a row broke out. With the Catholics then in the majority, and hoping to gain the

---

[39] Some authorities claim there were 3 000 inhabitants.

advantage over the city's defenders, one of them, Richard Taylor, a clothier, aimed his bow and fired. He accidentally injured his hand causing him to miss his target: his arrow lodged in the chest of his best friend, John Petre, brother of Sir William Petre, Secretary of State, who would have died had the arrow not struck a rib. Deeply distressed by the consequences of his action, Taylor made no further attempt to ignite a riot. Years later, when he died in a debtors' prison, those who possessed long memories claimed it was God's judgement on his actions. To prevent further trouble, a company of several hundred was created to patrol the streets day and night in order to prevent further treachery.

As Exeter waited anxiously for the non-existent royal army to come to its rescue, the conditions in the city deteriorated. The King seemed to have abandoned the citizens to their fate. As the days dragged on, there were fresh problems arising for both sides as dissensions between the citizens began to damage morale and weaken comradeship. Some of the Catholic majority in the city who sympathised with the rebels plotted to open the gates to give entry to the insurgents, and a number of them were bribed to smuggle in fifty of the enemy through the North Gate under the pretence of checking its security. The plot leaked out, however, and the patrol organised by the men at the Guildhall hid close by, ready to seize the invaders and the traitors who had opened the gate. Such betrayals inevitably further weakened the morale and confidence of the increasingly hungry citizens.

To make matters worse, rivalry broke out between the raiding parties that slipped out of the gates at night to harass the rebels. One particularly obnoxious individual, a servant of Russell, Bernard Duffield, who was in charge of Bedford House, made regular nocturnal expeditions into the rebel camp. One night, he left by the gate close to the House with several followers, killed some of the rebels, took others prisoner, and captured armaments. They did not all return home unscathed, however, as some were captured, a cook was killed, and others injured. One poor man, John Drake, struggled back into the city with an arrow lodged through both cheeks.

Pleased with his success, Duffield made further plans to conduct raiding parties, but his scheme was obstructed by John Courtenay, son of Sir William of Powderham, and step-son of the psychopathic Sir Anthony Kingston, who was later to play a brutal role as the executioner of the West. Duffield resented such interference and determined to defy the order but found himself swiftly summoned to appear before Mayor Blackaller at the Guildhall. After fully debating the situation with the man, the Mayor supported Courtenay's decision, and a row broke out during which Duffield became verbally abusive. He was rapidly dragged off to prison and probably cast into the dungeons beneath the Guildhall.

Blackaller, having already experienced a beating by a group of irate women of Exeter a few years before when foreign workmen were attacked by them at St Nicholas Priory, was about to discover that more of their ilk lurked in the city. As soon as Duffield's daughter heard of her father's imprisonment, she rushed to the Guildhall and demanded his release. When her request was declined, according to Hooker, she '*waxed so warm that not only she used very unseemly terms and speeches unto the Mayor but also, contrary to the Modesty and Shamefacedness required in a Woman, especially the young and unmarried, ran most violently upon him, and strake him in the face*'. It seemed that the long-suffering Mayor had a habit of being hit about the face by the spirited women of Exeter.

With nerves now very severely stretched to breaking point by events, one over-excited bystander rushed forward and declared that Frances Duffield had seriously injured or even killed the Mayor. The common bell, a signal to the people that Exeter was in immediate danger, rang out to alert the city to the catastrophe. At the sound of the alarm, men rushed from all around, pulling on their armour, as they ran to Exeter's defence. In the excitement, Frances escaped to Bedford House. When the men clattered breathlessly in through the entrance to the Guildhall, they were greeted by the Mayor, who was still very much alive. Furious that Blackaller had been attacked, the men were about to pursue Frances with the intention of teaching her to respect the civil authorities, but Blackaller instructed the mob to let the situation rest and told them to quietly disperse. With his wounds dressed, the Mayor returned to his home, but he had not yet heard the last of it. Minutes later, there was a pounding on his door. A group of agitated cathedral staff had heard of the affray and, after finding the Guildhall deserted, needed reassurance that the Mayor was still in good health. Blackaller thanked them courteously and calmly asked them to disburse. From that day forward, however, the archdeacon demanded daily reassurance that the Mayor was safe and well.

Soon the city was facing worse perils than those created by its feisty women: famine. The cost of food had escalated in recent times so the city had few reserves. As Hooker describes the situation: *'Albeit theare were good store of drye fishe, rice, prunes, raisons, and wine at [a] very reasonable price, yet bread was not to be had, so that in this extremity the bakers and householders were driven to seek up their old store of puffyns and bran wherewith they in times past were wont to make horse bread and to feed their swine and poultry and this they moulded up in clothes for otherwise it would not hold together and so did bake it up and the people well contented therewith.'* The situation was exacerbated by the usual collection of unethical individuals who profited from their neighbours' distress by exploiting the law of supply and demand by escalating the price of food stocks; but others were generous and prepared to share with their neighbours their own meagre resources.

The Mayor's greatest concern was the plight of the poorest citizens, and he arranged for them to be either given food or to purchase it for a very low price. In an effort to prevent Exeter from falling, the church plate was sold to purchase food for those in the greatest threat of starvation, and also to pay the defenders' wages. Meanwhile, there was still no sign of the royal rescuers who were promised. The plight of the city worsened. As the rumours of the increasing desperation of the starving inhabitants reached the army besieging the city, aided by their sympathisers within Exeter, they made strenuous efforts to increase the pressure on the people.

Outside the city walls, as the days dragged on, restless troops were finding it difficult to keep motivated and maintain discipline. The burning strategy they had adopted, although technically successful, had not been productive. Several attempts were made to scale the walls, but they, too, had failed. Their most promising line of attack was mining, but, for some reason, they had abandoned it. They, no doubt, still hoped for the sympathetic Catholics within the city to raise the gates, especially when driven by starvation. Certainly, time seemed to be on their side for there was no sign of the royal forces. The Government had apparently completely abandoned Exeter to her fate. It was clear that she could not withstand the siege for many more days.

With Exeter nearing defeat, an opportunity presented itself to the attackers. The gunner, John Hammond, a blacksmith from Woodbury, who had been prevented from blowing Sir Peter Carew to bits at Clyst St Mary, had yet another chance to make history. While he was occupied picking off a number of the inhabitants of the city from his vantage point at St David's, he boasted that he could use red-hot shot to burn Exeter to the ground within four hours. As most houses were of timber, he was probably right. A date and time were fixed for Exeter's destruction.

*

On the allocated day, a brisk wind was blowing, and hundreds of people in an inappropriate party spirit, assembled on St David's Hill to watch the spectacle. The priest of St Thomas, Father Welshe,[40] although secretly a rebel leader, was outraged by the plan and threw himself in front of the gun, saying, according to Hooker, '....*I will in no wise suffer so lewd an act – a wicked thing to be done. Do what you can by policy, or dint of sword and I will join you and do my uttermost, but to burn the city, which would be hurtful to all and profitable to none I will not consent to, but will withstand you with all my power.'* Thanks to the priest's intervention, Exeter was saved once again.

Among many attempts at espionage there was one where a man was caught red-handed. The way the rebels dealt with him was later

---

[40] Hooker writing in 1575, considered Welshe, a Cornishman, to be 'an arch captain and chief doer' of the Rising. Prof. Youings, writing in 1979, listed him as one of the main leaders.

used by the King's men to justify far worse brutalities of their own. Kingswell, a tinner, originally from Chagford, was in the service of a Tavistock JP called John Charles. One night, Kingswell was caught slipping out of the gate to take letters from his master to Lord Russell. He unwisely and forcibly voiced his strong Protestant opinions to the rebels, calling them traitors worthy of death. Father Welshe, who was in the rebel camp, lost all patience with him. The priest arranged a hasty and dubious trial which condemned the unfortunate Kingswell to death. The tinner was escorted to a great elm tree on Exe Island and hanged.

By the fourth week of the siege, with the people of Exeter starving and reduced to eating the few remaining scraps of animal feed, the city was about to surrender, giving the rebels the control of the South West. With no sign of an approaching royal force to relieve the siege, the peasant army only needed to wait for a few more days for victory. It was then that they made their fatal mistake.

Chapter Twelve

Lord Russell and the Royal Army Assemble in Honiton

With Exeter's citizens under siege and waiting for the royal army to rescue them, the man given the ultimate responsibility for suppressing the Rising was the Lord Privy Seal, John Russell, who was stationed in Honiton. Unfortunately for him, he had three problems. He had virtually

no money,

no weapons,

and

no army.

It was not surprising that Exeter felt deserted by the King. Russell had tried to raise a local army of two thousand, but the Devonshire men sympathised with the rebel cause and were not prepared to fight their neighbours. Probably, more to the point, they knew that Russell was short of money and might not be able to pay for their services.

The Lord Privy Seal's repeated requests to the King's Council for men, ammunition, and money were met with short-tempered replies. He was ordered to hang some of the local men for refusing to join the royal force, and those who showed any sympathy for the Catholic cause, even if they merely listened to the rebels' demands, were to be treated as traitors. Ammunition, Russell was informed by Protector Somerset, he could make for himself from the lead in Honiton's church roofs. Mercenary soldiers were promised, but they were far away, having been deployed in the war with Scotland.

As Exeter starved, waiting for the non-existent royal forces to rescue them, Russell became so despondent with the impossibility of the situation in which he was placed that, in despair, he retreated to the comparative safety of Somerset and Dorset. Sir Peter Carew, concerned by John Russell's withdrawal, immediately chased after the General. Catching up with him in the Blackdown Hills, he reasoned with him until he persuaded the exhausted King's General to return to Honiton.

Russell was at his wit's end when he was visited by three wealthy merchants of Exeter who, ultimately, changed the course of history. The three merchants: John Bodley, son of John Bodley of Dunscombe, Crediton, and Joan Hone, daughter of Robert Hone of Ottery St Mary; his half-brother, the ex-Mayor of Exeter, Thomas Prestwood, son of Joan Hone, and her second husband, Thomas Prestwood Snr; and his sister-in-law's husband, John Periam, had a plan to save Exeter.[41] They were all wealthy men whose prime concern was to rescue the economy of the city, and a royal victory provided the best chance of that. They explained to the General that they would canvas their business acquaintances in Taunton, Bristol, and other local towns, in an effort to raise sufficient funds which, if successful, would 'ease his grief'. At last, the Lord Privy Seal had hope of raising an army along with the necessary supplies, providing the merchants were successful in their appeal to the local businessmen. The future success of the King's forces depended on the generosity of this small group of men.

With the arrival of the news in London that Exeter was under siege, panic spread through the city and, determined to stop the ten thousand rebel army marching into the Capital, the Council ordered the destruction of the bridge over the Thames at Staines. On July 18th, a state of martial law was declared. Guards were placed at every gate to watch for the approach of the Western men while heavy ordnance was

---

[41] From a transcript of a lecture given at Sidmouth July 1903 by Frances Rose-Troup.

shifted from the Tower, and mounted in readiness on the city walls and gates. The news of the siege of Exeter and the surrender of Plymouth to the rebel forces finally galvanised the King's Council into action as the seriousness of the situation became apparent, even to far-away Londoners. Thoroughly alarmed, Lord Somerset then made a very unpopular move: he sent to the continent for yet more mercenaries, much to the fury of the citizens who loathed the foreigners. They threatened not to leave one of them alive if they landed on English soil.

There was indeed good cause to detest the foreign soldiers who had a terrible reputation for '*filling every place with death and slaughter*' and '*irrigating and inundating the ground with human gore*[42]'. Not surprisingly, the more efficient fighting men decided that they would rather forgo their pay than become entangled with the feisty, xenophobic, and aggressive English, and only the rougher sort of man signed up for the King's army.

Meanwhile, as Somerset was rustling up troops to send south, the sixty-three-year-old King's General became increasingly exasperated by the deluge of inappropriate advice that was showered on him, an experienced commander, by the Council whose responses clearly displayed both a lack of understanding and knowledge of the uprising and also of the local terrain. They not only rudely order him to make his own ammunition by using the lead from the local church roofs but when he needed infantry to negotiate the Devonshire lanes, they sent horsemen who were not capable of effectively manoeuvring in Devon's countryside. When he requested money, the Council sharply reminded him that the Treasury was broke and instructed him to seize valuables from the churches to make up the shortfall. Further orders, designed to inflame the hostility further, advised the exasperated General to busy himself by cutting off food supplies from the rebel troops and to prevent them from strengthening their numbers by spreading false claims of atrocities, allegedly committed by the local peasant army. Although secretly supporting the Catholic cause, certain towns such as Ashburton, which contributed two chalices and

---

[42] Quoted by the sixteenth-century Venetian diplomat Sebastian Guistinian

a pyx worth ten pounds, and Tavistock, where the loyalists sold enough plate to enable Russell to hire another twenty men, obliged the Council's orders, albeit with reluctance. The Earl of Warwick, meanwhile, who was to journey south to join Russell's ranks, was waylaid by fresh troubles in the South East.

While assembling his forces, Russell received for distribution two of the Council's responses to both the rebels' articles of June 8th and their second more belligerent demands[43] the tone of which reflected their renewed confidence, following the arrival of the Cornish during the second week of July. Somerset's first reply was partly conciliatory, but it carried the overt threat that '*we have condescended out of love to write rather than war against you as rebels, but unless you repent, we will extend our princely power and draw the sword against you as against infidels and Turks*'. He was not prepared to compromise on any article of religion.

With the rebels' failure to comply with his instructions, Somerset adopted a change of tactic and approached the headmaster of Eton, Nicholas Udall (1504-56), a classical scholar, playwright, cleric, alleged child abuser, and tutor to Edward VI. He appealed to the rebels to return to their homes and not be influenced by '*sinister persuasion of certain seditious papists, whelps of the Roman litter, abusing your simplicity and lightness of credit*'. The Council, he explained, had delivered them from the slavery of Rome with its superstitious and anti-biblical practices and they should obey the new Protestant laws, and disperse peacefully to their homes. Crucially, touching on a sensitive subject, Udall proposed that the King might be prepared to publish a prayer book in the Cornish language, and even forwarded a petition to them to be signed and presented to the Council. His letter ended with a plea: he strongly advised the Devonshire and Cornish men, both captains, and camp-men, to desert

---

[43] See Appendices

the '*few malicious papist agitators and return to the King's obedience*'.[44] His request was firmly rejected.

With merchant money now pouring into his coffers and having to appear to be doing something, Russell started a programme of reconnaissance. Starting out from Honiton, he headed towards Exeter but, fearing an ambush, he made a detour to Ottery, where he spent the night. The local men, hearing of his advance, swiftly felled trees and blocked the route between Ottery and Exeter. Russell retaliated by burning down some houses in the town but was trapped by rebels at Alfington[45], where he thrashed them in battle before returning to his quarters in Honiton. Here, he waited for the arrival of Herbert's Welsh force of five thousand men, Lord Grey and his army, and the first instalment of mercenaries.

Alfington: one mile from Fenny Bridges

As wild rumours were carried to London that Exeter and Plymouth had fallen to the rebel army, and the French were invading Cornwall with the intention of amalgamating their forces to conqueror the English, the Council made haste to ensure that the royal army arrived in Honiton with all possible speed. When the news of the imminent

---

[44] Sir John Frye in a letter to Sir John Thynne in 1549, attested to the involvement of the priests when he wrote, '*there were dyvers prystes in the fyld fyghtying ayenst us, and some of them were slayne at ever[y] fyghte*'.

[45] Rose-Troup suggests Alfington is the village where Russell is described as encountering a 'skirmish in the streights' when returning from a failed attempt to reach Exeter. On 27th July, a pamphlet provides evidence that Russell possessed an outpost described as '*a village nygh sainct Mary Otery*'. This is likely to be Alfington.

arrival of Lord Grey and the large contingent of Herbert's Welsh troops in Honiton reached the rebel leaders at Exeter, the Westcountry men felt compelled to make what was to be their fatal error: with Exeter about to fall into their hands, they determined to engage the royal army at Fenny Bridges.

A scene filmed in Feniton from the docu-drama,
'The European Reformation'.

The Battle of Fenny Bridges, 27th – 28th July 1549

On Saturday, 27th July, a breathless messenger brought the news to Lord Russell in Honiton that a contingent of rebels had seized Fenny Bridges[46] from the royal outpost there and were blocking the road to

---

[46] The rebels chose their battlefield well. According to Leland's earlier description of Fenny Meadow, after the King's troops had crossed the River Otter they would have been obstructed by a series of water courses, while the high hedges provided good hiding places for the Westcountry men. We know from an Order Book of 1711, and Hooker's writing, that the first phase of the battle took place partly in

Exeter. After hastily despatching further urgent requests to speed up the promised reinforcements that had not yet arrived, a Council of War was quickly organised with Sir Gawen Carew and his nephew Sir Peter Carew. The decision was taken to engage the rebel army the following morning.

A Lansknecht foreign mercenary
(15th - 16th century)

Landsknecht Mercenary

All was hustle and excitement in the royal camp as the news flashed through Honiton that the foreign 'rakehells', the mercenary army garrisoned in the town, would attack the next day. This was the first occasion that the Crown had employed a foreign - and partly Catholic - army to suppress an English rebellion, and like the rest of their countrymen, the Honitonians loathed the foreigners camped in their midst. They had well deserved their terrible reputation. Each year, it was said, they grew more ferocious, bloodthirsty, dishonest, and brutal. These men not only plundered the dead but destroyed the land, and, it was said, soaked the ground with human gore. The Landsknechts, who were sent by the King's Council to fight the Westcountry men, were the most feared mercenary soldiers of the sixteenth century. They had such a reputation for ruthless violence that one chronicler remarked that the devil so feared them that he refused to permit them to enter hell. These unprincipled men were known to even change sides partway through a battle if they were offered a suitable pay increase by those they were hired to fight. Their flamboyant, multi-coloured dress served as a means of intimidating their enemy, a privilege granted them by the Emperor

---

Gittisham parish. This determines the location of the site of the original bridge. Further archaeological work is required to ascertain the exact boundaries of the site.

Maximilian in compensation for their short, brutish lives. They made the most of the Emperor's concession to military dress by decking themselves in colourful slashed doublets, striped hose, tight or voluminous breeches, and outrageous codpieces, which were all worn in a deliberate attempt to flaunt their status, intimidate their enemies, and shock and terrify civilians. It was an army of these characters, hired by the King's Council, who were stationed in the East Devon town of Honiton to the distress and fear of the local inhabitants as they assembled in force to prepare to march on Fenny Bridges[47].

A Landsknecht mercenary taking his wife to war. The wives and daughters were often the first on the field after the battle to strip and plunder the dead.
Etching by Daniel Hopfer

To the Honitonians, who considered the inhabitants of Axminster ten miles away to be virtual foreigners, these wild, heavily armed, unprincipled strangers were indeed a threatening and alarming presence. They complained that the Government was trying to impose the new religion at the point of a foreign pike - a Catholic pike at that. The Crown, they grumbled, was '*subjecting the*

---

[47] The primary sources do not provide a consistent account of how many mercenaries had arrived by this time. Germany mercenaries appear to be present and some of Spinola's Italians. Four hundred horsemen and one thousand foot under Jermigny and Sanga and one thousand local men with seven hundred horse were also likely in Honiton. Lord Grey, some of Spinola's men, and Herbert's Welshmen had not arrived by July 28th. Russell's army was, according to the Privy Council, about three thousand and two hundred in strength and this suggests he was outnumbered by the rebels.

English to the insolence of the foreigner'. When these mercenary soldiers did finally engage with the Catholic rebels, their brutality was only matched by the outstanding bravery of the men of Devon and Cornwall.

[48]Early the following morning, a holy day, according to Hooker, the King's army assembled in the town to listen to a brief service by Myles Coverdale, Russell's chaplain. As the future Bishop of Exeter read the prayers for men entering battle from the new Book of Common Prayer, those of the Catholic mercenaries who

St Margaret's Alms Houses, part of the leper hospital founded by de Tracey, one of the murderers of Archbishop Thomas a Becket, sometime before 1307.

could comprehend English must have listened with scorn and impatience. When Coverdale completed the final words of the blessing for the battle, a flourish of trumpets heralded the beginning of the advance.

16th century St Margaret's Chapel

---

[48] Hooker informs us that it was a 'holy day'. According to the Catholic Encyclopaedia, July 29th was just a feast day, celebrating St Martha, leaving the only day that could be labelled 'holy' as Sunday 28th, under the Julian calendar. Hooker also refers to *'about six days later on Saturday 3rd August....'* that Russell and his troops left Honiton. July 25th, St James' Day, was a holy day, but a letter from Russell dated 25th July to the Privy Council makes no mention of the battle, so July 28th remains the most likely date, but uncertainty remains and some sources just state that it was late July.

THE BATTLE OF FENNY BRIDGES 1549
PRELUDE AND AFTERMATH

As the town reverberated to the sound of the beating drums of the infantry, the army splashed noisily through the little ford at the bottom of Bramble Hill. With the Royal Standard snapping in the summer breeze, the army made its way up the hill towards Fenny Bridges, past the leper hospital and on to the Turk's Head.

Part of Bloody Mead from the main bridge, and the River Otter.

When they reached the high ground over the Deer Park, the Royal army gazed down on the water meadow below where the people of Feniton washed their wool in the tucking mills and ground their corn. There, beside the little thatched chapel of St Anne's, they caught sight of the priests of the rebel army preparing to bless the men of Devon and Cornwall in readiness for the battle.

Arundell (Jonathan Cuming of Feniton,) leading the rebel charge with Feniton's banner in the rear.

Sir Gawen Carew

The army watched as the rebels sank to their knees before the elevated Host, bowing their heads in prayer beneath the banner of the Five Wounds of Christ.

Many of the Catholic mercenaries must have crossed themselves and offered a prayer for pardon as they prepared to slaughter their fellow believers on the field. When they returned home, many planned to request absolution from the Pope for the sin of killing their fellow religious in the battles; however, in the meantime, the lure of money conveniently dampened their consciences.

When the priests had completed the blessing, Humphrey Arundell rode up to the assembled men and addressed them as they prepared their weapons. His voice rang across the battlefield, '*Tus a Gernow, nyns yw homma batel ynter an Gernowyon ha'n Sowson, drefen bos lies Sows a omladh rybon an jydh ma. Nyns yw kas rag glori a'n bys ma ha tresoryow a wossen hag yw ledrys ha distruys gans ladron. Kas rag glori an nev na wra merwel nevra yw.*'[49] Then, raising his sword, Humphrey gave a rousing shout, '*Rag Kernow ha'n kryjyans gwir!*' The men lifted their weapons and responded in unison, '*Rag Kernow ha'n kryjyans gwir!*' As their voices died away,

---

[49] '*Men of Cornwall, this is not a battle between the Cornish and the English, for there are many English who fight by our side this day. It is not a fight for earthly glory and treasures that rust and thieves steal and destroy. It is a fight for the glory of heaven that will never die. It is a fight for Cornwall and the true religion.*' (Written by Stefano Mazzeo, film director, who used the first draft of this account for one episode of the documentary *The European Reformation*. It was kindly translated by Cornwall County Council, who also generously provided guidance with the pronunciation.)

a warning of Russell's advance brought an abrupt end to the speeches on the water meadow.

With the bridges strongly held by the rebels, Russell summoned the Carews to clear them. With the drumming of hooves, the flash of sunlight on metal, the clash of armour and harness, they led a terrifying cavalry charge, slashing their way through the rebel defenders[50] on the bridges. The Westcountry men held fast but, following a second cavalry onslaught, were swept aside, leaving the Westcountry men dead and dying on the field. After the charge, an ashen-faced Sir Gawen Carew reigned in his horse with one arm, an arrow buried deep in the other.

Russell urged his men onto the meadow, but a flight of arrows cut them down in scores. The arquebusiers opened a withering volley of fire as the cannons pounded the far end of the bridges. The Carews urged the infantry with their bills and pikes forward to engage in close combat, where they would be safer from

The hedge at Buckerell Cross where the rebels hid and also showing the corner of the battlefield

the deadly Cornish longbows. The fighting was fierce, but the superior weapons and training of the King's army forced the rebels

---

[50] There is little consistency in the primary sources of the numbers, military experience, and equipping of the rebel army. The Privy Council letters to Russell assured him there were only 7 000 'tag and rag' while the Spanish Chronicle states there were an improbable 30 000. They were wholly infantry armed with a combination of improvised weapons such as agricultural implements, and traditional bills, and bows of the county levies. Risdon also mentions that they had secured artillery from Plymouth.

back until they were beaten off the battlefield, leaving hundreds of their dead[51] and wounded on the water meadow. Then the mercenaries, like all of their kind, brutalised by their profession and underpaid, set to stripping the corpses, slitting throats, wrenching off jewellery, and seizing any spoils they could.

As the dispirited, bloodied remnant of the rebel army straggled wearily through Fairmile[52] towards Exeter, they met a strong contingent of two hundred and fifty giant Cornish archers, rushing to their aid. An officer at Fenny Bridges had sent for reinforcements. Under the command of Robert Smyth of St Germans, the strengthened force hurried back to the site of the battle, hid behind the hazel hedge that borders Buckerell Cross, and watched as the unsuspecting mercenaries continued their grisly task of plundering the dead.

A Landsknecht mercenary who fought at Fenny Bridges. One chronicler remarked that the devil refused to let landsknechts into hell because he so feared them.

---

[51] Hooker claims that 300 rebels were killed, while Hayward records 600 rebel fatalities and no royalist deaths. Brooks suggests that one to two hundred royalists were killed with many wounded, and Rose-Troup states that the fatalities were equal on both sides. Thus, although the battle marked the turning point of the Rising, it was not a clear victory for the King's army.

[52] It is possible that the rebels fled via the lane from Fenny Bridges to Alfington and on towards Exeter in the West Hill direction rather than through Fairmile where the Royalist cavalry could easily have cut them down.

Suddenly, at a given signal, a flight of arrows rained down on the King's men, throwing them into confusion as the rebels burst through the hedge and hurled themselves at the shocked mercenaries. Fleeing for their lives, they splashed across the River Otter, leaving many of their number dead, and the rebels in

Part of Bloody Mead with the Mill House in the background.

command of the field, at last. Their victory, however, was short-lived. Royal reinforcements arrived, and when Russell had reorganised his

According to local legend, the River Otter flowed red with blood.

troops, he charged towards his enemy. It was a fierce and brutal onslaught. According to Hooker, *'the Cornish were very lusty and fresh and fully bent to fight out the matter,'* .... and for a time, the conflict was *'very sharp and cruel.'*[53] The battle was renewed

---

[53] According to the Tudor Muster Rolls for Devon, the rebels were mostly armed with bows and bills, with the latter outnumbering bows by 2:1. (They did not acquire gunpowder or pikes until 1560.) Fewer than half of the Devonshire men possessed body armour, but the position of the Cornish was different on account of the persistent threat to their coastal defences. They had equal numbers of bows and bills, and they possessed much more body armour. To their great and continued disadvantage, they lacked a cavalry.

*Italian Mercenary
camped in Honiton*

again and again, but the professional soldiers gradually beat the rebels back, leaving hundreds more dead on the meadow.

In time, the Royal Standard was hoisted victoriously over the bridge above the carnage below, where about a thousand dead and injured lay on the field, giving substance to the local legend, which has been relayed down the centuries, that the field ran ankle-deep in blood, while the Otter flowed red.

Meanwhile, Smyth, '*with*', says Hooker, '*his comb cut, and showing a fair pair of heels,*' along with his broken army, trudged wearily back up the hill toward Exeter [54], many for the second time that day. They were, according to the chronicler, '*men of great courage, who in a better cause might have done better service.*'

Leaving the scene of the battle, Lord Russell hurried his army forward, eager to relieve the besieged city. According to Hooker, however, he had only travelled three miles up Straightway Hill to the ground above Fairmile when Joll, Russell's fool, galloped at full speed up to the King's General, having set out from Honiton. Screaming hysterically, and '*with a foul mouth*', he informed the alarmed General that the church bells were ringing backwards, a sign that the people of Devon were planning to attack the royal army.

As the Lord Privy Seal gazed anxiously over the panorama of the rolling countryside around him, he would have realised that the deep Devon tracks forged through the undergrowth were ideal for hiding a powerful force bent on ambush. The Carews encouraged him to

---

[54] This is according to Rose-Troup, but it is more likely they avoided the cavalry by fleeing via the back routes.

continue towards Exeter, and round up the battered remnants of the rebel army, but Russell feared that his lines of communications might be severed and, wary of further attacks, after sending a small boy ahead to the city to give news of his victory, he ordered his exhausted men back to Honiton.

With Exeter starving and failing to press on with his victory, Russell had, in fact, made a potentially fatal error that could have resulted in the fall of the city. However, the rebels failed to exploit his mistake and, although the royalist victory was only partial, the King's troops having probably lost as many men as the rebels that day, the Battle of Fenny Bridges, ultimately, proved to be the turning point of the Rebellion. Arundell had indeed made a gross miscalculation, although an understandable one, when he decided to engage the royal troops and their cavalry in open combat. Had he not done so, Exeter would almost certainly have fallen into rebel hands within a few days, leaving the South West in possession of the local Catholic army and London, which was hastily arming its citizens, within their grasp.

A scene from the docu-drama The European Reformation filmed in Ottery St Mary parish church where, according to a speech to the Ottery Institute in 1897 by Lord Coleridge, many of the (royalist?) dead from the battle are buried.

Between six hundred and a thousand men lay dead on the meadow and, with no firm evidence that the bodies were removed, they may still lay close to the old A30 where the road turns from Fenny Bridges towards the old village of Feniton.

However, recently, new light has been thrown on the possible resting places of the dead from the battle. While trawling through old books on the history of Ottery St Mary, I discovered a transcript of a talk

The Greyhound Inn where, according to local legend, the innkeeper was executed for giving aid to injured rebels.

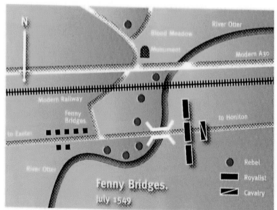

With thanks to the Battlefield's Trust. (Further evidence suggests that the second stage of the battle may have been closer to Bloomfield as a number of artefacts have been discovered in that area.)

given in 1897[55] by Lord Coleridge. He makes reference to a six-foot pile of bones which lie under the North Aisle at St Mary's, Ottery, and describes the bodies as lying in a heap as though cast there in a hurry. He states that, '*It is believed that the bones of the slaughtered soldiers have found in that sacred spot their last resting place.*' If Lord

---

[55] Lord Coleridge's talk in 1897 on the history of the town of Ottery St Mary was given to the Ottery Institute.

Coleridge is correct, these are probably the bodies of the royalists as the authorities would not have wanted to have been associated with the rebel cause. As we shall see later, the resting site of the Westcountry army might have been discovered close to Feniton.

Of those who were injured, a number were cared for at great risk by the people of Feniton, including Cecily Kirkham of the Manor of Feniton and sister to Sir Peter Carew. As a punishment for helping the injured Westcountry men, the royal forces burnt Feniton Manor to the ground. Six years later, Lady Jane Kirkham, Sir Peter Carew's sister's (step) mother-in-law died, and, in her will, left money for the upkeep of the bridges, perhaps in memory of the hundreds of men who had lost their lives there. Sir Peter Carew later made his sister's daughter a beneficiary of his will, maybe in recompense for the destruction of her home by the King's troops.

Some of the injured men were given shelter at the Greyhound Inn at Fenny Bridges, and, according to local legend, as a penalty for his kindness, the royalists later hanged the unfortunate innkeeper from a hastily-erected gallows.

Others, the unscathed and lightly injured, escaped through the village, and, to this day, there are reported sightings of a rebel soldier carrying a musket, fleeing across the fields and up Rutt's Lane that branches off from Broad Road, close to the Old Village. There are also tales of a priest, perhaps from the battlefield, who haunts a nearby farmhouse. One other oddity that may result from the battle is the peculiar numbering of the field system around that part of Feniton. The numbers

Rutts Lane where, according to local legend, a rebel is seen carrying a musket

are consecutive, apart from Bloody Meadow, which is listed in old records as 666, a number which does not synchronize with those of the surrounding properties and grounds. Was, perhaps, the Bible's Book of Revelation's number of *The Beast* allocated to the battle site to mark the loss of life that day?

A Sword Scabbard from the site of the Battle of Fenny Bridges discovered by Graeme Smith 2019.

Fifteenth-century German coin discovered in Feniton on Castle Hill in February 2019 that gives evidence of the presence of the Landsknecht mercenaries during the Battle of Fenny Bridges. (With thanks to Nigel Scarr).

*Bloomfield
(Bloo[d]field?)*

Repeated efforts have been made to unearth artefacts of the Battle of Fenny Bridges. An arrow head lodged in an ancient tree[56] that has now long disappeared was the first item to be found, but nothing else of interest has been unearthed on what has been accepted, historically, as the main battlefield site.

In recent years, metal detectorists have discovered other archaeological objects which suggest that the site of the final stage of the battle may have taken place around Bloomfield House rather than in the field through which the main course of the river now runs. The house, which was originally known as the Fenny Bridges Inn, is situated close to the turning into Feniton, which divides the ground surrounding the site of the present bridge into two separate parcels of land. Metal detectorists have located a pile of farm implements of the Tudor period in the grounds near Bloomfield: scythes, hooks, and other items, that were typically used by the peasant army. The implements have been smashed to pieces as though impacted by something far more powerful, such as the weapons belonging to the royalists and the mercenary army. Tudor chainmail and buttons have also been discovered just north of the site.

At this time, according to early maps, the river's course was different to that of today, and there is uncertainty as to the exact location of either the original Great Bridge or St Agnes bridge which collapsed ten years after the battle and was later reconstructed. According to an Order Book of 1711, however, the Great Bridge

---

[56] Memorials of the West, Historical and Descriptive by W. V. H. Hamilton Rogers F.S.A.

stood partly in Gittisham parish, while the remaining two stood entirely in Feniton. Thus, the initial stage of the battle took place on the edge of Feniton parish, and partly in Gittisham, while the implements have been found in Feniton parish, close by the parish boundary. The Royalist army probably beat the rebels back into the ground surrounding Bloomfield and in front of the medieval Skinner's Ash Farmhouse[57]. Could it also be that *Bloo[m]field* was originally *Bloo[d]field*?

Rosary Cottage stands close by Bloomfield, and it is conjectured that this building, of medieval origins, acted as a field hospital for the injured rebels. In the grounds, according to a previous owner, is a mound, which he believes is the burial place of the dead peasant army. This is a plausible suggestion for not only would it have been a formidable task to transport between six hundred and a thousand bodies the three miles to Ottery Church, the only one of sufficient size to cater for such a large number of burials, it is highly unlikely that any parish church of the period would have accepted Catholic rebels for burial for fear of punishment. Thus, it is feasible that the Westcountry fatalities were buried on the battlefield under the mound behind Rosary Cottage. The six-foot pile of bones, which, according to Lord Coleridge in 1897, was unearthed[58] during excavations in Ottery Church, meanwhile, possibly refers to the burial site of the royalist army[59].

Today, the one feature that distinguishes the water meadow from the old A30 is a Victorian chapel that has recently been converted into holiday accommodation; however, a short walk down the lane towards the Old Village of Feniton is a memorial set in a verge that was erected in the year 2000, one year after the 450-year anniversary

---

[57] Maps in subsequent centuries indicate that this area was used for orchards and gardens. If these were present in 1549, then this would make it unlikely that this area was incorporated into the battlefield.

[58] Renovations took place in Ottery parish church during 1849, so was this when the bodies were discovered?

[59] Primary and secondary sources claim that there were about two hundred loyalists killed. Haywood, meanwhile, maintains that Russell experienced no fatalities, but his account is markedly unreliable in certain areas.

of the bloody battle on Fenny Mead. On that day, a large number of Cornishmen, dressed in Cornish kilts, came to Feniton to honour those who had died to retain the old religion, Cornwall's semi-autonomy, and her language.

Any examination of the available primary sources in order to compile a coherent and logical narrative and to identify topographical features by which events might be located must be done with considerable caution. The above account draws on the most believable and logical aspects of the primary sources and is mostly based on Hooker, letters from the Privy Council, and Haywood. The latter provides the most material, but his accounts are apt to be conflicting and confusing, particularly in his geographical descriptions. Holinshed has little to offer here as he only has a rather short description of the battleground.

Commemorating the men who died at Fenny Bridges

'.........in this meadow on 29th July, 1549, Men from Cornwall and Devon fought and died to preserve their religious faith and practice and the language in which they had been brought up.'

N.B. Under the Julian calendar, the date was probably Sunday 28th, 1549, not Monday 29th. This was just a feast day, and not a Holy Day as Hooker describes it. The nearest Holy Day was July 25th, St James' Day, which was too early.

Chapter Thirteen

The Battle of Aylesbeare Common on Windmill Hill

Windmill Hill with its commanding view from Exeter to Lyme Bay.

A few days after the Battle of Fenny Bridges, on August 2nd, Lord Grey arrived in Honiton with a thousand troops. He had wreaked a terrible revenge on rebels in Bucks, Burks, and Oxford, leaving behind him their clergy hanging from their steeples. More German infantry, Spinola with the remainder of his foot soldiers, two hundred Reading men, and the advance guard of Sir William Herbert's fierce Welshmen arrived to further swell Russell's ranks[60]. Confidently, the strengthened royal army set out to rescue Exeter.

After a brief battle at Alfington, near Ottery St Mary, the King's men marched on past the Halfway Inn on the Exeter road and set up

---

[60] For a more detailed analysis of the military strengths of the armies, refer to Julian Cornwall's book, *Revolt of the Peasantry, 1549.*

camp on Windmill Hill owned by *'Gregorye Carey, gentleman'* where they had a commanding view that swept from the valley of the Otter across to Exeter. Just three miles away was the village of Clyst St Mary, where hundreds of rebels camped. Russell needed to seize mastery of the bridge at the village in order to gain access to Exeter and relieve the siege. With the men making camp beside the windmill, Spinola hatched a plan to lure the rebels into a confrontation.

The events at Fenny Bridges proved that the rebels were not equipped to engage the royal forces in a full-scale assault. Their skill lay in the use of guerrilla warfare, while ambush was a ploy in which they excelled and one that terrified the King's forces. As Spinola explained to Russell, his men, unlike the English, were accustomed to long, hot marches and were capable of remaining vigilant throughout the night. The rebel spies, it was reasoned, would assume that the royal forces were sleeping and spring a surprise attack by dawn. Russell approved of the ploy and gave his captains instructions that the men should feign sleep but keep awake all night, ready for a presumed dawn assault.

The Westcountry rebels did not disappoint. Assuming they had the advantage over sleeping men, they stealthily crept up to the windmill from Clyst St Mary under the cover of darkness. As they prepared to launch their 'surprise' assault, the royal outposts alerted the King's troops of the imminent attack. The rebels hurled themselves at their foe, and a fierce battle ensued. A storm of arrows rained down on Russell's army as the billmen charged towards their enemy. The royal arquebusiers lacked the time to wheel their match around to fire their shot.

For a time, Russell's troops could not withstand the onslaught of the Westcountry men as, with fierce yells, they fell onto their enemy in hand-to-hand combat. According to the contemporary chronicler, Hooker, they were *'of very stout stomachs, and very valiantly did stand to their tackles.'* After strong resistance, the rebels were driven back by Spinola's firepower and Grey's lances, sustaining heavy losses. Time and time again, they regrouped, and with suicidal bravery, they threw themselves at the royal troops. Eventually, with hundreds of dead on the slopes of Windmill Hill, the Westcountry men were finally forced to withdraw.

Surrounded by stiffening corpses and with their weapons still soiled from battle, the future bishop of Exeter Myles Coverdale paraded the troops for a service of thanksgiving. Giving thanks to God for the victory over their fellow religious was one thing but, to the restless Catholic mercenaries, having to endure a sermon in an incomprehensible tongue must have seemed tedious, especially when it took precedence over breakfast. They may not have been disappointed when Coverdale was suddenly interrupted by warning cries of, '*Bows! Bows! Everyone to horse and harness!*'

The surviving peasant army, empowered by religious fervour, with insane bravery and probably expecting their foe to be pre-occupied stripping the dead of their valuables rather than being engaged in prayers, launched a further suicidal attack. Repeatedly, they threw themselves at their enemy until most of them were dead or wounded. Finally, the few who survived the weapons of the mercenaries crept back to meet with their comrades at Clyst St Mary.

That night Russell's men made camp on the high ground near the village. From their vantage point, they would have seen the lights of Exeter flicker into life as darkness fell over the East Devon landscape. Perhaps the starving citizens took courage from the red glow of the distant campfires that heralded the presence of their would-be rescuers.

Meanwhile, the rebels in Clyst St Mary, on hearing of the slaughter of their men at the windmill, sent out a call for assistance. With remarkable speed, several thousand reinforcements gathered to fight from all around and set to fortifying the village behind a defence of ramparts with the bulk of their army congregating on the green, anticipating the return of Russell's troops. They did not have long to wait.

Chapter Fourteen

Battle of Clyst St Mary, August 4th – 5th, 1549

Next morning, Myles Coverdale rallied the sleeping Catholic troops early for a further homily and morning prayers. Perhaps the mercenaries, by this time, were growing accustomed to the eccentricities of the English. Overnight, while the King's army was sleeping, according to Hooker, six thousand rebels had erected three great rampires, probably along the three roads surrounding the village of Bishop's Clyst. The area of marshland alongside the medieval bridge, which was barricaded with large felled trees, also provided further protection. Then they quietly laid in wait for their enemy.

At 9 a.m., Russell's troops attacked at full gallop, breaking through the rebels' defences, driving the defenders back to the bridge. Swiftly, a flight of arrows from the surrounding houses where Westcountry men were hiding cut down the royal army, killing many. Then, from behind them, the King's men heard the alarming flourish of trumpets and the roll of a drum. Panic-stricken, fearing yet another ambush, the royal troops fled in confusion, trampling each other to death in their terror as they ran hell for leather back towards the heath, probably to an area east of Mill Down. Others were picked off by the Cornish archers who hastened after them. In reality, however, the 'ambush' consisted only of Sir Thomas Pomeroy[61], a solitary trumpeter, and a drummer, with a few armed men, hiding in a *'furse close'*.

---

[61] Sir Thomas was married to Lord Russell's niece and it was probably this connection that enabled him to be spared the executioner's axe after the Rising, although he was incarcerated for about three years.

THE BATTLE OF FENNY BRIDGES 1549
PRELUDE AND AFTERMATH

Catching up with the royal wagons straggling behind the fleeing troops, the rebels captured great quantities of ammunition and guns, which they dragged back to the village. The King's General soon discovered the deception, rounded up his terrified army, and marched them back to Clyst St Mary with Sir William Francis leading the way down Bishop's Court Lane.

As they approached the village, they had to traverse a sunken road above which the villagers waited, armed with boulders. As the troops passed beneath them, the Westcountry men hurled the stones down upon them. One boulder landed on Sir William's head, driving his helmet down into his skull and fatally injuring him.

Following the death and realising that the area was now strongly garrisoned, Russell gave orders for the houses in which the rebel forces were hiding to be set alight. As the village blazed, those escaping the flames, villagers and rebels, were slaughtered indiscriminately by Russell's troops. They did not run, however, but with remarkable bravery fought to the death. *'Cruel and bloody was that day,'* wrote Hooker, *'for some were slain with the sword, some were burned in the houses, some shifted for themselves and were taken prisoner, and many, thinking to escape over the water, were drowned, so that the dead that day by one and other* (was) *about one thousand.'*

Russell may have seized the village, but the skilled gunner, John Hammond, was still guarding the bridge behind the barricade of trees. Russell, not able to find a volunteer to challenge the lone rebel, offered a reward of four hundred crowns to the first man who overpowered Hammond. One individual, who, says Hooker, *'was more respecting the gain than forecasting the peril, gave adventure.'* A swift movement of the hand, a flash, and an explosion despatched the reckless adventurer to eternity, leaving the bridge still under rebel control.

While everyone's attention was fixed on the drama, John Yarde, a man familiar with the area quietly crept up on the unexpecting defender who was just reloading his gun - and Hammond was no more.

*

125

Lord Grey rounded up the nine hundred survivors and marched his prisoners up to the high ground over the heath. According to

Lord Grey

contemporary writers who sought to justify the appalling act that took place, when he paused and looked back, he thought he saw, in the evening light, the sun's shimmering rays reflect off weapons in the distance, and jumped to the conclusion that they were about to be attacked again. If they had had to make a hasty retreat, the royal apologists claimed, their nine hundred prisoners would be a burden, and there was also the possibility that they would round on their captors during a fresh onslaught. It was then that a brutal order was given *'Slaughter all the prisoners!'* According to Hooker, it took only ten minutes for the cries of the dying men to fall silent. The mercenaries, no doubt, enjoyed taking revenge on the peasants who had humiliated them earlier that day.

Three hundred years later, a plough unearthed a vast quantity of bones at this spot[62], giving evidence of the mass killings that took place on the heath - an event that was one of the worst atrocities in English military history.

Bodkins from Windmill Hill and buckle, musket balls and cannonball from the Battle of Clyst St Mary discovered by William Churcher.

[62] See Rose-Troup *The Western Rebellion of 1549*, page 276.

Chapter Fifteen

Battle of Clyst Heath

News of the mass murder was carried with all speed to the rebel force laying siege to Exeter. Enraged by the brutal killings on the heath, a strong contingent of two thousand men hurried down the Topsham Road to check the progress of Russell's men. With them, they brought a large crucifix and religious regalia hoisted on a cart to remind them of the cause for which they were fighting. All night long, the peasant army worked silently around their unsuspecting sleeping enemy, preparing for a fresh attack. At dawn, they released a rain of shot that fell into the middle of the royal camp from the guns stealthily arranged around its perimeter. Taken by surprise, the King's men hastened to fight in three directions while the Royal

Landsknecht weapons

Engineers busily made a way of escape through the hedges between Clyst Heath and the Topsham road. Over this route, Russell swiftly advanced, cutting off the peasant's army line of communication with the city, and followed up on their rear guard. Surrounding them front and back, the King's General demanded their surrender. The rebels refused and, although outnumbered, outgunned, and outmanoeuvred, they continued to fight with suicidal fury. Appalled by the previous day's atrocity, they were determined to die rather than give way. According to Hooker, the ensuing attack by Grey was more of a carnage than a fight with the few survivors of the onslaught immediately executed by martial law. Such was their bravery, even their opponents admired them. Hooker says, *'Great was the slaughter and cruel was the fight and such was the valour and stoutness of these men that the Lord Grey reported himself that he never in all the wars he had been, did he know the like.'* An accolade indeed.

As evening fell on yet another bloody massacre, with two thousand more Westcountry men dead, the royal forces drew off to Topsham, carrying the body of Sir William Francis with them. That night the news of the catastrophic defeat was carried to the remaining rebels surrounding Exeter. Realising that all was lost, they released their prisoners and silently stole away in the darkness, heading west. Their cause was completely lost.

Two-handed Landsknecht swords which exceeded six foot in length. The mercenaries were paid more to wield these heavier weapons.

Chapter Sixteen

The End of the Siege of Exeter

August 6th, 1549

It was the prisoners in the tower of St Sidwell's Church, including Walter Raleigh, who first realised that the rebels had dispersed. They pounded at the East Gate but were initially ignored, the citizens thinking it was another rebel ploy. But, when they finally convinced the city's guards, they were taken straight to the Mayor, who, with great relief, spread the news. Not waiting for daylight, the starving citizens flocked out of the gates, searching for food. Such was the feasting that night, Hooker tells us, many ate themselves to death before the morning[63].

It was early, about eight the following day, when the sound of trumpets and drums warned the hollow-eyed people of Exeter that their rescuers were approaching the city. Crowds flocked to every vantage point to witness the grand procession as the King's army approached the city gates.

The victorious Carews, in full armour, on their war-horses were at the head of their servants and tenantry dressed in the heraldic colours of their house, yellow and black. Following them was the royal infantry in their brilliant livery, their coats 'guarded' with red, and their body-hose with the right leg, red, and the left, blue. The Alwayn soldiers with their long bills and staves, and the Italian and Spanish

---

[63] This was probably a result of 'Refeeding Syndrome' whereby a person suffering starvation experiences a fatal shift in electrolytes if food is introduced too rapidly.

arquebusiers, wheel-locked guns gleaming in the summer sunlight, marched beside the cavalry, under the command of Lord Grey. In all, with the arrival that day of the Welsh contingent, who turned up just in time to gather the spoils of battle, the royal force numbered about ten thousand men. Behind them were the captured weapons and wagons, stained and soiled from battle. Above the large army billowed the Royal Standard, which was hoisted victoriously beside Bedford House.

Russell's immediate problem was to replenish the city's food supplies and to provide for the hungry troops, who were camped in and around Exeter. Herbert's Welsh troops, many of whom had only joined up at the last minute when they heard of the Lord Russell's imminent victory, therefore missing the fighting but arriving in time to enjoy the plunder, added to his troubles as they rampaged through the city, sacking homes, killing livestock, and treating the inhabitants with considerable barbarity. The Welshmen's behaviour was as contemptible as that of the loathed mercenaries; however, in their greed they gorged themselves with so much bounty that they couldn't transport it out of the city, and so sold it cheaply at the local markets, thus providing Exeter's starving population with a source of supplies.

Russell set to speedily balancing the city's books, restoring the administrative lines of command that had been severed while ignoring the plundering of the churches. Those who had stayed loyal to the King were granted the lands that had been seized from the Catholic army, while those who had fought or had shown any sympathy for the insurgents were savagely treated. Many local men, even some who had been confined to bed for months and had taken no part in the Revolt, were handed over to individual members of the King's army for use as ransom as a reward for their efforts in defeating the rebels. Others, like Sir Hugh Pollard, used the situation to settle old quarrels. Families were left bereft not only of their men but were deprived of all their lands and property, leaving the county devastated and many of its people impoverished. Gallows were set up at every crossroads right across Devon, and many were hanged, drawn, and quartered in order to strike terror into the hearts of those who had supported the rebels.

THE BATTLE OF FENNY BRIDGES 1549
PRELUDE AND AFTERMATH

One of the first to be executed was the vicar of St Thomas's Church, Father Robert Welshe, a Cornishman, who, although a rebel leader, had saved Exeter from being burnt to the ground by John Hammond, the gunner from Woodbury. Hooker obviously witnessed the event and has documented it for us.

St Thomas's tower, Exeter, from where the priest and rebel leader Father Welshe was left to hang for several years. It was destroyed in 1645 during the Civil War, and rebuilt in 1657.

Bernard Duffield, whose behaviour during the siege proven him to be an unpleasant character, was appointed executioner, a position which, apparently, he enjoyed. He, says Hooker, *'....caused a pair of gallows to be made and set up on the top of the tower of the said vicar's parish church of St Thomas, and all things being ready, and the stage perfected for the tragedy, the vicar was brought to the place, and by a rope about his middle, drawn up to the top of the tower and there in chains hanged in his popish apparel, and having a holy water bucket, ... a pair of beads and such other popish trash hanged about him, and there he, with the same about him, remained a long time. He made a very small or no confession but very patiently took his death.'*

It is not recorded how long Robert Welshe took to die, but his corpse was left to dangle from the tower for several years as a warning of the fate of those who rebelled against the king until it was taken down during the reign of Queen Mary.

With the executions and reprisals in full swing, Lord Russell was shocked to be informed on August 16th, probably by the treacherous Kessell, Arundell's trusted secretary, who had always kept the King's General informed of his master's activities, that a thousand rebels had re-grouped at Sampford Courtenay. It is astonishing that they were prepared to engage the vastly superior royal troops yet again. Russell immediately set out with his entire army. The slaughter was not yet at an end.

Chapter Seventeen

The Second Battle of Sampford Courtenay

On August 16th, the King's General divided his forces into three divisions and headed for Sampford Courtenay. With Russell's arrival delayed by the heavy artillery that he hauled twenty-six miles from Exeter to the village, Lord Grey with the Italian mercenaries[64], Sir William Herbert and his troops still unscathed by battle, and a number of local people eager to purge themselves of any accusations of disloyalty to the Crown, all arrived ahead of the General. In total, his forces numbered about eight thousand.

Arundell, after fortifying Sampford Courtenay with chains stretched between the buildings as a snare for the cavalry, made excellent use of the topology of the area and planted his main force on the hill half a mile to the east of the village. He directed the remainder of his troops to stay near the church from where they attacked the royal forces at the rear. Unfortunately for Arundell, his army was greatly depleted after the heavy losses in the battles of the last few days, while others had melted away after the defeat of the siege of Exeter, hoping to lose their status as rebels against the Crown.

The two royal forces led by Grey and Herbert assailed the rebels on both sides. While Arundell's men bravely fought back by throwing themselves at their enemy in hand-to-hand combat, the defenders in the village crept up to the rear of their enemy, and, wrote Russell, *'wrought such fear into the hearts of our men as we wished our power a great deal more.'* With Arundell on the defensive, Russell arrived

---

[64] The Landsknechts had been summoned north to deal with the situation in Norfolk in early August and so played no role in the second battle of Sampford Courtenay.

Okehampton Castle

equipped with heavy artillery, and all three sections of the royal army attacked simultaneously. For an hour, the battle raged but outgunned and outnumbered, the result was inevitable. Making a brave last stand

at the end of the village, they continued to fight on, refusing to give way until nearly all of them were killed or captured, including the important rebel leader Underhill. Leaving about six hundred dead behind them, those few remaining limped away to join fresh forces at

Sampford Courtenay Church

Okehampton. Here, the royal troops slew a further seven hundred.

The Westcountry men, although outnumbered, fought with such bravery that their professional and better-equipped opponents regarded them with considerable respect. When Sir John Smythe in 1589 wrote[65] a defence of the use of the longbow, he selected the rebels of the west as providing impressive evidence of the continued

---

[65] His work was entitled: *Certain discourses written by Sir John Smythe, Knight: Concerning the formes and effects of divers sorts of Weapons, and other verie important matters Militarie, greatlie mistaken by divers of our men of warre in these dates; and chiefly, of the Mosquet, the Caliver, and the Long-bow.*

effectiveness of the weapon. He describes how Spinola and many of his mercenaries were injured while, *'The archers of the rebels did so behave themselves with their volleys of arrows against* (the) *Italian harquebusiers* (...) *that they drave them from all their strengths* (.........) *to the great effects of the archers against harquebusiers I* have heard the Lord of Hunsdon (Herbert) aforesaid (who was an eyewitness) *very notably reports: Beside that, many years past I have heard Captain Spinola, an Italian, who was a very brave soldier and wounded with arrows* (............) *give singular commendation of the archery of England.'*

That night, as Russell's men remained sitting in their saddles too fearful to dismount in case of ambush, the surviving rebels, along with Arundell, slipped away through the darkness to Launceston. There they made one more last stand, refusing to surrender. Finally, they were taken alive, their cause lost, and the male population of Devon and Cornwall left literally decimated.

Launceston Castle

Old postcard showing the rebels at Sampford Courtenay

'...........the wind fretted and wept, whispering of fear, sobbing old memories of bloodshed and despair...........In her fancy she could hear the despair of a thousand voices and the tramping of a thousand feet, and she could see the stones turn to men beside her.'

The words of Mary Yelland on Bodmin Moor from 'Jamaica Inn' by Daphne Du Maurier

Chapter Eighteen

The Captured Prisoners taken for Trial

With their feet tied underneath the bellies of their horses, and their hands secured behind them, the captured prisoners began their last journey from Cornwall. As the horses made their way over the desolate moorland and on to Exeter, the crossroads presented a grim spectacle: the corpses of their comrades garnished every hastily erected gallows in the county.

On entering the city, they passed by the tower of the church of St Thomas, where the priest dangled high above them, slowly dying of thirst, starvation, and exposure. As the procession of prisoners moved

Rougemont Castle, Exeter

up the High Street, the mercenary soldiers kept back the jeering crowds until they reached their temporary prison at Rougemont Castle.

On September 3rd, the prisoners continued their humiliating journey to the Tower of London, passing the site of the first mass slaughter of their comrades at Fenny Bridges. Here, the decaying remains of the owner of the Greyhound Inn revolved slowly in the wind as it hung from its gibbet. The Manor of Feniton, the home of Carew's sister, who was married to the Lord of the Manor, Thomas Kirkham, was burnt to the ground as a punishment for the family's aid to the injured rebels. The prisoners knew that they, too, at the end of their journey, faced the most unpleasant death that this barbarous age could devise.

This was not quite the end. A thousand more rebels made their way up the valley of the Exe, heading for Somerset. The King's army pursued them, catching up with some at Tiverton, where they were hanged, drawn, and quartered. Others were caught at King's Weston, where there was another great slaughter, followed by many executions from Dunster to Bath on August 29th.

Executions and Reprisals

Sir Anthony Kingston, a veteran of the Pilgrimage of Grace where his savage suppression of the rebels had earned him a knighthood, was a vicious and sadistic executioner who enjoyed inflicting extreme punishments with a cruel and twisted humour. Kingston was sent to the Westcountry to ensure that the people would never rebel again. Styled Provost Marshall in the Field, he had earned himself a notorious reputation for savage and twisted cruelty by contemporary writers such as Richard Grafton (c1507-1572) who, despite not being sympathetic to the rebel cause, recorded examples of the brutality Kingston displayed when acting as the executioner in the West.

The son of Sir William Kingston, Lord of Painswick Manor, Gloucestershire, Kingston had gained himself a reputation for his sadistic behaviour in the locality at an early age, and was hatred by his neighbours. One little vignette mentioned by Rose-Troup well describes the character of the man. One day, Kingston was riding past a churchyard when he witnessed several people standing there with a corpse. Upon questioning them, he learnt that the vicar had refused to bury the body until he had been paid his dues. Kingston dealt with the situation in his customary manner. He summoned the clergyman to appear before him immediately and, after a short conversation with the man, ordered that the mourners toss the parson into the grave, and bury him alive, instead of the corpse. This clearly was not a man who would deal compassionately with the Westcountry men.

Further insight into his character is provided by his involvement with the torturing of the famous Protestant, twenty-six-year-old Anne Askew. After preaching on the streets of London and leaving her Catholic husband on the grounds he was not a Christian, she was imprisoned in the Tower of London where Sir Anthony was Constable of the Tower. He was ordered to ensure that she confess the names of her fellow Protestants, possibly in the hope of implicating Queen Catherine Parr, Henry's sixth wife. Kingston put Anne to the rack where her ankles and wrists were tied and the wheel turned until she was held taut a few inches above the table. In her own account, she says she fainted from the pain and was twice revived so the procedure could be repeated. She bravely endured the torture and refused to surrender the names of her fellow Protestants. Even the sadistic Kingston, however, declined to continue the brutality, and left the chamber to seek an audience with the King to request that he not be forced to continue. Henry VIII granted his wish, but Lord Chancellor Wriothesley and his side-kick, Richard Rich had no such scruples, and continued the grisly work. Anne's cries could be heard, it was reported, in the garden next to the White Tower where the Lieutenant's wife and daughter were walking. She gave no names, and her ordeal ended when the Lieutenant ordered her to be returned to her cell. Anne was the only woman recorded as having endured

The Tower of London

torture in the Tower, and maybe this was one novelty that even Kingston could not relish.[66]

Three years after the torture and burning of Anne Askew, Kingston was despatched to the Westcountry to inflict the King's justice, with his own original brand of cruelty, on the people of Devon and Cornwall. Grafton, despite his lack of sympathy for the rebels, reported the following two stories about Kingston's behaviour, when fulfilling his duties in the West.

Mayor Bowyer of Bodmin was thrilled and honoured one day, Grafton informs us, to receive a letter from Sir Anthony inviting himself and others to dinner. Bowyer had been forced, it was said, to support the rebels under threat of the destruction of his property, and it was the former mayor, not Bowyer, who had actively and willingly taken part in the Rising. Bowyer felt no fear of punishment as he naively believed that Kingston would sympathise with the fact that he had only supported the rebels as he was under duress. On the day of the visit, he welcomed Kingston and his party by supplying an impressive spread for dinner, but before the Provost Marshall sat down to dine, he took Bowyer to one side. He whispered to him that an execution was to take place of a rebel sympathiser that evening, and he would appreciate the Mayor's co-operation in the proceedings.

---

[66] Anne was burnt shortly after at Smithfield, London, on 16th July 1546, along with John Lascelles and two other Protestants. She was carried to her execution in a chair wearing just a thin garment as she was unable to walk. Anne was dragged to the stake that had a small seat attached to it, which she sat astride. Chains were used to bind her body firmly to it at the ankles, knees, waist, chest, and neck. Because of her refusal to recant, she was burned alive slowly rather than being strangled first or burned quickly. Those who witnessed her execution were impressed by her remarkable courage and reported that she did not scream until the flames reached her chest. The execution lasted about an hour and Anne was unconscious and probably dead after fifteen minutes or so. Prior to their death, the young Protestants were offered one last chance of pardon. Bishop Shaxton mounted the pulpit and began to preach to them. His words were without impact, however. Anne, in spite of her sufferings, listened carefully throughout his sermon. When he spoke the truth, she expressed her agreement, but when said anything contrary to Scripture, she called out, '*There he misseth, and speaketh without the book.*' Immediately after, the fire was kindled.

Bowyer, delighted to be presented with the opportunity to ingratiate himself with his important guest, readily agreed to erect the gallows for the Provost Marshall. After the lavish meal, Sir Anthony asked the Mayor if he had done as requested. Bowyer, no doubt curious to know which of his neighbours was about to be dragged to his execution, enthusiastically agreed that the scaffold was ready. Rising from the table, the executioner took him by the hand and led his host to the site prepared for the execution.

'*Do you think they are strong enough?*' said the Provost Marshall to the Mayor, when they arrived at the site.

'*Oh yes, Sir!*' said the Mayor.

'*Well then,*' said Kingston to the Mayor, '*Get you even up to them for they are provided for you.*'

The Mayor, horrified, cried out in shock and distress, '*I trust you mean no such thing to me!*'

'*Sir,*' said Kingston, '*there is no remedy, you have been a busy rebel, and therefore this is appointed for your reward.*'

Without further hesitation, the poor Mayor was hanged until dead.

Leaving the Mayor swinging from his own gallows, Kingston moved on to a nearby town where a miller had taken part in the Rising. The miller had warning of the visit, however, and planned to be out of town. Before his departure, he instructed his servant to tell Kingston that he was the miller and had been so for the past four years. When Kingston asked the question, the servant obediently replied, '*I am the miller, Sir, and have been these last few years.*'

The servant was grabbed by Kingston's men and dragged to a nearby tree.

'*You have been a rebellious knave, and therefore here you shall hang,*' said Kingston to the terrified servant.

'*But Sir, I am not the miller, but just his servant*' the poor man blurted out in terror.

'*Well then,*' said Kingston, '*you are a false knave in two tales, therefore hang him up.*' After he was hanged, a spectator is reported to have said to the Provost Marshall, '*Surely this was but the miller's man?*'

'*What then,*' jeered Kingston, '*could he ever have done his master better service than to hang for him?*'

Kingston continued to travel throughout the area, performing executions characterised with his sadistic humour. He then set loose the royal troops to rape and cause desecration in the region on whomever or wherever they chose, whether rebel or loyalist. '*Such was the trail of death and terror,*' says Rose-Troup, '*with gallows scattered plentifully over the two beautiful counties, putrefying bodies polluting the atmosphere, a veritable shambles on an enormous scale; the people cowering in hiding places, the innocent fearing that some spiteful neighbour would accuse them, and the guilty.....those who remained true to the faith in which they had been nurtured.........seeking refuge in vain.*'[67] It is no wonder that from this time people dated all further events as either before the Commotion Time or after it, and the term became the stock phrase in the law courts, and elsewhere.

By the time that he and Russell had carried out their grim task, about one-tenth of the entire male population, and as many as one-fifth of the men of Cornwall, and possibly one-half of those of fighting age, had been killed in battle, murdered by their captors or executed in the subsequent reprisals. Such was the extreme cruelty inflicted on the Cornish in particular that for a hundred years after the Commotion Time people would spit on the ground at the very mention of Kingston's name. Even today, the Cornish have not forgotten the brutality they suffered at the hands of the executioner of the West.

---

[67] *The Western Rebellion of 1549* by Frances Rose-Troup, p.311

The true English judge delivers the sentence of law, which he is compelled to pronounce, with the most impressive solemnity and pities those whom he condemns to die. An assassin may laugh in the midst of murder, but few can practise the deliberate barbarity of Sir Anthony Kingston.

(The History of Cornwall: From the Earliest Records and Traditions, to the Present Times. Published 1824 by Fortescue.)

*

Such was the combined death toll from the battles during the three summer months of 1549 and the executions that followed that some Cornish today regard the slaughter as a case of ethnic cleansing by the English and refer to the Cross of St George as the Butcher's Apron.

Warning:

The next chapter is not for the squeamish.

Chapter Nineteen

The Significance of Punishment by Hanging, Drawing, and Quartering

This brutalising punishment, the most barbaric ever devised by an English government, was meted out regularly over a period of five hundred years, and all who rebelled against the monarchs, including the Westcountry men, risked this form of execution. It was a punishment excessively used by Judge Jeffreys a century later, following Monmouth's rebellion in 1685 when he sentenced hundreds of Westcountry prisoners to be hanged, drawn, and quartered. At least ten from the neighbourhood of Feniton, which included nine who were working on the building of Escot House, and John Lee from the neighbouring village of Payhembury, likely suffered this extreme form of punishment for supporting Monmouth. Following those executions, the body parts, including the head, were boiled in the vast sizzling cauldrons of pitch that lined the streets of places such as Honiton, and Dorchester, to preserve them, giving rise to the saying, *'Go boil your head!'* The body pieces were then displayed on trees and poles, while church steeples and houses were covered with the heads, rendering the illusion from a distance that a flock of crows had settled on the buildings. This form of punishment enabled Jeffreys to boast that he had more men sentenced to a barbaric death than any judge since the invasion of William the Conqueror. By the time he had completed his grisly work, Jeffreys had turned the West Country into a scene straight from hell. This most repulsive form of execution was continued until 1782, when David Tyrie, a Scottish naval clerk of Portsmouth, was the last victim to suffer.

To appreciate the significance of the stages of hanging, drawing, and quartering to the English, it is necessary to understand that when this form of execution was first introduced the people were steeped, through the influence of the Catholic Church, in a culture of ritual and symbolism. The practice of heraldic display, for instance, included much symbolism that was associated with rank and status. The whole intention of hanging, drawing, and quartering was to symbolically obliterate the victim's physical, social, and spiritual standing, literally, bit by bit with the purpose of completely erasing all evidence of the individual's existence from the earth.

At the first stage of the execution, a man was relieved of his horse, weapons, coat of arms, and, if he was of an appropriate rank, his knighthood, thus removing from him all symbols of his earthly status. He might then be tethered onto a starved and skeletal horse that further emphasised his fall from the higher echelons of society. Any remaining finery was stripped from him, and he was forced to wear a surcoat with his arms reversed to show that he no longer qualified to bear a coat of arms, a powerful symbol of social status and respect. In a mocking parody of his claims, which might be to the throne, a crown of weeds was placed on his head. The meaning of these symbols would have been obvious to the large crowds who gathered to enjoy the spectacle. A man who previously had had complete authority over them became the target for their wrath as an expression of both their real and perceived injustices. He was now totally defenceless to their taunts, insults, jeers, missiles, and the blare of horns and trumpets that accompanied him on his agonising journey to his assumed hellish eternity.

Hanging was a sentence usually suffered by thieves in the Middle Ages. The felon was made to stand on the back of a cart, chair, or ladder and a noose placed around his neck. The stage beneath his feet was then pulled away, and the rope sharply tightened around the victim's throat as his body sharply plummeted its full length. Death was either caused by asphyxiation or by the restriction of the blood supply to the brain through the carotid arteries. In either case, the hanged person might remain conscious for a few seconds or even minutes, depending on the noose and the way they dropped. When the prisoner became semi-consciousness, his body would start to spasm, all control would be lost over the bowels and bladder, and his face became blue with the tongue and eyes protruding. To ensure that life was extinguished, the man was left to hang for an hour. In the case of hanging, drawing, and quartering however, the short drop was used from a high platform so that the victim could be revived for the next part of the procedure, which would be highly visible to the thronging crowds, eager for the next stage of the entertainment.

Cold water would be thrown over the man to revive him, and he would regain consciousness to the sight of the leaping flames of the cauldron of fire placed before him, waiting to burn his entrails while he remained alive. At this stage the victim was at times castrated, symbolically removing his claim to masculinity and power, and metaphorically ending his lineage and name[68] from the earth.

Many medieval scholars maintained that once a man was corrupt then that corruption resided in his bowels and heart. The heart was also associated with love and passion and, therefore, with the crime with which the victim was accused. A skilled executioner aimed to keep his victim alive as long as possible as he cut through the abdomen and removed the bowels, thus revealing the source of corruption to the crowd and the victim. If the executioner had accomplished his task successfully, the dying man's last image before he was cast into a hellish eternity was that of his entrails being tossed into the waiting cauldron for the corruption to be obliterated by the purifying flames.

The head was then removed and, at times, thrown to the waiting crowd who kicked it around like a football and desecrated it by decorating its sockets with weeds and rubbish. It was then placed on a pike and sent to London or a nearby place of local importance where it would be paraded up and down to the usual fanfare of horns and drums before being hoisted onto its final, and very public, resting place.

Finally, the body would be chopped into four quarters for public edification in various places to serve as a warning of the fate awaiting those who were a threat to the king either by accident, birth, or by rebellion.

---

[68] Based on *Anatomy of an Execution* by 'Jules' in '*Lady Despenser's Scribery*'.

The integrity of the body at death was very important during the Middle Ages and Christian belief to many dictated that it was crucial for spiritual reasons that the body remained complete. According to Christ's teaching, at the time of the resurrection, the spirit of the Christian would become reunited with the physical remains again and would rise from the dead. Therefore, to have one's corporeal parts littered about the country was tantamount to being denied a chance of salvation in eternity - a devastating concept to the poor individual who faced such a barbaric death, and a consequence that is often forgotten by writers of history. The condemned man or woman[69] not only faced social and physical obliteration in the most brutal way that man could devise but spiritual obliteration as well. Hanging, drawing, and quartering, therefore, effectively evicted the victim not only from their class or cause, and the earth, but also, devastatingly, from heaven.

It was on January 27th, 1550, that four rebel leaders of the Western Rising, Humphrey Arundell, John Wynslade, John Bury, and Thomas Holmes were taken to their execution by hanging, drawing, and quartering. Others, including several priests, met a similar fate later. They had to endure being dragged three miles at the heels of horses over wet, muddy ground and rough cobbles to the jeers of the waiting crowd until they reached Tyburn. When the sentence was completed, the Rising was finally at an end. Devon and Cornwall were completely crushed.

Such was the severity of the reprisals taken against the Westcountry that neither county ever rose in a county-wide revolt again. It had been the first and the last time that Devon attempted a full-scale rebellion.

---

[69] The elderly Lady Lisle was condemned to this form of execution by Judge Jeffreys, but the King intervened and ordered that she be merely hanged.

THE BATTLE OF FENNY BRIDGES 1549
PRELUDE AND AFTERMATH

When Arundell and his fellow prisoners were finally brought to trial in London it was ordered that *'....on that gallows (they were to be) suspended and while yet alive to be cast down upon the ground and the entrails of each to be taken out and burnt before their eyes while yet living and their heads cut off and their bodies to be divided into four parts.'*

Chapter Twenty

Aftermath

Only three years later, on July 6th, 1553, Edward died, and Catholicism was briefly restored under his sister Mary I. She had suffered long imprisonment under both her father and half-brother and was even cruelly prevented from visiting her dying mother. Resolutely determined to return the realm to Rome, her policy was supported by some vengeful Catholic subjects who had some old scores to settle. Her victims, which numbered nearly three hundred, included Bishops Ridley, Latimer, Hooper, and former Archbishop Cranmer, who, for their refusal to recognise the Mass, were consigned to the flames for their faith.

Bishop John Hooper who was burnt in 1555 for his criticism of the doctrines of the Catholic Church and a piece of the actual stake upon which he died.

More than two hundred lay people also suffered the grim penalty, including pregnant women, blind children, old men and women, and even a baby, whose mother, Perrotine Massey, through sheer terror, gave birth as she was burning. The baby was thrown into the flames.

If Mary had not died prematurely at forty-two years old and, especially if she had produced an heir, England would almost certainly have been returned to the Catholic fold, and her remaining Protestant population would not have escaped the bloodbaths that plagued Europe during Rome's counter-attack when she determined to restore her jurisdiction over those who had escaped from her totalitarian state.

For more than a hundred years until near the closing decade of the seventeenth century, Rome's determination to re-establish her power base that had been greatly weakened by the Reformation resulted in Catholic monarchs promoting severe persecutions and mass killings of Protestant Christians, including the French St Bartholomew's Day Massacre in 1572. These murderous onslaughts on Protestants continued in Catholic countries until the end of the seventeenth century, and resulted in the near-genocide of an entire Christian people, the Waldenses, who experienced the worst atrocities ever known in history at the instigation of the papacy[70]. England was spared this terrible fate by the premature death of Queen Mary, and her failure to produce an heir, which removed any chance of the papacy creating an English bloodbath as it did in countries that had

---

[70] The details of these persecutions are well-recorded and based on reports from eyewitnesses. The historian Leger whose family witnessed the events that took place during the papal-inspired and orchestrated attacks on the European Protestants recorded the tragic and terrible history of the persecutions of these people and their forerunners, both prior to and after the Reformation. The descriptions of the barbarous attacks on the Christian people of Europe who for centuries led lives based on the teachings of the Bible are too horrible to describe here. Leger, who records the dreadful acts says, '*My hand trembles, so that I scarce even hold the pen, and my tears mingle in torrents with my ink, while I write the deeds of these children of darkness—blacker even than the Prince of Darkness himself.*' The crimes exceed those inflicted by the Roman Empire on the Christians of the first three centuries. They are described by Wylie in his nineteenth-century volumes on the History of Protestantism which are freely available from the internet.

not separated itself from papal jurisdiction. We also owe Henry a debt of gratitude as his ejection of the papacy played a crucial role in protecting England from this bloody backlash. Maybe we should even review the reputation or at least temper our opinion of the irascible and tyrannical king.

*

In 1558, Mary was succeeded by Queen Elizabeth I and the Church of England became established. She, while wisely keen to not create a window into men's souls, was forced to protect herself from the very real threat of Catholic assassination which became severe after 1570 when Pope Pius VI proclaimed Elizabeth to be excommunicated. This action served to declare open season on the Queen by encouraging any Catholic determined to drag England back under papal domination to commit regicide without fear of condemnation by Rome. The several plots against Elizabeth, including that of the Northern Earls 1569, Ridolfi 1571, Throckmorton 1583, and Babington 1586 - were all Catholic-inspired or attracted Catholic support. The three Armadas, similarly, were sent by Catholic Spain to invade England and overthrow her monarch, while there were numerous rumours of plots to place Catholic Queen Mary Stuart or Arabella Stuart on the English throne. Such treasonous activities troubled loyal English Catholics, placing them at risk, and hardened Protestant resolve.

Catholics suspected of treason were confronted with what was known as 'The Bloody Question' which asked, *'If the Pope invaded England, would you support him or the Queen?'* An honest Catholic could, unhappily, only provide one answer which made them guilty of treason and, therefore, subject to the death sentence. Their situation, perhaps, can be regarded as analogous to that of Germans living in Britain during World War II. Just as they were regarded as a potential threat, and ran the risk of imprisonment, so, to the Elizabethans, any Catholic was also naturally a potential traitor and had to be dealt with in the customary way. Inevitably those who were prepared to remain loyal would be regarded with the same suspicion, and became a persecuted minority, as the official Church of England became established.

The very real Catholic threat to England triggered ten years of tyrannical suppression that led to priests, Jesuits, and the laity, including children, being hauled from their homes and locked away in dungeons and jails, such as the Bridwell. Here they were subjected to severe cruelty typical of the age. Priests and laity were strung high by their hands for many hours a day till driven mad with pain and kept without sleep until they lost their wits prior to interrogation on the rack. Such were their sufferings, their ultimate fate of hanging, drawing, and quartering was regarded with anticipation as a final escape from their sufferings.

The situation of the English Catholics was expressed well by one onlooker at the execution of Jesuit Edmund Campion in 1581, one-time favourite of the Queen. As Campion died by hanging, mercifully, by design or miscalculation, before he was dismembered, a witness cried out: '*In your Catholicism, all treason is contained.*'[71] Even those who gave shelter to the priests, including poor Margaret Clitheroe who, with appalling cruelty, and against the wishes of Queen Elizabeth, was crushed to death with heavy weights on the scaffold in 1586, suffered terribly for their devotion to the papacy.

It is perhaps a stretch for the Catholic Church to dignify many of those executed during this time with the title of 'martyr' as they were, under the law, criminals, and some were certainly a proven threat to the life of Queen Elizabeth. They played a role in the twenty-five known Jesuit-led assassination plots. This does not, however, detract from the undoubted fact that a number lost their lives as a consequence of being unhappily torn in the conflict between their religious allegiance to the pope and their political allegiance to a queen they respected. They died on account of their consciences rather than any act of deliberate treason.

The sons of those who had taken part in the Western Rising, even during the reign of Elizabeth, still maintained their Catholic roots and produced a number of young men who went overseas to train for the

---

[71] *The Catholics* by Roy Hattesley, p.148

priesthood. When they returned, they were secretly appointed as priests in the large houses owned by Catholic landowners. It was rare that they could return to Devon or Cornwall, though, for the large landowners of the South-West peninsular were staunchly Protestant. Consequently, by the mid-seventeenth century, Westcountry Catholicism had died out, and the region became firmly Puritan.

Of those who took part in the Western Rising, Russell was granted extensive properties, including those confiscated from Lord Protector Somerset, Edward VI's uncle, and an earldom. Somerset was thrown into the Tower for his inept management of the Rising. He was released but was rearrested and executed on 22nd January 1552. The psychopathic Sir Anthony Kingston, the brutal executioner, was arrested for his treasonous role in the Dudley Plot that aimed to overthrow Queen Mary. He committed suicide, some say by throwing himself and his horse into the Thames rather than face the gibbet, thus denying history a piece of poetic justice. Cranmer, the author of the Prayer Book, was burnt at the stake in 1553 for his Protestant faith.

Exeter's Mayor Blackaller was rewarded with a knighthood for his skilled and successful management of the siege. The city, meanwhile, was granted both the Manor of Exe Island and the title of *Semper Fidelis* - For Ever Faithful, by Queen Elizabeth I for its consistent loyalty to the throne. For a further three hundred years, on August 6th, the city and her dignitaries in full regalia celebrated the relief of Exeter in a service of thanksgiving in the cathedral.

Elizabeth Arundell lost her husband to the executioner's axe, while her sons were deprived of their inheritance, and Humphrey's property transferred to Sir Gawen Carew. Within a few years, Elizabeth married Thomas Cary of Cary and had a further eight children. She died on 24th November 1565.

A short time after Mary I ascended the throne, and with plans made for her to marry King Philip of Spain, a warrant was sent to the Sheriff of Devon, Sir Thomas Denys, for the arrest of the two Carews, Sir Gawen and his nephew Sir Peter. They were both implicated in Wyatt's plot to overthrow the Catholic Queen and charged with high treason. Sir Gawen and his co-conspirators were caught, and two were imprisoned in the Castle of Exeter, while one was placed in the dungeon of the Guildhall before they were transported to the Tower of London. Sir Peter escaped by posing as a servant and made his way to France. Later, his uncle and his companions were surprisingly acquitted and were fortunate to escape with their lives. Sir Gawen was to survive to the age of eighty. John Bodley, one of the wealthy merchants who provided the funds for the royalist army that led to the rescue of Exeter, fled abroad with his family to escape the Marian persecution of Protestants. He lived first in Frankfort before moving to Geneva, where he joined Myles Coverdale and John Knox. Bodley and Coverdale must have been close friends as he named one of his sons after the Bible translator. Bodley became a printer and, with his friends, translated and printed a new version of the English Bible which bears his name. The fresh translation was circulated throughout England when the ascension of Elizabeth I made it safe for the Geneva reformers to return to their homeland. Bodley settled in London, where he returned to his previous occupation. In 1588, he provided the Crown with two hundred pounds to contribute towards the cost of protecting the nation against the Spanish Armada, so he must have been a successful businessman. The name of his son Sir Thomas Bodley is immortalised today as Oxford's famous university library was named after him.

The execution of the rebel leaders was not quite the end of the Rising: there was one other important aftermath that was played out forty-six years after their death that has received little attention.

The story is to be found in a Latin document written between 1594 and early 1595 by Tristram Wynslade, grandson of William Wynslade, the executed rebel leader[72]. It is held in the Library of Congress's Rare Books and Special Collections, which is part of the Hans Kraus Sir Francis Drake Collection and is called *The Present State of Cornwall and Devon*. It is a 'top secret' document written for King Philip of Spain, which describes the benefits of invading England and converting it back to Catholicism.

---

[72] *Tristram Winslade – the desperate heart of a Catholic in exile:* a thesis written by Cheryl Hayden. N.B. The name is spelt as either Winslade or Wynslade in the literature.

Tristram was the grandson of John, the rebel leader, and son of William Wynslade and Jane Babington, a former nun, of Ottery St Mary, Devon. Like the other sons of the executed leaders of the Western Rising, William lost his inheritance and was reduced to eking out an existence by wandering around the countryside, earning an impoverished living as a minstrel. Tristram lived with his parents until he was ten and was then sent as a gentleman-servant to the house of Sir John Arundell at Lanherne. Here he probably became friends with the two landless sons of Humphrey Arundell, Richard and Humphrey.

By 1574, the documents prove that Tristram was in the service of Philip of Spain, and, by 1583, he was a student at the English College of Douai, an establishment for the education of well-bred English Catholics who desired to train for the English Mission that aimed to restore England to the Catholic fold.

In 1588, he was aboard the Armada ship *Nusetra Senora del Roscino,* which foundered off the coast of England. Tristram was captured by Sir Francis Drake and taken to London where he was racked by the Queen's master torturer, Sir Richard Topcliffe, yet bravely stuck to his fabricated story that he had been forced aboard the Spanish ship to act as an interpreter, following the invasion. After his torture, he was kept prisoner for nearly two years until the Privy Council finally ordered his release. Tristram immediately embarked on a legal battle to be recognised as the new Earl of Devon, but he lost his fight and returned to Brussels, the heart of English Catholic resistance.

By 1595, Tristram, destitute, starving, and desperate for the restoration of his family's lands, devised a plan for King Philip of Spain that supplied him with sufficient intelligence to lead a successful invasion force into Cornwall, recapture England for the Roman Catholic Church, and set an English Catholic ruler on the throne of England. According to Tristram's document, he was determined to rid England of the Protestantism that had *'taken the profane and heretical rites.............(from)...............the stinking pit of the Calvinists'.* Crucially, however, he did not plot for the assassination of the Queen but intended that an Englishman should succeed following the natural death of Elizabeth I.

Surprisingly, given that the document is unencrypted, it lists Tristram's main conspirators. This includes Gabriel Denys, who had strong connections not only with the English Privy Council but also with the Catholic families of the Westcountry. Denys had also been an advisor to Don Juan, brother of Philip of Spain, and was, by 1598, serving Father Hart, who was one of two priests described as determining *'all courses for England'* with responsibility for collecting money to fund the English Catholic exiles. One other co-conspirator was the popular Richard Bray, who had strong connections with Cornwall. Tristram also had an affiliation with one of the Council's most wanted traitors, the head of the Catholic Mission, Robert Parsons, with his network of spies. The other notable conspirators listed in the document were none other than Sir William Courtenay and Sir Francis Godolphin, the very men charged with the responsibility for defending the West against Spanish attack.

In 1596, the Privy Council received alarming news: King Philip was about to use *'all his force for the recovery of England from heresy'* and install his intended bride, the *infanta* of Spain, and Cardinal Albert of Austria as joint rulers of England. One hundred Spanish ships set sail for the Cornish coast, where their allies waited anxiously for a view of the approaching armada and its nine thousand men, intent on conquering the island, deposing the Queen, and presenting England for conversion to the Pope. There must have been much excitement when the men keeping watch at Plymouth and Penzance caught the first sight of the approaching galleons, heading for the Cornish coast. However, a strong north-easterly wind developed at the crucial time to batter the harbours which were waiting to receive the invading force. The large fleet struggled to lay anchor close to the shore, but the wind was so strong that it beat the invaders back. Forty of the ships sank, causing great loss of life, while the rest were forced to retreat. This time, it was her notorious weather, and not Britannia, that saved England, her Queen, and the Protestant Reformation from destruction.

No evidence exists that suggests that the Crown ever discovered that one of the chief conspirators of the treacherous plot to invade England and overthrow the Protestant Reformation was a disgruntled descendant of one of the executed leaders of the Prayer Book Rebellion.

The Spanish King had, in fact, behaved duplicitously. He had used Tristram's intelligence and his network of co-conspirators but had failed to follow the arranged plan. The Westcountry men were anxious not to act as traitors: they were Englishmen first and Catholics second. Their intention was not to threaten the safety of the Queen, and they intended that the invasion should wait until she had died of natural causes. They also planned to replace her with a Catholic Englishman. Philip, however, had clearly dispensed with their main tenets of the invasion plan and plotted to depose and, perhaps, assassinate the Queen and replace her with a Spanish Catholic monarch. In these circumstances, would the English conspirators, such as Godolphin and Courtenay, have resisted the Spanish as they marched through the Westcountry on their way to London? Alternatively, would they have acquiesced and offered no resistance to the invaders? If the English plotters had kept their part of the bargain, despite the King of Spain's premature invasion, Elizabeth would have been made a prisoner in the Tower or even executed. A Spanish queen, and her Catholic husband, would have then replaced her on the English throne, and England would once again be under papal domination. Following the success of the invasion plans, if Philip kept his promise, Wynslade's fortunes, too, would have been reversed, his family lands restored, and he would have been able to return safely to his own country at last. There is evidence that Philip would have honoured his part of the bargain as he later endowed Tristram with money in 1597 in recognition of his sufferings, despite the failure of the invasion plan.

Tristram, before his (supposed) death in 1606[73], continued to champion the Catholic cause and planned to establish a new secure

---

[73] His 'death' may have been one of convenience, given the dangers created by the Gunpowder Plot 1605 as it was reported that certain 'dead' men were seen walking about in Brussels after that time. It may also explain the statement in the Douay College Diaries which states: '.......on 31 January 1611, Mr Winslade, "*a nobleman" arrived at the Douai College from England and stayed with us here for*

homeland for persecuted Catholics in America. However, he failed to accomplish his ambitions and never managed to regain his family's lands and wealth, nor the title of Earl of Devon. At least, on his death, he was honoured by the Catholic Church by being buried in the English College, Douai.

Whether Wynslade's attempt to restore his family's lands and wealth to his possession and England to the jurisdiction of Rome would have been successful had his plans not been dashed by the strong north-easterly wind that defeated his cherished ambitions, we shall never know for sure. However, we can be certain that the failure of his treasonous activity marked the closure of the final chapter of the Prayer Book Rebellion.

---

three or four days then on account of some business he left from here to Brussels from which parts he returned to us again and on his return stayed with us for three or four days'. Tristram probably lived for several more years in peaceful obscurity, perhaps in Cornwall.

Chapter Twenty-One

Rebels or Heroes?
Developing the Rebels' Perspective.

Throughout the ages, the reframing of a historical narrative by the victorious parties nearly always ensures that the voices of the defeated are obliterated from the public consciousness. The courageous local men who fought in the Prayer Book Rebellion, over the centuries, have been denigrated by England's historians who followed in the tradition of the contemporary chronicler Hooker. Writing many years after the event, the security of the Elizabethan Settlement gave him free rein to colour the interpretation of the Rising with heavy Protestant overtones. He readily dismissed the local men of the South West as being mere ignorant rebels against the Crown. He refers to the Westcountry peasants and their gentry leaders who beseeched the Council to respect the terms of the old King's will by maintaining the *status quo* until Edward reached the age of majority as '*refuse, scum and rascals,*' and the '*worse the man…the greater his authority.*' Relying on Hooker's account, English historiography for centuries has consistently dismissed the story told by the voices of the men in their Articles to the King, and it has repeatedly failed to recognise that the Cornish not only fought to retain their religion but also their culture and heritage. Consequently, the account of their terrible suffering, high principles, outstanding bravery, and brutal suppression has largely been expunged from the history books.

Throughout the last two hundred years, it has been made easy for the reader of modern histories to align themselves with the Government cause and approve the ruthless determination to eliminate the challenge to its policies. Even historians of the stature of Professor Mackie, in his great tome on the early Tudors in the Oxford History of England, ignores the significance of the movement and dismisses the greatest threat to the Edwardian Reformation in just five lines, while writing off the brave Westcountry men as mere troublemaking rebels. Similarly, the importance of the outcome of the Battle of Fenny Bridges, which had the potential to change the course of English history, has consequently been unappreciated.

The men who took part in the Prayer Book Rebellion certainly did not view themselves as rebels but rather as petitioners. They believed that a young king was being manipulated by powerful advisors, and they sought to take legal action to persuade the Government to respect the old King's will, an action sanctioned, in certain cases, by English constitutional law. In this belief, they were mistaken. Edward was a Protestant by conviction who read ten chapters of the Bible every morning, and is described as being more determined in his Protestant zeal than was his uncle.

The 'petitioners' of Devon and Cornwall, inevitably, did not comprehend the wider picture that dictated the necessity of reform[74], and it is open to debate just how much they understood the issues at stake. The contemporary documents at the time repeatedly accuse the priests of taking advantage of the peasants as a means of securing the situation to their own advantage, and they make it clear that the rebels did not understand the theological reasons for the great change. This general view was encapsulated in the Elizabethan *'Homily against Rebellion'*. The document criticises the rebels for using the banner of the Five Wounds as their emblem because they had no understanding of the meaning of the wounds of Christ as depicted on the *'ragge'* by some *'leude paynter'* for they did not *'haue the cross of Christ painted in their hartes'*. What they certainly did comprehend was something much more mundane: the move to return to a purer version of early biblically-based Christianity, which stripped medieval Catholicism of a number of its traditions, would fundamentally change every aspect

---

[74] See *The Historical Context: the Protestant Perspective of the Western Rising* in the appendix.

of their existence and abolish the structures on which their society was based.

A document entitled, *La Response du People Anglois a Leur Roi Edouard*, published in France in 1550, the year of the execution of the leaders, clarifies the intentions of the Westcountry petitioners and describes their views of the situation. It was written, it is believed, by the leaders of the Rising or was certainly condoned by them. It describes their distress at the King's accusation of rebellion and raises their concern that Edward should respect his father's will by leaving the Act of Six Articles on the statute book until he reached the age of twenty-four. This would have ensured the continuation of Catholic doctrine for another twelve years. The document also reasonably emphasised the dangers of alienating Catholic Europe at a time when England was vulnerable and not in a position to successfully withstand an invasion from her European Catholic neighbours. It ends with a patriotic plea to the King: '....*accept your very humble and very obedient subjects, whose desire is to be dogs appointed to keep your house and your kingdom and the oxen to cultivate your land and the asses to carry your burdens. We will pray the Lord God, who holds and turns the heart of kings where he wills to watch over and conduct your young age.*' They continue to beg the King to understand that..... '*it is not the devil's persuasion, it is not the light headedness of the people, the simplicity of the ignorant, nor the temerity of the seditious which caused us to assemble. It is more the particular responsibility each of us owes his friend, the common displeasure at seeing the religion that our ancestors, so greatly revered over the past twelve hundred years, is now, at the caprice of two or three, so much changed and reduced by new ways, that the old men amongst us will die, and the young people will reach extreme old age before understanding that which commends them for salvation.*'[75] These were not the words of rebels, but of reasonable subjects

---

[75] While this illustrates their attitude prior to the siege of Exeter, it is important to note that their tone changed as the city weakened and their new demands were prefaced with the words: '*We will have...*' At this juncture, it would be difficult to maintain they were merely petitioning the King. From this point, they crossed the line.

pleading, according to the law, to their king who they believed was under the evil influence of men motivated by self-interest.

To understand the motives, laudable or seditious, that drove the Westcountry men to resist the new policy of the Crown and to assess the veracity of the French document, we need to briefly review the main events that had sculptured their mindset by 1549. There can be no question that the situation in which they found themselves and that threatened all they held dear must have seemed very unjust and the culmination of two decades of bewildering royal vacillations of policy. During the first two decades after the Reformation parliament first sat, the tales of the twists and turns of events that marked the King's attempt to struggle free of the influence of popes and emperors trickled down to the people of the South West. His treatment of his queens, his vacillating policy, and his contradictory religious positions in response to the political need of the day inevitably eroded the respect an effective monarch required from his subjects. The duplicitous terror-tactics and vicious cruelty employed by the King following the pre-cursor of the Western Rising in 1536 further soured the peoples' view of their monarch. Henry had also exacerbated the resentment towards the Crown by reneging on the compensation owed to the people of the peninsular for the loss of their horses commandeered to defeat the rise of the northern men. The whispers of the unsavoury courtly intrigues that marked the vacillating progress of the King's Great Matter fuelled village gossip, further eroding the respect for those responsible for the implementation of Tudor law. The execution of their popular Marquess of Exeter, Henry Courtenay, first cousin of the King, and virtual local sovereign of the South West, played into this narrative and served to further alienate the Westcountry men from the throne. As his reign drew towards its end in 1547[76], Henry continued to undermine the Englishman's respect for the Crown by exterminating his subjects with such enthusiastic gusto that it was said that their children merely existed to decorate the

---

[76] In all, it is estimated that Henry alone sent approximately seventy-two thousand Englishmen to their death during his reign which totalled about 1/32 of every person in the land. This figure includes those who died in battle fighting Henry's wars.

King's 'gallows trees'. His legacy was a country reduced to penury and ripe for rebellion.

The Tudor Brexit, of course, not only rid England of the popes[77] but gave rise to what was, in the view of Catholics and the Westcountry men, the greatest act of cultural destruction and vandalism in English history on a scale that would have made Oliver Cromwell proud. By plundering his way through the wealth of their ecclesiastical institutions, Henry created deep hostility, particularly in the Cornish who greatly mourned the loss of Glasney College, a calamity that further exacerbated their historic festering resentment towards the English king. His looting of his peoples' ecclesiastical valuables and treasures, meanwhile, provided the Crown with the opportunity to bribe the support of wealthy men, a number of whom feigned Protestantism by making it a political rather than a spiritual choice in order to wax fat off the spoils. This naturally secured Protestantism's future firmly in the pockets of the wealthy and influential, who would, after the Rising, seek to exterminate the survivors as they defended their newly acquired wealth.

Thus, when Edward came to the throne, determined to institute Protestantism on Catholic England, although the Pope was no longer an obstacle, there was a ready-made festering cauldron of resentment brewing in the South West that provided a formidable threat to the roll out of Protestantism.

In determining whether the Devon and Cornish men should be viewed as rebels or as innocent petitioners, at least in the early stages of the Rising, it is important to remind ourselves of the immense impact that the imposition of the Act of Uniformity had on the individual. In one swift blow, not only was his spiritual community destroyed but his hopes of salvation abolished; his ability to relieve the suffering of his loved ones in purgatory was stripped away, leaving him, too, to face a prolonged period of unrelieved anguish when his time came; his secular life was also undermined with the erosion of his welfare and working community while his parish

---

[77] Henry's eviction of the popes from England probably saved the country from experiencing the bloodbaths inflicted on Protestants on the continent where the popes still held sway.

church was stripped of its sacred images, further divesting his spartan existence of colour and replacing it with shades of grey. It must have seemed that the essential structures that made life endurable for the Tudor man were shattered. England's first Brexit was indeed devastating and revolutionary. The transformations in church and state, the architects of which were controlling events in far-away London inevitably left the Westcountry peasant impoverished in every facet of his precarious life. What options did the poor man have but to either acquiesce and accept the stripping away of the necessities of his life that made his existence tolerable, or risk what he had left, his life, to fight to regain what he viewed as fundamental for his spiritual, economic, and social survival? The common man was also about to be confronted with the complex issue of the life-and-death debate about the validity of the Real Presence in the Eucharist as the country at this time was also becoming increasingly split over the crucial question of the nature of the Lord's Supper. One person's true faith was becoming another's pernicious treason and blasphemy, with both sides prepared to die for their preferred sacred interpretation.

The complex theological disputes that were at the core of the Reformation and the passions they engendered in the hearts of the Westcountry men are, indeed, hard for our secular, largely atheistic society to comprehend. For kings, princes, popes, and those in the higher echelons of society, who were quick to seize any opportunity to land grab, their concerns at this time were more obviously materialistic as they jockeyed to either retain or extend their power base. Some would benefit from the newly-released wealth as the ecclesiastical institutions were closed, and the Church's finances diverted. This much is easily understood. Meanwhile, for the academics, educated churchmen, and even the ordinary people, especially the Devonshire men, it was largely the religious causes of the movement, and their alleged consequences, that were pre-eminent in the Western Rising. The crucial doctrinal issues, particularly concerning transubstantiation, which engendered such passions and high-minded ideals are apt to be unappreciated by our largely secular society of today. We witness the stark consequences of this debate, of course, during the reign of Queen Mary I, who earned her reputation as 'Bloody Queen Mary' for the barbaric burning of just under three hundred Protestants, largely for rejecting the doctrine of transubstantiation, when she came to the throne in 1553.

While the above engenders sympathy for those who rebelled against the imposition of the Prayer Book, we must also consider a further less laudable motive that has been assigned to the rebels. Over recent decades, historians, by rejecting the mono-causal explanations of rebellions, have diminished the role that high-minded ideals played in the Western Rising. While acknowledging that conservative religious adherence and anti-Protestantism inflamed by Cornish cultural sensitivities were predominant causes of the Rebellion, historians from the beginning of the twentieth century have increasingly posited the idea that alleged resentment against the gentry by Westcountry peasants created an army of rebels who viewed themselves as class warriors, a phenomenon, it is claimed, that was a subsidiary but significant cause of the protest. By promoting the notion that class hostility played a substantial role in triggering the 'Commotion Time' or the 'Insurrection of Devon and Cornwall', the appellations assigned to the event by the Victorians and their forebears, modern historians have added a further and less commendable motive which changes the character of the Rebellion and, perhaps, our view and understanding of the insurrection and the people involved. This argument is allegedly underpinned by two factors: the circumstances surrounding the murder of William Hellyons at Sampford Courtenay, and, secondly, the wording of a particular accusation found in the indictment of the two leaders Arundell and Wynslade which claimed that the rebels' slogan was, allegedly: *'Kill the gentlemen!'*

This view, which, although not a dominant one until recent years, was, in fact first mooted in the 1590s, further reinforced by Carew in his *Survey of Cornwall* in the early seventeenth century, revived in the nineteenth century, and further developed by the scholar Rose-Troup in her very influential book *The Western Rebellion of 1549* (1913). In her descriptive account, she paints a vivid picture of rebellious and angry Cornishmen marching through Bodmin chanting, *'Kill the gentlemen!'*[78] Her interpretation of events was echoed later by such respected scholars as Professor Sir Geoffrey Elton, whose books were standard reading for undergraduate students in the 1970s. In the 1990s, Loades[79] even posited that the Devonian of the period harboured more hostility to the gentry class than any other man in England.

Certainly, some of the Protestant gentry were roughly treated by the Westcountry men while their petitions to the King and Council contained a clause that demanded a reduction in the number of serving men a gentleman could retain, thus curtailing their local influence[80]. Their demand that half of the monastic land should be restored[81] would also have been viewed as an attack on the gentry and aristocracy who held them. The story of Walter Raleigh, whose rough and unwise admonishment of an elderly woman at Clyst St Mary for carrying a rosary angered the villagers to the point that he apparently feared for his life, also plays into the class war narrative. Similarly, Carew, in his 1602 *Survey of Cornwall,* reinforces this view where he states, regarding the gentry families who were held captive following their defence of St Michael's Mount, that they were in danger of being slaughtered by their captors who *'rather by God's gracious*

---

[78] Rose-Troup *The Western Rebellion of 1549, p.* 127 *'.........the restraints of camp-life became quite irksome, and some of them got quite out of hand, threatening the lives of the imprisoned gentlemen: according to the Indictment, they tumultuously paraded the streets of Bodmin, crying - Kill the gentlemen and we will have the Six Articles up again, and ceremonies as they were in King Henry the Eighth's time.'*

[79] See *The Mid-Tudor Crisis*, by D. Loades 1545-65 (1992)

[80] The demands that the rebels sent to the King during the siege of Exeter reflects their growing confidence in the strength of their position. Their demands included: .... *'we will that no Gentylman shall haue anye mo seruantes then one to wayte vpo hym excepte he maye disepende one hundredth marke land and for euery hundredth marke we thynke it reasonable, he should haue a man.'*

[81] Again from Exeter they demanded of the King that: ' ......we wyll that halfe parte of the abbey landes and Chauntrye landes, in euery mans possessyons, how so euer he cam by them, he geuen again to two places, where two of the chief Abbeis was with in euery Countye, where suche half part shalbe taken out, and there to be established a place for devout persons, which shall pray for the Kyng and the common wealth, and to the same we wyll haue al the almes of the Churche boxe geuen for these seuen yeres.'*

providence, than any want of will.....[or] purpose.......restrained from murdering the principle persons' whom they had made their prisoners. Carew pushed his accusations of rebel cruelty and barbarity further when he described the plight of the gentry at Trematon Castle, but even he had to temper his allegations by acknowledging that not one of the captives were killed, and all survived their capture at the hands of the rebels.

Regarding the evidence supplied by the murder of William Hellyons, there are few concrete facts available, although his murder in Sampford Courtenay is certain as Hooker confirms the event. We know he was murdered on Whit Monday 1549, and it is believed that he was a farmer of the wealthy yeoman class or even a member of the lesser gentry. However, little conclusive contemporary evidence has been discovered to confirm either of these two suppositions. We can be certain that a man named William Hellyons existed for, apart from Hooker's evidence, according to a London ballad that appeared in the immediate wake of the Rising:

> *They [the rebels] put some in person, & sume to greate payne,*
> *And sume fled a waie or else they had bene slayne*
> *As was Wyllam Hilling that marter truly*
> *Which they killed at Sandford mowre in the playne.*[82]

There is no reference to his social status, but the mention of martyrdom suggests that he died for the Protestant cause rather than as a victim of class hostility. If class warfare did play a role, then Hellyons' death was not evidence of it as he did not represent the wealthy gentry class, and, therefore, was not an obvious target. The class war hypothesis certainly isn't supported by Hooker's contemporary accounts, whose description of Hellyons paints a picture of a pugnacious, quarrelsome, and tactless individual whose abrasive conduct added much fuel to the fire of inflamed emotions of villagers enraged by the abrupt stripping away of their cherished

---

[82] British Library in *A Short-Title Catalogue of Books Printed in English, 1475-1640.*

beliefs, and the way of life that it supported. We can identify the cause of Hellyons' murder solely in the words of Hooker. His abrasive manner and his Protestant faith, rather than his social class, undoubtedly, triggered the ire of the villagers, which the farmer then exacerbated by continuing to berate his audience until his words ignited a murderous rage in his listeners. The facts do not provide support for the claim that his death was a consequence of local hatred of the gentry.

The balladeer, however, does suggest that others might have met a similar fate if they had not made their escape, and, in this sense, the writer hints that class warfare may have played a role in the revolt, even if not in Hellyons' death. However, the timing and location of the ballad suggests that caution is advised when evaluating its worth as supporting evidence for the hypothesis that class hostility played a role. It was written by a pro-government supporter who wrote after the event in London when the process of framing the nature of the Rising by the victors to their best advantage was in full swing. The notion that class warfare was a feature of rebellions in general at the time was a popular one and so endowing the Western Rising with a similar characteristic was a natural development, despite the lack of evidence to support the proposition.

The second strand of evidence that is added to the story of Hellyons' murder to support the claim by modern historians that the Rising was an expression of class warfare are the words that are used in the indictment of the two rebel leaders, Wynslade and Arundell. The relevant part of this document charges the two men with having levied war against the King, and then goes on to state that they and their followers had imprisoned many Cornish gentlemen and kept them in prison, crying out, '*Kyll the Gentlemen and we wyll have the Acte of Sixe Articles uppe agayne and ceremonyes as were yn Kyng Henry th'eighths tyme.*' As mentioned above, Rose-Troup imaginatively elaborated on the claim by setting the scene in Bodmin with the band of rebels marching around the town '*tumultuously*', crying out: '*Kill the gentlemen..............!*' Other notable historians, like Julian Cornwall, echoed and reinforced this legend until it has become accepted as a historic event which adds weight to the view that the rebels regarded themselves as class warriors. There is no contemporary evidence, however, to support this particular depiction of the early days of the Rising in Cornwall by Rose-Troup while a careful consideration of the unfolding of events suggests that there was no significant class hostility in operation from June to August 1549. In some modern-day sources, such as Wikipedia, the rebels' alleged cry has even been subtly changed to '*Kill ALL the Gentleman'*, which reinforces the claim that the rebels were motivated by hostility towards the gentry, whereas the indictment omits ALL, thus downgrading the threat to only certain gentleman rather than the whole class. Even this, however, is an unlikely scenario, based on the evidence and events.

In his published paper, *Kill All the Gentlemen?* (2019)[83], Professor Mark Stoyle emphasises that it is significant that the indictments of Arundell and Wynslade were written on the same day as that of Robert Kett, who led the Norfolk Rising and he too was accused of adopting the cry '*Kill the gentlemen!*' This was being composed at a time immediately following the series of revolts that had threatened to de-stabilise the Government, and the case had to be made against the leaders in the strongest possible terms. Accusing the leaders of seeking to overthrow the established hierarchy of government, a clear charge of treason, would strike fear into any who considered following their example, while also ensuring the death penalty. Accusing two members of the gentry, such as Arundell and Wynslade, of such motivation, however, is a little strange. Even though such sentiments may have been more likely to have been expressed during the Norfolk Rising, we know that Kett did his best to protect the lives of the gentry, so the accusation is even suspect, or at least exaggerated, in his case and suggests the alleged cry of the rebels was an attempt to re-frame the revolt by government lawyers to make it appear as a class war. The fact that all three leaders of the two discrete revolts were arraigned before the judges at Westminster on 26th November 1549 on the same indictment, certainly rouses suspicion

---

[83] *'Kill all the gentlemen?' (Mis)representing the western rebels of 1549,* Professor Mark Stoyle (Institute of Historical Research, vol.97, no.255, February 2019)

that the accusation that class warfare and the wish to murder the gentry was a motivating factor in the two rebellions was indeed contrived with the purpose of reinforcing the rebranding of the revolts to accord with the victor's purposes. The circumstances suggest that the charge that they planned to 'Kill the gentry' was probably no more than, to quote Professor Stoyle, a 'formulaic fiction' that was invented to serve the Government's political agenda at the time and did not reflect actual events or motivations.

Certainly, according to Hooker's accounts of the Rising, there was no evidence of rebel hostility to the ruling classes apart from that directed at individual members who were supporters of the Protestant cause. Indeed, Hooker's accounts of the gentry and magistrates' dealing with the rebels at Sampford Courtenay suggests that the gentry were not necessarily altogether opposed to letting the rebels have their head as a number sympathised with their demands; some, such as John Bury of mid-Devon, the mayors of Torrington and Bodmin, and others, even provided leadership for the rebel army. Hooker certainly suspected that the ineffectual actions of the official royalist Westcountry gentry were evidence of their collusion with the rebels. The hostility towards the Carews, meanwhile, can be easily explained by their clumsy handling of the Crediton debacle rather than any general resentment towards them as representatives of their class. The collective evidence supports the view that those who suffered at the hands of the rebels were Protestants of any social standing, whether gentry or peasant. These included the Protestant Kingswell, a tin-miner, during the siege of Exeter, who was executed by the rebels under the direction of the priest of St Thomas' church, Robert Welshe, and those local men who joined Russell's army, as well as Raleigh, and the Protestant and/or royalist gentry who defended St Michael's Mount and Trematon Castle. Meanwhile, Hellyons, ultimately the only one to be murdered by the petitioners, was of a dubious and undetermined social standing, and likely a yeoman or perhaps, at most, a minor member of the gentry, and therefore not an obvious target of class hostility. The motivation for his murder must lie elsewhere, no doubt, in retaliation for his Protestant sympathies and his unwise and overbearing attitude towards the crowd at Sampford Courtenay. In conclusion, his death provides no more evidence for the claim that class war was a factor in the Prayer Book Rebellion than does the unpersuasive accusation in the indictments that the rebels determined to 'kill the gentlemen!'

Ironically, however, the situation changed markedly after the Rebellion as the local gentry, perhaps eager to avoid the fate of the Northern Men a dozen years before and keen to prove their loyalty to the Government fell on their poorer powerless neighbours like a pack of wild animals. Cruelly inflicting barbaric punishments, seizing their lands and goods, destroying their families, and hunting them down like prey, the gentry drove them to desperation and destitution. Even Russell complained of the cruelty demonstrated by the gentry classes in the wake of the Rising and wrote saying: *'that sythe your departure from me ther hath passed no daye in the whych I have not hard sondry ... horryble complayntes from ... Cornewall: some pore men oppressed withe extreame and unreasonable composicions; some greved withe unjust exactions by ther land lordes; some spoyled by one gentylman; som utterly undone and impoverished by another; some forced to entre in to bondes; some emprysoned and threatened with deathe for their goodes ... some persecuted withe one crueltye; som withe another; and the hole Comyns universally vested withe such extreamitye, wronge and oppressyon as ... no slaunder or reproche was ever hard or reportyd lyke unto this, whych at the present to the great dysworshippe and discredyt of all the gentylmen of the shyre is generally spred and brutyd in every honest mans mowthe.'*[84]

The accusation that the insurrectionists were motivated by a desire to 'Kill [all] the gentlemen' is, therefore, without historical foundation. The evidence strongly suggests that it was merely a false portrayal of them deliberately connived by the royalist lawyers of the day, so the Rising could be reframed as a class war, rather than a religious revolt by desperate people who only wanted to defend their faith and culture. Given the barbaric punishments inflicted on the

---

[84] This theme is further developed by Prof Mark Stoyle of Southampton University in the published paper: *Kill all the gentlemen!* See bibliography, p.251.

THE BATTLE OF FENNY BRIDGES 1549
PRELUDE AND AFTERMATH

Devonshire men and, especially on the Cornish, maybe, too, it was less embarrassing for the Government to be seen brutally suppressing the Westcountry for treasonable activities which aimed to overthrow the middle level of government than for merely seeking to reason with the King to restore their faith and way of life. It is a double injustice that not only were they misrepresented as enemies of ordered government, and bore the pejorative label of 'rebels', which they arguably did not deserve, certainly in the initial stages of the Rising until they laid siege to Exeter, but that it was the gentry class, the alleged target of their rebellion, who ultimately displayed excessive class hatred towards them during the suppression of the Rising.

The reframing of the Rising as being, in part, a class war against the gentry has encouraged historians down the centuries to tarnish the Westcountry men with accusations of subversion. This has played into the popular narrative that they were a mere ignorant rabble of peasants challenging the rule of lawful government under the direction of seditious priests. This depiction of the Westcountry men, while undeniably partly rooted in truth, has enabled historians to judge them harshly while ignoring the devastating effects on them by the revolutionary laws that ushered in the new prayer book, and to further sully their reputations by misconstruing their motives. By so doing, history has virtually airbrushed these brave men and their sufferings out of existence.

It has often been ignored that a prime motivator of the people of the far South West was their strong resentment of the interference of a dominant central government in their affairs and the destruction of their privileges that had been granted by former monarchs. Indeed, Cornwall's history through the centuries repeatedly reveals more an allegiance to their Celtic roots in opposition to the English, rather than to their current denominational preference: just as the Welshman would later adhere passionately to Methodism, the Irishman, to Catholicism, the Cornishman would cling fiercely to his Celtic heritage and was determined to oppose rule from the foreign Englishman, whatever his religious persuasion. Thus, for Cornwall, the enforced introduction of the Protestant Prayer Book on June 9th, 1549, not only destroyed the warp and weft upon which the fabric of its society was woven but also eroded its status as a nation separate from England. Crucially, with the abolition of the Latin Mass, the services had to be conducted in English and not in Cornish, a concession that had been granted by the popes. This ultimately resulted in the eventual demise of Cornwall's language and, consequently, of its identity as a nation separate from its more powerful neighbour over the Tamar.

England's last act of revenge following the Western Rising was to obliterate all evidence of Cornwall's semi-autonomy from the map. From this point on, the term *Anglia et Cornubia* was no longer used on official documents and, significantly, the British Sea became the English Channel. As a further punishment, unlike the Welsh, the Government also denied the Cornish the right to have a prayer book in their own language, thus further encouraging the decline of the Cornish tongue. Therefore, the new law enforcing the implementation of Protestantism by the boy-king's government effectively marked the final absorption of Cornwall into England.

Today, nearly five hundred years later, it is indeed telling that whereas the Scots have their Braveheart, and the Cornish their An Gof, Arundell, and Wynslade, that films are made of the former, while the Celtic Westcountry champions have been almost erased from history. Instead of being hailed as heroes, these courageous men who sacrificed their lives to defend their culture, language, and faith have been relegated to obscurity, and the obliteration of a whole generation of men is recorded as no more than a mere footnote in the history of the establishment of the Church of England.

It is only now that the heroic Westcountry men are being repatriated back into their own history from which they have been banished, and their reputations besmirched, for nearly five hundred years by the dominant rhetoric of the government-sanctioned victors. At last, too, their great suffering has also received official recognition: in 2007, the Bishop of Truro, Bill Ind, apologised to the people of Cornwall (and Devon?) for the '*brutality and stupidity*' that was perpetrated on them in the name of the Church of England. Perhaps that apology will go some way to heal the wound that has been left, particularly in the Cornish psyche, by the brutal events of 1549.

Some of the Men who fought in

The Western Rising

Thomas Leigh; John Wynslade; William Wynslade; Humphrey Arundell; William Alsa; Sir John and Sir Thomas Arundell; Peter Bellameye; Roger Baret; John Barrow; Richard Benet; John Bochym; Robert Bochyn; Humphrey Bonville; Nicholas Boyer; Henry Bray; Richard Bray; John Bury; Thomas Calwen; …..Coffin; Crispyn; John Croker; John Donne; Thomas Dowrish; …Drewe; Stephen Foole; William Fortescue; John Furse; William Geste; William Harris; John Hamon; Robert Hayes; Richard Hayman; Thomas Holmes; Thomas Hooper; Stephen Hore; William Hore; Edward James; Henry Lee; …Lethbridge; George Martin; …Maunder; William Mayow; John Moreman; Gabriel Mourton; James Mourton; Simon Mourton; Thomas Osbourne; John Payne; Robert Paget; Edward Parker; Anthony Paw; Robert Perin; Sir Thomas Pomeroy; John Prideaux; Roger Quiarme; Nicholas Reve; Richard Rosecarrock; James Rosogan; John Rosogan; Robert Royes; William Seger; John Sharke; John Shere; John Sloeman; Robert Smyth; Richard Taylor; John Thompson; Henry Tredynnyck; William Tredynnyck; Thomas Underhill; William Viell; John Vincent; Robert Whettell; John Wolcot; William Wykes

(In Cornish, then in English
A dhew Ollgallosek, Tas Mapden-Oll,

y commendyn Dhys trobels an Norvys;

Yn le cas gwreth (gorryth) kerensa.

Yn le brew grontyth gyvyans.

Yn le dycrysy restoryeth fyth.

Yn le trystans daswreth gwaytyans.

Yn le tewlder gesyth golow,

dhe Jesu Cryst agan Sylwyas ha Redemyer.

Amen

Almighty Father, we remember before Thee the troubles of the world.

Where there is Hatred, give Love.

Where there is Injury, grant pardon.

Where there is Doubt, grant Faith.

Where there is Despair, restore Hope.

Where there is Darkness, let there be Light.

Through Jesus Christ our Saviour and Redeemer.

Amen

The People who Lived in the Village of Feniton at the Time of The Battle of Fenny Bridges

Lady Joan Kirkham	Gawen Conant
Cecilia Kirkham	John Salter of
(sister of Sir Peter Carew)	'in the corner'
Thomas Kirkham	Henrye Till
James Kirkham	Ellis Forde
John Pringe (Priest)	Mycaell Searell
John Salter	William Salter
Joan Salter	Ellis Hellier
Henry Manley	Stephen Pringe
John Colbear	John Sherforde
John Coterell, the elder	Margaret Lucas
Robert Bounde	Andrew Thorne
John Skinner	William Smith
William Lucas	John Tocke
Robert Baker	William Gold
Peter Saunder	John Bowne
Robert More	Edward Ingelbye
Thomas Pringe	Joan Pringe

Appendices

1. The Battle of Fenny Bridges
   Round Two
   September 1st and 2nd, 2018

2. A Protestant View of the Western Rising

3. A Catholic View of the Western Rising

4. The original Flyer 1913 for the book 'The Western
   Rebellion of 1549' by Frances Rose-Troup

5. The Rebels' Articles sent from Exeter in July 1549

THE BATTLE OF FENNY BRIDGES ROUND TWO 1ST AND 2ND SEPTEMBER, 2018 FILMED AT FENITON AND OTTERY ST MARY FOR A T.V. SERIES ON THE EUROPEAN REFORMATION.

Battle of Fenny Bridges
Round Two, 2018

In 2017, The Battlefields' Trust was contacted by Stefano Mazzeo, a film director for a US TV company. He wanted information about the Prayer Book Rebellion for his new series on the European Reformation, which he was planning to film in 2018. He read a draft copy of this book and decided to devote one episode to the story of the Rebellion.

The film became a community project for Feniton. For six months, members of the village, and nearby communities worked extremely  hard making their magnificent banner of the Five Wounds of Christ, the battlefield pennants, and dozens of peasant costumes made from fabric that was generously donated by villagers. Piles of old duvet covers and curtains were to be found deposited on various doorsteps whenever we ran out of supplies. The ladies of the Feniton Art and Craft group, aided by the talented Alma, worked hard researching Tudor patterns, designing, and stitching. Pam and RoseMarie spent five hundred hours alone making the banner, now a village heirloom.

On Friday 31st August 2018,[85] villagers, who had volunteered to be 'extras' with some Cornish reinforcements, turned up at the village hall to prepare for the dress rehearsal. They were soon stripped of their clothes and turned into Tudor peasants and gentry. Andrew Moulding, Chairman of the East Devon District Council, armed with a pitchfork,

---

[85] The text is an abbreviated account of the filming written by the author that was printed in the local media.

looked particularly striking in a pair of pink brocade breeches, the fabric of which, in a previous life, must have adorned someone's windows. A pink Tudor flat cap, white shirt, and black jerkin completed his ensemble. Local Conservative M.P. Neil Parish, armed to the teeth and keen to attack the Government forces, was attired in a similar outfit in green and looked impressive as a Tudor gentleman.

Meanwhile, the wives of the gentry struggled into very heavy Tudor dresses and looked stunning. The majority, however, were

peasants dressed in breeches or long flowing skirts, many of which had spent their early lives as Feniton duvet covers, and jerkins. Their outfits were completed with hats, bonnets, and various accessories that Rosanne, with the help of a few of us, had made over the previous months.

Later in the afternoon, Ellen, the very hard-working producer, arrived with a rail of costumes, hired at the eye-watering cost of over a thousand pounds. All was going well. Then we discovered a problem: our six-foot pennants, beautifully made by RoseMarie, didn't fly. There was no wind, which was just as well as our two banner holders would have been seen soaring over Feniton rooftops had there had been a breeze, such is the weight and size of our new village heirloom. Stefano, therefore, despatched George, dressed as a rebel, to Homebase for longer poles. No doubt, any visiting

grockles must have been amused to see how some of the native yokels still dress in the heart of Devon. Eventually, with the aid of yards of wire, and much persistence and ingenuity, Andrew and Alma had our pennants flying proudly over the battlefield.

At 6 p.m., everyone made their way to Feniton Court for a short dress rehearsal in preparation for the cameras to start rolling by 8.30 a.m. the next morning. The horses also needed to be prepared for the

shock of being confronted, not by the usually refined people of Feniton, but by an army of angry Tudor men who noisily clanked with armour to the accompaniment of a beating drum as they waved their weapons menacingly against a skyline decorated with flying pennants. In the middle of all this was the huge eight-foot banner that bore down on the poor horses, who had never encountered such an alarming scene in their lives. Quigley, and his lovely companion packhorse, however, proved to be

built of sterner stuff and didn't bat an eye as they found themselves in the midst of mass killings while serenaded by a cacophony of drum beats, yelling, cries of the dying, and the clashing of weapons that broke out around them. They were probably extras in War Horse and took it all in their stride.

On Saturday, a bunch of us were already hard at work by 7.15 a.m. in the hall, preparing for the first whole day of filming. The weather, always a concern, was perfect. One of us changed gender with the aid of a painstakingly applied beard, make-up, and wig. Others were turned into priests. Soon, a motley looking army of people were winding their way down to the entrance of Feniton Court for an experience of their lives.

After arriving at the field, all the men were rounded up to re-enact the opening scenes of the battle. Jonathan, as Humphrey Arundell, looking every inch the dashing country gentleman, rode up to the rows of Westcountry men to deliver a rousing speech, first in Cornish, and then in English for the Devonshire men. He did remarkably well - his beautiful horse, however, was panicked when the mass crowd roared back at him, '*RAG KERNOW HA'N KRYJYANS GWIR!*' [86] at the top of their lungs while threateningly waving their weapons and hoisting the eight-foot banner in preparation for the charge. Many takes later, with Jonathan still amazingly remaining in the saddle, the scene was completed to Stefano's satisfaction.

This was followed by a charge down the rough field to annihilate the royalists who were lurking in the trees. Dave Retter, Honiton's town crier, wisely decided to die early and threw himself down on the field as the first fatality. The terrain was rough, and dying prematurely was preferable to suffering a twisted ankle.

Those surviving were taken prisoner by the royalists, had their hands bound behind them, and were forced down on the ground in

---

[86] For Cornwall and the true religion!

preparation for a scene of the murder of the nine hundred, one of the worst atrocities in English military history. One by one, each man had his throat slashed and was thrown to the ground as the body count mounted. It looked a painful experience. Of course, they had to do it again,…. and

again. *Ouch!* Only one of the executed had to pay a visit to the hospital afterward.

This time, the women and children were needed to join the men as the clock was wound back to the time of the Pilgrimage of Grace in 1536. In that year, forty thousand rose in protest against the religious changes of Henry VIII and they adopted the banner of the Five Wounds of Christ as their emblem for the first time. Robert Aske was filmed reasoning with the people and then, of course, he

joined them as leader. We all looked forward to the scene of his hanging, drawing, and quartering later that afternoon.

Fiona, dressed in a beautiful gold gown and long headdress, completed the day's shoot by presenting her colours to a knight who was leaving her to fight the Government's troops. Fiona

wanted to keep the gown, but she had to part with it as Queen Elizabeth I, apparently, was waiting for it in another location.

The following day, we gathered in Ottery churchyard as we waited for the Lady Chapel to be stripped of any signs of post-Tudor furniture. After the radiators, pipes, and other signs of modernity, were camouflaged, the Protestant table converted to a Catholic altar, and George had unscrewed the Tudor pews from the main body of the church floor and hauled them to the Chapel, we were ready for the off.

Next, baby Thomas stole the show as he and his mum wept and prayed before a crucifix as his father, Alex, was fighting on the field. I suspect he survived as I found his costume neatly folded in the hall afterward.

This was followed by the knight's vigil, and then the women and more senior men were called. They knelt on the stone floor, praying and weeping as their husbands, sons, brothers, and fathers were being killed outside. Daniel, meanwhile, died beautifully of head wounds on the steps of the Lady Chapel as his mum, in a widow's veil and his wife mopped up his blood. Both collapsed in tears as he passed away. A sharp-eyed viewer may notice that the grieving new widow had been presenting her colours to her dashing knight only the day before.

Next up was the now Rev. Dave Retter to deliver the first Protestant service to his scandalised Catholic congregation. Stefano instructed them

to look horrified at the words of the new service and to walk out of the church in protest. Dave, however, needs his spectacles to read. He could not see the print, as, obviously, he couldn't wear them during the filming. Stefano gave the not-so-brilliant instruction to Dave to just repeat the Bible verses he knew by heart. There was a long pause - then Dave began. '*We are gathered today in Bethlehem to welcome the donkey*'. If we weren't prepared for that, we were less prepared for Dave's next piece of improvisation. He proceeded to regale his now genuinely shocked congregation - with the football scores and the history of his favourite football club - it was no wonder his Catholic audience stormed out - trying to suppress their giggles - .which was more than those of us behind the cameras could do. I think Stefano may add a slightly different script over the Retter version of the New Protestant service. I just hope there won't be too many lip readers amongst the viewers.

All in all, we had a fabulous weekend and one which we will always remember.

APPENDIX

THE HISTORICAL CONTEXT

OF

THE PRAYER BOOK REBELLION

The Historical context
of
The Prayer Book Rebellion
A Protestant View of the Western Rising

It is the last Thursday in May in 986 A.D. A small group of men, a young bishop, a jailor, and the 15-year-old Emperor Otto III make their way to the lowest basement in the strongest fortress in Rome: the mausoleum of Emperor Hadrian, over which a bronze statue of Michael the Archangel stands guard. The jailer unlocks a cell door, and the three enter, their candles casting watery pale pools of light across the cold stones that form the tiny prison. As the stench of fetid air assails their nostrils, they peer into the eerie darkness to where the flickering flames trace the barest outline of a mound of rags piled on a thin bed of straw. Huddled beneath is a woman who has lain there for many years, a prisoner of her son Alberic. Marozia does not rise[87].

The bishop addresses the mound of rags: *'Marozia, daughter of Theophylact, are you living?'* The old woman does not move. *'Yes,'* she whispers, although she knows that the visit heralds her imminent demise, but she has no reason to care. After reading the charges against her, the bishop offers her absolution, and then, the task accomplished, hastily leaves the dank atmosphere of the cell for the fresh air of the outer yard, leaving the way clear for the next stage of the plan. Shortly, two cowled men slip quietly into the prison. One of

---

[87] The exact age and length of imprisonment of Marozia varies according to the historical source with a range from five to fifty-four years. For the facts contained in this appendix pertaining to the story of *The Rule of the Harlots*, I have drawn from the writings of Jesuit Fr. Malachi Martin, who died in 1999, aged 78 years. He claims Marozia was ninety-four when she was murdered, although it is difficult to believe she would survive so long in such dire circumstances.

them bears a red velvet cushion, which is all that is required to fulfil the final act.

Marozia hears the clunk of the key and the creak of the cell door as the cold draft of air that is sucked into the cell chills her old bones. The straw crunches under her executioners' feet as they pull back the filthy rags to reveal the frail old lady cowering beneath. She knows not to struggle or resist as the dark shadow looming above her lowers the velvet cushion. Within minutes her many years of imprisonment are over. Marozia, the pope-maker, is dead.

During her life, she had been the mother of one pope, whom she conceived by another, the grandmother of a third, the aunt of a fourth, and the creator of nine more of whom she had two strangled, one suffocated to death, and four disposed of in questionable circumstances. Her reign, along with that of her mentor and predecessor, and then that of her mother, which turned the papacy into a pornocracy, known as *The Rule of the Harlots,* was over. The hierarchy that ruled the Christian people of Europe had now reached its nadir, the causes of which would eventually lead to its partial collapse when educated and courageous churchmen ultimately challenged and rejected the rule of a corrupt religious system that refused to reform itself from within.

Her career had begun when she was a mere six years old in 897 A.D. when Agiltruda, the Queen Mother of Spoleto, took her hand and led her through the crowds assembled around the Lateran Palace to the inner room where an astonishing drama was being played out. The child clutched the Queen Mother's hand tightly for reassurance as she watched Pope Stephen VI, the 'Trembler', raging at the eleven-month-old corpse of his predecessor, Pope Formosus, whose decayed and fragile remains were precariously propped up in a chair in front of Stephen. Standing beside the body stood a young man of about eighteen who was answering the questions on behalf of the deceased.

Formosus, who had crossed Agiltruda a year earlier, died, it was said, by poisoning, his mode of death arranged by the Queen Mother herself. He had deprived her son of the emperor's crown by rewarding it to her hated rival, Arnulf, in 896 A.D., a rebuff she would not tolerate as she connived to jockey her family into power. She and her family had attempted to seize Rome herself, but Emperor Arnulf and the Pope sent her packing, and she had returned to her homeland in defeat. Naturally, she could not forgive such a slight. By denying her son the position of emperor, which was now in a pope's power to bestow, Formosus had made himself her bitter enemy and her enemies had short life spans. Within weeks, he was dead. An armed group of Roman citizens replaced him with Boniface VI, but, within a fortnight, a vengeful Agiltruda, unhappy with their choice, successfully packed him off to his Maker and connived the appointment of her own puppet pope, the insane Stephen. His insanity made him an easy target for Agiltruda's scheming and, within months, her faction had manipulated him into a position where she could use him to satisfy her determination to avenge her son's failure to achieve the position of Holy Roman Emperor. Now, Agiltruda was keen for her protégé, the child Marozia, to witness the total degradation of her bitter enemy.

At Agiltruda's bidding, Stephen ordered the corpse of Formosus dug out of the ground where it had been rotting for eleven months, dressed it in pontifical robes and had it propped up on the papal throne where it would be cross-examined by cardinals and bishops. To circumvent the awkwardness of the prisoner actually being dead and, therefore, at something of a disadvantage, the nervous young deacon was ordered to stand beside the corpse and respond in a previously choreographed desired manner on behalf of the deceased.

Clasping the hand of the small child beside her, a smiling Agiltruda surveyed the dramatic scenes unfolding before her with satisfaction. It had been months in the planning, but, finally, her need for vengeance was about to be satisfied.

She watched with pleasure as Stephen, notorious for his black uncontrollable rages, addressed the corpse propped precariously in the chair before him, *'Why did you usurp the See of the Apostle?'* he snarled, spitting out his words with venom.

Hesitantly, the cowed deacon stuttered a shaky reply on behalf of Formosus: *'Because I was evil,'* he conveniently answered Stephen. With the confession in the bag, the case against the deceased was proved beyond all reasonable doubt. He was guilty!

With the verdict declared, the small child watched in fascinated horror as the cardinals rushed on the corpse, ripped off the pontifical vestments, prised off the first three fingers of the right hand that had been used in pontifical blessings from its remaining sinews, and dragged the corpse from the hall. As the body was hauled along the streets, the citizens yelled abuse and hurled rubbish and mud at it until, after being re-buried and dug up yet again, it was ultimately tipped into the River Tiber where it was, finally, left to decay in peace. Agiltruda's thirst for vengeance was finally satisfied, and the child Marozia had had her first lesson in power politics.

As instructed, Stephen proceeded to pass the severed fingers to the thirty-six-year-old Cardinal Sergius, who, in turn, presented the gristly trophy to Agiltruda Suddenly, the ground shook beneath their feet as a thunderous roar echoed across the city: with extraordinary timing the Basilica of St John next to the palace crashed, ominously, to the ground.

Agiltruda continued her scheming and plotted the seizure of the city of Rome again in 897 A.D. Pope Stephen, meanwhile, was thrown into prison, strangled, and replaced by another of her puppets, Pope Romanus. After failing to satisfy her expectations, within a few weeks he too was dispatched to clear the way for another of her choosing: Pope Theodore II. He lasted only twenty days before he annoyed Agiltruda, who wasted no time in arranging his death. This time his murder, however, marked a turning point in her fortunes for it was swiftly followed by the death of her son and heir when a fall from his horse resulted in a gangrenous broken hip. To make matters worse, the German emperor imposed a Roman-born German cardinal as Pope John IX, much to Agiltruda's annoyance. Nevertheless, he managed to survive for two years and, to everybody's surprise, died naturally in his bed – a rare achievement for a pope. These events, while eclipsing Agiltrude's power, heralded the entrance of Marozia's family to the business of pope-making, a profession in which Marozia excelled - for a time.

Marozia had learned valuable lessons from Agiltruda, and her education in power politics and pope-making was reinforced by her scheming mother, Theodora. Mother orchestrated the placement of the gentle Benedict IV on the throne, but he lived only three years and two months, dying in the summer of 903 A.D. Theodora's next two popes lasted only weeks. Leo V was pope only for July of 903 A.D. and then was imprisoned by Cardinal Christopher, who replaced him. He, in turn, was imprisoned by Cardinal Sergius, who arranged for him and all cardinals who opposed him to be assassinated. All further opponents who challenged Sergius, were, with Theodora's connivance, strangled, leaving the way clear for him to grab the papacy for himself. With his opposition dead, removed, or intimidated into silence, he was declared Pope Sergius III. Theodora's determined attempt to manoeuvre her family into a position of power was soon accomplished by playing her final trump card: she pimped her daughter, now aged fifteen, to Sergius. This arrangement resulted in a child, John, who was later to be jockeyed into position as Pope John XI[88].

Sergius died in 911 A.D., and Mother manipulated the appointment of the next two popes, Anastasius III, who survived for two years, and Lando, who only managed to stay alive for six months before Theodora allegedly despatched him with methods of her own design. Next time, she chose more carefully and, with force of arms, according to the writings of Lliutpranda, Bishop of Cremona, arranged the installation of her alleged lover, Bishop John of Ravenna, as the next pope, John X. At least, if the accusation of Lliutpranda is to be believed, he promised to be more biddable and malleable to her whims and ambitions.

By now, Marozia was twenty-two and lived a life of sumptuous decadence either in the Lateran Palace or in her own family mansion where walls were draped with purple and velvet and the evidence of vast wealth surrounded her. After Mass was said, the clergy and their patrons would mount their horses for a day's hunting and return to tables laden with golden goblets where they feasted, were entertained by dancing girls and musicians followed by dice-playing until they retired for an evening of lechery and silken pillows. Marozia, well-

---

[88] Some sources claim that Marozia was the aunt and not the mother of Pope John XI who, it is thought by some, was the result of the rape of Theodora, Marozia's young sister, by Pope Sergius.

instructed by Mother, loved her extravagant life of privilege and was more than adequately qualified to ensure she could appoint and control those who conferred and secured it. The life-styles of the leaders of Christendom were, indeed, in stark contrast to those of the genuine followers of Christ.

Then a potential problem arose. An unknown Lombard prince, Alberic, suddenly appeared in Rome, and he was gaining popularity. He was not under their control and the threat of his presence alarmed Pope John X so much that he and Theodora delegated Marozia to take care of him. Marozia, therefore, married Alberic, and a few months later they had a son, which they named after the father. Alberic, however, was not so easy for even his wife to control, so something more drastic had to happen. It did, and, before long, Marozia was arranging the burial of the mutilated body of her husband. This was followed by Theodora's own death by poisoning and the marriage of Marozia to Guido that marked the beginning of the waning of the family's successful pope-making business.

After the marriage, Marozia plotted against Pope John, had him flung into prison and arranged for him to suffer the same fate as she many decades later in similar circumstances.

Following John's murder, she and her powerful allies arranged for the enthronement of Pope Leo VI. His appointment, typically, resulted in his death sentence, and, by some unknown means, he was 'dispatched' and replaced by another of Marozia's choosing, Pope Stephen VIII. Stephen typically failed to live up to expectations and was soon disposed of in 931 A.D. and replaced with Marozia's own sixteen-year-old son by Sergius, who was made Pope John XI.

Guido did not live long after his step-son became pope, and his widow chose King Hugo of Tuscany for her next spouse. Inconveniently, he had a wife at the time, but Marozia had means of dealing with such an encumbrance. With the impediment to their plans removed, she and the newly-created widower were married by her son with extravagant pomp and ceremony in Rome.

The ambitious couple then devised a new scheme: she would arrange for her son to make her empress and her new husband, emperor, with her son Alberic as his successor. She was about to realise the summit of her ambition. Agiltruda would have been proud of her protégé.

However, her hopes were dashed when Alberic revolted with the Romans in 932 A.D., became ruler of the city, and opposed his mother. Hugo, clad only in his nightshirt, panicked, scrambled into a basket, was lowered over the city walls, and fled for his life back to his homeland. Alberic had his half-brother Pope John XI placed under house arrest in the Lateran Palace, where he died five years later, and flung his forty-year-old mother into prison. Never again did she see the light of day, and remained there until her murder more than half-a-century later[89].

During the twenty-two years from 932 A.D. that Alberic, who unsuitably self-styled himself as *'Alberic, by the Grace of God, humble Prince and Senator of all the Romans',* ruled Rome, he appointed five popes of his own choosing. As his death approached, he met with Pope Agapitus II, one of his own appointees, along with the clergy and city dignitaries and had them swear that not only would they elect Alberic's son, Octavian, aged fifteen, as the next pope but that the papacy was then to be inherited by his descendants, making it a hereditary dynasty. All present swore the oath. Marozia's power politicking had seemingly paid off.

One year later, Marozia's grandson was made pope on December 16th, 955 A.D. as Pope John XII. His promotion did not motivate Octavian to clean up his act, and he continued his debauched lifestyle, bringing in prostitutes for the amusements of his teenage friends and himself, while they feasted and lived lives of total depravity. As a counterbalance for his immoral lifestyle, he arranged for the monks of Subiaco Monastery to chant one hundred Kyrie Eleisons every day to ensure his free pass to heaven, and, clearly not a man to take risks with his immortal soul, he ordered a further one hundred *Christe Eleisons* for good measure. According to rumour, though, the monks were said to pray more fervently for his death than his salvation. He was to die as he lived: in 964 A.D., he was killed by an infuriated husband who caught him in the act of an adulterous liaison with his

---

[89] According to the writings of Jesuit Malachi Martin

wife. Marozia and her machinations had, indeed, brought the papacy to its nadir. The Christian peoples of Europe were no longer ruled by worthy leaders but by those who were a complete anathema to their predecessors of the early centuries.

How had the church leadership of the Christians of Rome sunk so low? For the first two hundred and fifty years, following the death of the last apostle, the bishops of Rome rarely, if ever, experienced the luxury of dying in their own bed, but for entirely different and far nobler reasons than those of their successors of later centuries. Evidence from early documents suggests that the church in Rome continued for several years as a true church, and the timing of its departure from the New Testament model is difficult now to determine. They followed the teachings of the early church and faced bitter persecution for proclaiming the gospel of Jesus Christ during the first two centuries. Every day, they lived under the threat of arrest and faced appalling deaths. Christians were tarred in pitch and used as living torches, while others were thrown to the wild beasts to the delight of tens of thousands of excited screaming fans in the Roman theatres or sent to work in the Roman mines of Sardinia. Unlike their successors, they were men of integrity and faith who were prepared to die in the most dreadful manner for the sake of spreading the gospel message of salvation through faith in Jesus Christ.

Pontian, who was made bishop of Rome in 230 A.D., was a typical example. Born into a family of slaves, he had received little education but was a faithful Christian deemed fit for the leadership of the congregation of Rome. He was, at this time, only one of a number of bishops who were elected by their individual local congregations while under him were presbyters and deacons, according to the New Testament model. Pontian, however, already in his seventh decade of life, fell victim to Emperor Maximinus when, on September 27th, 235 A.D., the order was given to arrest all Christians, burn their buildings, close their cemeteries, and confiscate their goods. Rome did not like those of its citizens who refused to worship its pagan gods.

Pontian was seized and endured torture for ten days as the Romans sought to extract from him the names of other Christians, but he bravely refused to oblige his torturers, despite the horrible suffering inflicted on him. Finally, with terrible injuries, the elderly bishop was hauled aboard a ship bound for Sardinia, where he was destined to provide slave labour for the Roman mines. For many days, he endured pain, starvation, thirst, and severe seasickness, while chained to his desperate fellow convicts. On October 12th, the ship docked in Sardinia just before the cold, windy winter weather struck the area.

The frail, sick bishop then had to endure the usual brutal induction to life as a Roman slave. After his left eye was gouged out and the socket cauterized with molten iron, the joints of his left foot were burnt, followed by the slicing of a nerve at the back of the right knee. He was fortunate that his age spared him the next stage in the induction process: the castration which all prisoners under thirty endured. After his forehead was branded, iron rings soldered around his ankles and linked together by a six-inch chain, a tight chain was placed around the waist that was attached by a third to the ankle chain in such a way that the prisoner could never straighten up again. He had to bend down, anyway, for twenty out of the twenty-four hours per day, and so was now permanently forced into this position. Locks were unnecessary as all chains were soldered permanently onto the prisoner's body. Finally, every new prisoner was tied to a large pillar and given sixty strokes of the lash. With the induction ceremony now completed, the prisoner, if he survived the introduction to life as a slave, was given his shovel and set to work in the mine until he dropped dead which, in the case of the strongest, took a few months. Understandably, many, in sheer desperation, sought their escape during the times they were not at work by filling their nostrils with soil until they asphyxiated. By February of the following year, the bishop's dead body had been disposed of in the usual way by his Roman slave masters, and those who came to collect it dragged it out of the cesspool so to return it to Rome where he could be given a Christian burial.

Pontian was in the mode of his predecessors[90] who had become leaders of their local Christian congregations. Unlike the official

---

[90] The Roman Catholic author Eamon Duffy provides a comprehensive and entertaining account of the popes in his book: *Saints and Sinners: A History of the Popes* by Yale University Press.

medieval church of later centuries, these early disciples revered the Word of God in its oral and written form and recognised its supremacy. This comprised of the Old Testament, in which they found the coming of their Messiah prophesied in meticulous detail, and the later gospel accounts of Jesus Christ, first verbally relayed by the apostles, and then in written form short decades later, which gave evidence of the precise fulfilment of the Scriptures. In their reverence for the Word, they followed in what was called '*The Way*' of Jesus Christ, who instructed his followers to appeal constantly to the Jewish Scriptures which he came to fulfil.

During the first three hundred years, the zeal of the disciples, their heroic deaths, and the translation of the Scriptures resulted in the rapid and extensive spread of Christianity. The faith was spread across continents, watered by the blood of its martyrs who, like Pontian, suffered appallingly, especially under Emperor Septimius (193-211 A.D). One hundred years later, their persecution became even more severe under Emperor Diocletian and his co-regent, Galerius (303 A.D. to 311 A.D). All their property was confiscated, and their refusal to obey the compulsory order to sacrifice to the gods led to a terrible death; yet, despite the bloodshed, the faith continued to spread across the empire during the early centuries. In the epistle of Peter, we read of the success and extent of the first missionary endeavours of the early disciples that resulted in the planting of Christian churches in Africa and across large swathes of Europe and Asia.

Finally, early in the fourth century, life for the Christians was revolutionised. No longer were they a persecuted minority for the Emperor Constantine claimed he had received a vision that made him sympathetic to the Christians, and the Edict of Milan in 313 A.D. ended their persecution. After three centuries of barbaric suppression, Christians were finally able to practise their faith in peace, but the Edict was to prove both a blessing and a curse. The succeeding centuries revealed that those who were at the heart of the Roman Church's organisational structure, by their determination to maximise the benefits of the emperor's gift, made a fatal mistake: they harnessed the gospel message of Jesus Christ to the political and socio-economic system which, for the following thousand years, immoral, corrupt, and ambitious men would seek to exploit for their own gain. In essence, by accepting Constantine's gift, they ultimately exchanged the red of the blood of Christ for the purple of the emperor's robes. The old centralized political system of the Roman empire was to become the earthly model of Christ's kingdom. All the attributes of classical Rome would be seen as attributes of Roman Christianity. It was a fatal amalgamation the ugly fruit which ripened in future centuries.

The emperors proceeded to organise the Christian churches on the model of the secular empire. Under the four vice-prefects in Alexandria, Jerusalem, Rome, and Antioch, who governed the Roman empire under Constantine, the Edict of Milan established the policy of religious freedom, not only for Christianity but for paganism. According to Protestants, this led to certain aspects of the latter being progressively assimilated into the former and, therefore, contaminating the pure message of the first century Apostles.

The bishops of Rome, as they ruled over the most important city in the empire, emerged at this time as the leading influential figures in the church. As the bishop of this great city naturally attracted honour, the other bishops also sought similar prestige and respect. The Apostles' model of pastors and the accepted priesthood of all believers, under the jurisdiction of overseers, who were men with families, was replaced with a hierarchy of ambitious men who, increasingly, built a temporal empire to accompany the consolidation of the ecclesiastical jurisdiction.

As the power and exalted position of the Roman hierarchy increased, a system of ritual and ceremony replaced the original worship of God and the work of the Holy Spirit as practices tinged with paganism were introduced, disguised with an external shell of Christianity. From the beginning, the gospel had produced an internal unity among the believers, but, as it was replaced by ritualism, the flame of spiritual regeneration was almost extinguished by a new emphasis on an external visible unity of the church. Increasingly, this came to replace the invisible church made up of all regenerated men as founded by Christ and the Apostles.

Significantly, in 378 A.D., Damasus, the Bishop of Rome, took on the title of Pontifex Maximus, the office of the High Priest of the Babylonian religion that had previously been the prerogative of the emperor, thus arguably further combining Christianity with the pagan religion.

Meanwhile, as the Roman Catholic Church was ultimately brought to birth in the vacuum created by the demise of the empire, a number of other Christian churches, which originated from the earliest times, continued to spread the message of Jesus Christ to Egypt, France, Germany, Britain, the Iberian Peninsula, and the Byzantine Empire. All attempted to be faithful to the teachings of the Apostles, used essentially the same scriptures, and were dedicated to spreading their understanding of the gospel message to far-away lands. A number of these, whom the Roman Church would later label heretics as she sought to bring the world under papal jurisdiction, held to beliefs that resembled those which would later be known as Protestantism. Rome was not the only Church that claimed to date her existence back to the first century.

By the turn of the sixth century, the Church's priesthood, in which the priest claimed to mediate between God and men, had replaced the early teachers of the gospel, who had taught the Scriptures. No longer, as it morphed over the centuries into an institution dominated by a hierarchy of popes, cardinals, and bishops who competed for power and temporal influence, could the evolving church's organisational structure claim to promote a fellowship of Christians on the New Testament model, united by the gospel, and individually filled by the Holy Spirit.

In the fifth century, Bishop Leo (440-461A.D.) seized the chance to exploit the opportunity presented by the decline of the empire by proclaiming himself ultimate head of the Roman Church. Inevitably, given the political void created by the fall of the empire, Leo, effectively, became Caesar's successor. In practice, the Roman Empire did not perish but merely changed its shape as the bishops of Rome neatly filled the increasing power vacuum left by the shrinking strength of the emperor, a move which completely contradicted the teachings of the New Testament and provided the seedbed for the causes of the Reformation.

Protestants maintain that the Roman Church of this period essentially lacked the original gospel as it struggled to accommodate the hordes of pagan barbarian princes that invaded the empire. As the Church hierarchy sought to assimilate the various conflicting belief systems under its jurisdiction, Rome compromised on the personal commitment required of a new disciple and permitted those who made a mere nominal conversion to regard themselves as Christian. No longer were alleged followers of Christ required to follow the New Testament's costly pattern of discipleship.

Within three centuries, the Roman Church transformed the administrative organization of the Roman Empire into an ecclesiastical system of bishoprics, dioceses, monasteries, schools, libraries, administrative centres, envoys, legal courts, and a criminal system of complex laws that were all under the direct control of the bishop of Rome. The Lateran, his Roman palace, effectively became the new Senate and cardinals replaced the Roman senators. With this fundamental change in the structure and administration of the Roman church, the message of salvation became further subsumed beneath power politics, which served to dilute the heart of its message. Temporal power and ambition increasingly eclipsed the spiritual, and the Christians under Roman jurisdiction were ultimately betrayed by their new overlords who preferred a life of comfort, power and wealth to that of spreading the message of Jesus Christ. Families squabbled over the acquisition of the papal throne, each wanting to install their own favoured candidate who would bolster their privileged positions. Repeatedly, they shunned any opportunity to reform. As centuries passed, the church drew nearer and nearer to the precipice, but leading Roman churchmen were not prepared to pay the price of reform and ultimately left the task to a '*smelly, ignorant, vulgar, superstitious, ungodly, and obstinate* '[91] monk from Whittenburg who, with his hammer, nailed his ninety-five theses to the church door. By so doing Luther was to accidently begin the Reformation at the time that

---

[91] The description was given by Pope Leo X who excommunicated Luther in 1521.

growing numbers of people were becoming increasingly scandalised by the corruption and cruelty born of the deadly mix of politics and religion that had been inflicted on the Christian peoples living under papal jurisdiction. As yet, however, that was far in the future.

Meanwhile, Clovis, King of the Franks, was the first prince to accept the Roman Catholic religion. He was baptized in 496 A.D. in the Cathedral of Rheims for which he was rewarded by the Bishop of Rome with the title of '*the eldest son of the Church*'. Others followed the King's example: the Burgundians of Southern Gaul, the Visigoths of Spain, the Suevi of Portugal, and the Anglo-Saxons of Britain. This development served to increase the power and prestige of the city's bishops. Furthermore, Rome's historic position as the seat of authority of the emperor made it acceptable to the barbarian rulers to accept it as the new power base as the bishops replaced the Caesars. This amalgamation of Church and State was an error which some early Protestant reformers were to later follow, much to the detriment of the success of the reforming movement of the sixteenth century.

It was in the sixth century that the supremacy of the bishops of Rome was finally consolidated under Emperor Justinian I in 533 A.D., although it would not be until 1073 under Gregory VII that the title of pope was formally declared to be the sole monopoly of the bishop of Rome.

As Justinian determined to shore up his failing political power by using force to achieve ecclesiastical unity, he, by so doing, ultimately bestowed on the bishops of Rome the power to use the sword of civil coercion to achieve their aims which led to the Roman Church's severe persecutions of both Christians and non-Christians of the next millennium just as its predecessor, the Roman Empire, had done to the early Christians.

Ultimately, the temporal rise to power of the bishop as his office evolved into that of 'pope' resulted in the official faith[92] of the early Christians of the Roman Church no longer being recognisable, as it was harnessed to power politics and became the pawn of secular

---

[92] Throughout this appendix, the description of the Roman Church refers to the papacy and not, in the main, to the individuals who were under its jurisdiction.

ambition. The evolution of the bishop of Rome from spiritual leader to a temporal lord with the attendant ceremonial worldly pomp that accompanied the papacy was a development which was forbidden in Luke 22 v 25-26[93].

The power of the Roman Church continued to wax as that of the empire waned. In the seventh century, the cunning seventh-century pope Boniface III shrewdly took hold of a familiar measure to secure papal hegemony in the ecclesiastical domain of the failing empire by making excellent use of the conjecture that Peter was the first bishop in Rome.[94] This claim was based on a particular interpretation of Matthew 16 but is contradicted by a number of respected linguistic and theological scholars and also by several of the early Church Fathers[95], including the most respected of them all, Augustine, who, in later life, confirmed it was Christ who was the 'Rock' of the church and not Peter but did acknowledge that others might think differently. Matthew 16, in view of the interpretations of the writings of some

---

[93] *And he said unto them, 'the kings of the Gentiles exercise lordship over them…but ye shall not be so.'*

[94] Roman Catholic author Eamon Duffy in his book *Saints and Sinners: A History of the Popes*, points out that there was no papal tradition following the death of Peter during the first two centuries.

[95] A number of the early Church Fathers regarded the rock and foundation of the Church as either Peter's confession of faith or Christ himself. Protestants argue that the Church Fathers, as a whole, did not interpret Matthew 16 in a pro-Roman sense. It was the views of Origen and Tertullian that were foundational for the interpretation of this important passage for many centuries, and their writings, as a whole, do not provide support for the papacy's continued exalted claim to spiritual power. By selecting isolated phrases and ignoring context, the Catholic Church has persuaded its members that the opposite is true. Meanwhile, Augustine, who is regarded as the greatest of the Church Fathers by Catholics, in his Retractations, withdrew his support of the suggestion that the bishops of Rome were the successors of Peter, but left it open for personal interpretation. Augustine, in fact, in his later life, supported the understanding that Jesus Christ was the Rock, and not Peter. In the view of the majority of Protestants, both history and Scripture indicates that the claim for papal supremacy is not based on sufficiently sound evidence to support the dogma that dictates that the popes are Peter's successors.

Church Fathers at that time, was being misused in order to raise the profile of the bishop of Rome so to, according to Protestant opinion, falsely endow him with power over other bishops, and Augustine wrote to correct this misapplication of their writings. There is also no clear supporting evidence in Scripture, including by Peter himself in his letters, for Rome's claim. It would be thought that he would know whether Jesus Christ had intended him to be the head of the church. There would be some evidence of that in his writings, and by his treatment by the other disciples, but there is none to be found, although he held an influential position. Nevertheless, despite the controversy over this issue, Boniface acquired the acquisition of the title 'Universal Bishop' that was granted to him by Emperor Phocas. This accorded him dominion and power to reign in ecclesiastical supremacy from the city of Rome to the far-flung reaches of the empire. The combined disputed interpretation of Matthew 16, and the claim that this also instituted an inherited apostolic succession, has served to enable the popes to assert dominance throughout history.

By the eighth century, the politicisation of the empire-sanctioned church that forged an organisation in the spirit and pattern of Imperial Rome, in sharp contrast to the persecuted church of the first three centuries, was nearing completion. Pastors were replaced by priests who, Protestants argue, positioned themselves between God and man, while the bishops of Rome increasingly usurped the role of the Holy Spirit in the lives of those who were drawn under their jurisdiction. Celibacy of the priests became a law of the Roman Church, despite the Scripture stating that the 'elders' must be men with one wife. As barbarian invaders, the Goths, Vandals, and Huns, who overthrew the Roman Empire, continued to accept its version of Christianity, their 'conversion' remained mostly nominal as they meshed their pagan practices and belief systems with those of Christianity, thus further diluting the gospel message as the years passed. Increasingly, those whom Rome deemed to be heretics led lives which more resembled those of first-century disciples than did the occupants of the papacy and its attendant hierarchy.

In the eighth century, the fraudulent claim was made by the growing Roman Church that the Emperor Constantine had transferred his authority, power, and palace to the popes. The document, known as the *Donation of Constantine,* was claimed to be a legal transaction in which the Emperor had bestowed on Bishop Sylvester (314 A.D. - 335 A.D.) much of his property and invested him with considerable spiritual power. The scope and significance of the bequest allegedly granted in this forged document is seen in the following quotation from the manuscript:

'We attribute to the See of Peter all the dignity, all the glory, all the authority of the imperial power. Furthermore, we give to Sylvester and to his successors our palace of the Lateran, which is incontestably the finest palace on the earth; we give him our crown, our mitre, our diadem, and all our imperial vestments; we transfer to him the imperial dignity. We bestow on the holy Pontiff in free gift the city of Rome, and all the western cities of Italy. To cede precedence to him, we divest ourselves of our authority over all those provinces, and we withdraw from Rome, transferring the seat of our empire to Byzantium; inasmuch as it is not proper that an earthly emperor should preserve the least authority, where God hath established the head of his religion.'

The *Donation of Constantine,* in which the Emperor allegedly refers to Bishop Sylvestor as 'Prince of the Apostles, Vicar of Christ' is now known to have been forged in about 750 A.D. Throughout the Middle Ages, the papacy exploited this alleged deed of gift, inserted it in her laws, and burned alive those who questioned its authenticity. It was not until the sixteenth century that Rome was forced to acknowledge that the Donation was, indeed, a forgery.

Five years after the creation of the fake document, when the kings of Lombardy were attempting to suppress Italian power, and the Moors were conquering Spain and Africa, the son of Charles the Hammer, and father of Charlamagne, Pepin of France, seized the throne from Childeric. To secure his power base, he determined to seek the blessing of the papacy. To this end, he and his army marched over the Alps, conquering the Lombard towns, which he presented to Pope Stephen, thus greatly increasing his power over the Catholic church.

A further milestone was passed on Christmas Eve 800 A.D. when Charlemagne, as master of nearly all the Romano-Germanic nations, knelt before Pope Leo III, who placed on his head the crown of the Western Empire, an act which, in total contradiction of the teaching of Christ and his apostles, highlighted the pope's increasing secular power. In 538 A.D., Emperor Justinian had given the Bishop of Rome the title of Pontifex Maximus, the title of the High Priest of the pagan Babylonian religion; now, significantly, it was the Pope who was crowning the Emperor.

The fraudulent *Donation of Constantine*, less than half a century old at this time, was already proving to be one of a number of very useful tools in the papal armoury. In a move revealing how far the papacy had evolved from its Christian roots, Pope Nicholas I seized the advantage in 865 A.D. and used the document and other forgeries[96] to demand submission from bishops and princes while

---

96 During the ninth century, major changes took place in the Roman Church that significantly altered its constitution and laid the foundation for the full development of the papacy in later years. This radical revolution in ecclesiastical government that changed the character of the Roman church was enabled by a mid-ninth-century forger who created the *Pseudo–Isidorian Decretals*, which were a fictitious account of church history. They created fabricated precedents for the exercise of sovereign authority of the popes over the Church prior to the fourth century and made false claims to the effect that the popes had always exercised sovereign dominion and had ultimate authority even over Church Councils. Pope Nicholas I (858A.D.– 867A.D.) was the first to use them as the basis for securing his claims of authority, but it was not until the eleventh century that they were utilised by Pope Gregory VII to change the government of the Western Church in a very significant way.

By combining the forged documents of the Donation, the Decretals, and other fraudulent historical accounts, and incorporating them into Church law, the popes were elevated into the position of absolute monarchs over the Roman Catholic Church. This made them, effectively, the temporal lords of Western Europe. Gratian furthered their power-base with the composition of his *Decretum* of 1151. This aimed to provide alleged foundational precedents for the claim of papal primacy with claims to tradition. His scheme was successful and this fraudulent ploy became the basis of all canon law and academic theology.

A highly-regarded Roman Catholic scholar Johann Joseph Ignaz von Döllinger when referring to the forgeries makes this comment, '*In the middle of the ninth century—about 845—there arose the huge fabrication of the Isidorian*

amassing tremendous riches to the papacy. These forgeries enabled the papacy of the second millennium to claim power and position that would have been considered blasphemous by earlier incumbents of the bishopric.

From this time, the arrogance and corruption of the popes escalated to new heights, as did their financial fortunes. Intoxicated with their own power, pride, and position, they participated in nefarious and immoral practices as they ruled a very unholy and corrupt see which had become one wild party of debauchery. Immoral women, as

---

Decretals......About a hundred pretended decrees of the earliest popes, together with certain spurious writings of other Church dignitaries and acts of Synods, were then fabricated in the west of Gaul, and eagerly seized upon by Pope Nicholas I at Rome, to be used as genuine documents in support of the new claims put forward by himself and his successors. That the pseudo–Isidorian principles eventually revolutionized the whole constitution of the Church, and introduced a new system in place of the old...on that point there can be no controversy among candid historians…Gratian's work displaced all the older collections of canon law and became the manual and repertory, not for canonists only but for the scholastic theologians who, for the most part, derived all their knowledge of Fathers and Councils from it. No book has ever come near it in its influence in the Church, although there is scarcely another so chockful of gross errors, both intentional and unintentional.' (Johann Joseph Ignaz von Döllinger, *The Pope and the Council*, (Boston: Roberts, 1870), pp. 76-77, 79, 115-116).

The Protestant historian George Salmon in his book, *The Infallibility of the Church* (London: John Murray, 1914), explains the importance and influence of *Pseudo–Isidore* in these words: *'In these are to be found precedents for all manner of instances of the exercise of sovereign dominion by the pope over other Churches. You must take notice of this, that it was by furnishing precedents that these letters helped the growth of papal power. Thenceforth the popes could hardly claim any privilege but they would find in these letters supposed proofs that the privilege in question was no more than had been always claimed by their predecessors, and always exercised without any objection...On these spurious decretals is built the whole fabric of Canon Law.'*

Thomas Aquinas was also misled by the forgeries and used them as almost his entire reference for his writings on the rights and authority of the popes, which became foundational teachings of the Church. These spurious quotations had enormous influence on many Western theologians and were regarded as an undisputed authority throughout successive centuries until the Reformation.

described in the story of Mazoria above, for many years governed the papal throne while they installed and deposed their favourites and their family as rulers of the Church during the so-called *Rule of the Harlots*. The papacy continued its descent over the years into the dregs of iniquity as it revealed how far it had departed and separated itself from the early Church of Rome. Those who were genuine Christians, as described by the apostles, remained separate to this powerfully corrupt system, or quietly existed within it. It is difficult to imagine a greater contrast than that which existed between the Christian Church of Rome of the first centuries, and the papacy, by the turn of the millennium.

For two hundred years, therefore, the papacy remained an unsavoury scene of immoral behaviour during which popes led corrupt lives in complete contrast to that required by the followers of Christ. They shored up power and wealth for themselves as the most powerful families of Italy disputed and squabbled over it like a possession with as many as three 'popes' at one time claiming to be the official occupant of the Chair of Peter. Judging by their behaviour, the incumbents of the papacy could be viewed as being completely apostate by the beginning of the second millennium.

Twenty years after the schism split the church into two institutions, one in the East that became the Eastern Orthodox Church, and the other in the West that was ruled from Rome, it finally experienced a partial reformation, and some measure of discipline was imposed. The changes did not, however, challenge the pride of the popes whose secular ambitions rose to new heights as they jockeyed to fill the power vacuum created in the wake of the waning authority of the descendants of Charlemagne. Pope Gregory VII (1015-1085) proved to be even more ambitious for political power than his predecessors. Incredibly, perhaps, pathologically, Gregory went so far as to decree, blasphemously, that the reign of the pope was the reign of God on earth. To this end, he determined to subject all spiritual and temporal authority to himself and his successors. It was Gregory VII who, enabled by the collection of forged documents, envisioned what was to become of the vast structure of the papacy. His ambition was to be the supreme ruler and judge of all leaders of both Church and State.

World domination was clearly part of his agenda. It is difficult to imagine a greater contrast with the early church of Rome and the other first century churches that were based on the Apostolic teachings.

By laying claim to the concept that the pope is Christ's Vicar, Gregory VII, in the Protestant view, created a papacy that rivalled or even occupied the position of the Holy Spirit of Christ in Scripture. This supremacy, which Gregory claimed by divine right, demanded ultimate dominion over both emperors and kings. His promotion of this concept and his relentless ambition, in conjunction with the enormous wealth that the Roman Catholic Church possessed, brought his desires to fruition. The original Church of Rome now no longer existed in the heart of the papacy. Instead, it was replaced by a monstrous megalomaniacal regime. Far divorced from the teaching of Jesus Christ, it would for centuries wield the papal sword, instigate massacres and sanction the widespread use of the most terrible tortures ever devised as it sought to accumulate wealth and increase or maintain its jurisdiction over mankind. It is little wonder that some now began to claim parallels between the Antichrist of Scripture and the papacy.

The pontiffs that followed him, by the use of deceit and crusades against Christians who were not under the jurisdiction of Rome, as well as non-Christians, sought to further papal domination. For hundreds of years, the papacy increased in power and glory at the cost of thousands of lives as popes deposed kings and princes, destroyed lands, committed virtual genocides, ruined numerous cities, and countless homes.

*

Some Papal Facts

Boniface VIII (1294-1303), in his 'Unam Sanctam', declared salvation was not possible for non-Catholic Christians. After massacring the entire population of Palestrina in Italy, he indulged in a ménage à trois with a married woman and her daughter. He also earned the reputation throughout Rome for being a shameless paedophile. Meanwhile, Dante, who visited the Vatican, observed that it was a 'Sewer of Corruption'.

John XXIII (1410-1415) had an adulterous relationship with his sister-in-law, sold Cardinalates to children of wealthy families, and openly renounced the teaching of Scripture.

Nicolas V (1447-1455) empowered the King of Portugal to make war on African peoples, steal their property. and enslave them.

Sixtus IV (1471-1484) announced that money rescued souls from Purgatory and was involved in plots to murder any who opposed him, including Lorenzo de Medici. He sanctioned the Spanish Inquisition—the murder and torture of Christians and others with appalling cruelty that had not been witnessed before in history.

Innocent VIII (1484-1492), whose rule is known as the Golden Age of the Bastards as he had so many illegitimate children, sold off church offices for vast profits. He also appointed Thomas of Torquemada, who tortured many Christians, the Inquisitor General of Spain. He ordered the genocide of the Waldenses, known as the Poor in Christ, by sending an army against them. When on his death bed, it is alleged that he ordered an attractive wet nurse to supply him with milk fresh from her breast.

Alexander VI (1492-1503), the most corrupt of the Renaissance Popes, bought the papacy, appointed Cardinals for financial gain, openly had many illegitimate children whom he later appointed to high church offices, and, together, they murdered anyone who stood in their way.

Leo X (1513-1521) offered offices and church honours for sale and appointed Cardinals as young as seven. He was constantly jockeying for secular power with kings. Leo also supported Unam Sanctam, and declared the burning of heretics to be a divine appointment.

Pope Paul III (1534-1549) produced many illegitimate children, and offered Charles V an army to exterminate Protestants.

Julius III (1550-55) inspired the poem 'In Praise of Sodomy' after he fell in love with a teenage boy whom he appointed as a cardinal. For six hundred years, the papacy sanctioned torture, murder, burning at the stake, and the confiscation of the property of both Christians and non-Christians who refused to accept papal jurisdiction or who recognised the primary authority of Scripture.

*

*Pope Formosus and Stephen VII (Cadaver Trial) 1870
by Jean -Paul Laurens*

Christians and Heretics

Assessing the veracity of the opposing claims of scholars concerning the early beliefs of various Christian or heretical groups is problematic: there are a number of obstacles that hinder our attempt to provide a valid interpretation of historical evidence relating to these early Christian communities. A significant collection of foundational documents that the Roman system used to advance and give historical justification to her power, both temporal and spiritual, are now known and acknowledged by the Catholic Church to have been forgeries. In addition, most of the written evidence concerning the early non-Catholic Christian and heretical groups whom Rome ultimately persecuted nearly to extinction were mainly written by their opponents, inquisitors, and executioners, who were keen to label them as heretical Manicheans. We are unable to examine their own views as the Inquisition destroyed their victims' documents just as they destroyed their authors, thus denying future historians a valuable contemporary resource.

In recent years, records from the Inquisition have been released and have been examined by historians; however, the voices of the accused have been largely expunged on account of the destruction of their own written works. and so, again, we only have accounts as recorded by their inquisitors and persecutors. We are thus left with biased documents and fragments of contemporary records upon which we must strive to present a valid narrative of the history of Christianity. As always, we also must be mindful, too, of the need to judge the situation in the context of the period and not from the perspective of our present age. Fortunately, however, we do have detailed records of the lifestyles and attitudes of the Waldenses, the forerunners of Protestantism, from eye witness accounts which we can compare with their papal opponents. The existence of these records and eye-witness accounts enable us to make a fairer assessment of the conduct of people from earlier centuries.

It may be challenging to assemble the pieces of the historic puzzle together, but it is clear that, from at least the fifth century, many Christians recognized the increasing apostate nature of the Roman

Catholic Church and spurned it. The character of the Church of the twelfth century, and later, is not that of the Roman Church of the first two centuries.

Heresy also flourished from the days of the New Testament, and it is difficult to determine which groups were, despite some unorthodox beliefs, yet still deserving of the title 'Christian'. Perhaps it is reasonable to assume that the various groups contained a mixture of heretics and authentic Christians, as is true today of various denominations. As Rome sought to draw all these varieties of believers under her sway, she attempted by various methods, culminating in torture and death, to persuade the people of Europe, heretic and Christian, to accept her as the ultimate authority of God on earth and to capitulate to her demands.

One of these successful and very influential groups who challenged papal demands was known as the Paulicians, followers of Paul, the Apostle. Their leader was Constantine[97], who was converted to Christianity from Manichaeism in 660 A.D. by studying the Gospels and Epistles given to him by a Christian to whom he gave shelter.

Constantine spread the message of primitive Christianity and won many people to the faith, including large numbers of those who had previously sworn allegiance to the Roman Church. They disseminated the Apostles' teachings on the need for repentance before baptism and demanded a genuine experience of conversion; they maintained the equality of all believers, condemned the use of images, maintained the Lord's Supper as a memorial only, and promoted the necessity of the simplicity of the Christian life as set out by the early church. Their doctrines, which heralded many of those of later Protestantism, were protected through the Dark Ages by similar groups, until a coalition of circumstances a millennium later, finally, enabled them, with refinements, to come to fruition in the Protestant Reformation.

The Paulicians spread the primitive faith across parts of Italy and France, reaching England in large numbers by the beginning of the second millennium. Passing under various names and with some

---

[97] Constantine is not to be confused with the emperor of the same name.

variation in doctrine - Paulicians, Bogomils, Waldenses, Albigenses - most of whom, as far as we can judge from contemporary evidence being clearly godly men - kept alive some glimmer of light amongst all the spiritual darkness of the Medieval Age as the Roman church passed through *The Rule of the Harlots,* and beyond. Thus, like a golden thread reaching from the time of Christ to the Reformation, we can catch glimpses of the true church via some of these groups, which included many in the Roman Church who just kept their head down. This continued until Lutheranism, with all its serious faults, and without a doubt in need of further refinements that were yet two hundred years in the future, finally entered the European stage, and gifted its greatest contribution to the medieval church by directing people back to their foundation: the gospel of Jesus Christ and the Scriptures.

As the Roman Church evolved her new persona and departed from its original foundation and structure while her power base expanded across the empire, she ruthlessly persecuted the Paulicians and their spiritual descendants, and all who withstood her advance. While the apostles emphasised the need to root out heresy from the Christian church, Rome broadened this to all who opposed either her doctrines or her temporal power. Paul taught that Christians must disassociate from heretics; however, Rome believed in torturing and killing not only them but scripturally-based Christians who withstood her temporal rule. She accused the Paulicians, according to respected sources, erroneously, of being a heretical branch of Manichaeism, which was a tactic Rome frequently used to discredit those who criticised the evolving papacy for its temporal ambitions and what they viewed as its increasing departure from its scriptural roots.

From the twelfth century, the papacy ordered the Alpine communities of the followers of Christ who had escaped from being brought under either the Roman or the Constantinople yoke to be exterminated as the crusading popes increasingly turned their attention to those Christians who were not part of the Catholic fold.

It is claimed by Rome that one of the groups, the Albigenses, was heretical and, certainly, their alleged beliefs, as recorded by Rome, would exclude them from the title of Christian. Nonetheless, they led lives and held beliefs that more resembled those of the disciples of the first century than did their persecutor. Meanwhile, one group, the Waldenses, recognised as being the forerunners of Protestantism with their Christ-like lifestyles, good citizenship, trustworthiness, and honesty that resulted in prosperity for their regions, attracted an increasing number of disciples who were impressed with their example. They maintained that there had been no true pope since Sylvestor and espoused many of the beliefs that were later held by Protestantism. They opposed temporal offices and the extravagant lifestyles adopted by the Church that were inappropriate for preachers of the gospel. They taught that a pope's pardons were worthless, proposed that purgatory was a fable and that relics were simply rotten bones of uncertain origin. Pilgrimages were simply a papal money-making racket, holy water was no more efficacious than rainwater, and prayer in a barn was as effectual as that offered in a church. Crucially, they held that the doctrine of transubstantiation was unbiblical and even accused, as did the sixteenth-century reformers, the Roman Church of being the harlot of the book of Revelation. Not surprisingly, given the aspirations of the papacy, the popes sought to annihilate these non-Catholic Christians and, by so doing, strangle the prototype of the Protestant Reformation while still in its infancy.

Like the Paulicians, who probably influenced them and by now had been slaughtered in hundreds of thousands for their faith by the papacy and its puppets, the Catholic princes, the Waldenses are also understood to have possessed the New Testament in the vernacular. This enabled them to derive their beliefs directly from the Scriptures and base the structure of their churches upon its model in stark contrast to the hierarchy of the Church of Rome at this time. They committed large portions of the Scripture to memory, became missionaries to foreign lands, and even penetrated Rome with the gospel. Their simple dress and lifestyle attracted admiration from those who encountered them while their example and evangelistic zeal drew many converts to join them, much to the alarm of the papacy, which determined to exterminate them.

The popes proceeded to entice and cajole men to eradicate these sincere Christian people by offering free tickets to heaven and forgiveness of sins as a reward for annihilating them. This, with the opportunity to loot the prosperous Christian communities without the hazardous journeys that the Crusades had entailed proved too tempting to the popes' thugs to refuse.

Repeatedly, for four centuries, French and Italian communities were drowned in blood, as many thousands of men, women, and children were butchered, entombed alive in the walls of newly constructed homes, and burnt to death. As the pope's men rampaged across large swathes of Europe, significant areas of the continent were destroyed, civilization ruined, art treasures dismantled, and the progress of the world rolled back centuries as large populations of Christians were cruelly butchered in the name of the papacy[98].

The Waldenses, known alternatively as the Poor of Christ, or the Vaudois, together with the Albigenses, suffered terribly during the papal persecutions. The genocides were then followed by a deliberate attempt by the papacy to erase them from history by derogatory and slanderous misrepresentations. Simultaneously, with the beginning of the papal-driven massacres, the Inquisition was created with the aim to stamp out whatever the Roman Church chose to call 'heresy' using torture, imprisonment, and even death when it suited its purpose.

In 1252, Pope Innocent IV solemnly authorized the establishment of the Inquisition and confirmatory or regulatory decrees about it were issued by Alexander IV, Clement IV, Urban IV, and Clement V. No other power in history has devised such acts of dreadful cruelty against their fellow man. Even the tortures suffered by those in the Tower of London could not compete with that inflicted under papal jurisdiction. The instruments employed were terrible, and it is difficult to even read the description of the manner in which all who disagreed with the popes – including Christians who wanted to follow the New Testament teachings of Christ whom Rome called 'heretics',

---

[98] The history of these proto-type Protestants can be read in J.A. Wylie's book on *The History of the Waldenses* which is freely available from the internet.

were brutally tortured. The historian Wylie[99] describes the methods used by Rome to shore up her power and influence in this manner:

'We pass on into the chamber, where more dreadful sights meet our gaze. It is hung round and round with instruments of torture, so numerous that it would take a long while even to name them, and so diverse that it would take a much longer time to describe them. We must take them in groups, for it were hopeless to think of going over them one by one, and particularizing the mode in which each operated, and the ingenuity and art with which all of them have been adapted to their horrible end. There were instruments for compressing the fingers till the bones should be squeezed to splinters. There were instruments for probing below the finger-nails till an exquisite pain, like a burning fire, would run along the nerves. There were instruments for tearing out the tongue, for scooping out the eyes, for grubbing-up the ears. There were bunches if iron cords, with a spiked circle at the end of every whip, for tearing the flesh from the back till bone and sinew were laid bare. There were iron cases for the legs, which were tightened upon the limb placed in them by means of a screw, till flesh and bone were reduced to a jelly. There were cradles set full of sharp spikes, in which victims were laid and rolled from side to side, the wretched occupant being pierced at each movement of the machine with innumerable sharp points. There were iron ladles with long handles, for holding molten lead or boiling pitch, to be poured down the throat of the victim, and convert his body into a burning cauldron. There were frames with holes to admit the hands and feet, so contrived that the person put into them had his body bent into unnatural and painful positions, and the agony grew greater and greater by moments, and yet the man did not die. There were chestfuls of small but most ingeniously constructed instruments for pinching, probing, or tearing the more sensitive parts of the body, and continuing the pain up to the very verge where reason or life gives way. On the floor and walls of the apartment were the larger instruments for the same fearful end—lacerating, mangling,

---

[99] The volumes on *The History of Protestantism* by J.A. Wylie are freely available from the internet.

and agonizing living men; but these we shall meet in other dungeons we are yet to visit.'

One of the best summary statements on the papacy's Inquisition is that of the renowned Catholic historian Lord Acton. He writes:

'The Inquisition is peculiarly the weapon and peculiarly the work of the popes. It stands out from all those things in which they co-operated, followed or assented as the distinctive feature of papal Rome. It was set up, renewed and perfected by a long series of acts emanating from the supreme authority in the Church. No other institution, no doctrine, no ceremony is so distinctly the individual creation of the papacy, except the dispensing power. It is the principal thing with which the papacy is identified, and by which it must be judged. The principle of the Inquisition is the pope's sovereign power over life and death. Whosoever disobeys him should be tried and tortured and burnt. If that cannot be done, formalities may be dispensed with, and the culprit may be killed like an outlaw. That is to say, the principle of the Inquisition is murderous, and a man's opinion of the papacy is regulated and determined by his opinion of religious assassination.'

According to these accounts, by its infliction of excruciating torture and cruel death on Christians, and others, papal Rome even exceeded the barbaric cruelties of those of pagan Rome. However, since the turn of the present millennium Catholic writers have been promoting a revision of the history of the Inquisition following the release of records that were made by the inquisitors and, certainly, our view of the Inquisitions must be tempered by the context of the period in which they were functioning.

The officials of the Church believed that the heretic was destined to hell and sought to win them back to orthodox Catholicism; however, when they failed, they had no compunction in giving them over to the secular arm to sacrifice in, according to their view, the interests of the spiritual wellbeing of the community, which would be terrified into conformity by the ugly scenes of people being burnt alive. Impossible as it is to imagine today, the fact that this was in complete defiance of the teachings of Christ never gained any traction in the minds of the alleged Christian inquisitor, torturer, or executioner[100].

Into this dangerous world, John Wycliffe was born in 1330. He became a theologian at Oxford University who maintained, contrary to the Roman Church, that Scripture must be the primary authority and that everyone who could read should have access to it. Wycliffe began the movement that translated the Bible into English so that people, known as Lollards, who were eager for a more biblical-based Christianity in England had access to the Scriptures. Pope Alexander's persecution of the followers of Wycliffe included Jan Hus, a Czech scholar at the University of Prague. Czechs were critical of the immorality of the clergy and demanded that the Scripture be translated into the vernacular. Hus, unlike Wycliffe, however, did not escape the stake and was burned in 1415. Although deceased by this time, Wycliffe was declared a heretic, his corpse disinterred and

---

[100] The Church's apologists emphasise that the aim of the Inquisitions was to save the soul of the accused, and, more importantly, to protect Catholics from the spread of heresy. Some promote almost benevolent motives to the Inquisitions and compare them favourably with the secular courts of the time while maintaining that the stories of the tortures were a fiction, part of the so-called Black Legends, spread, according to Roman Catholics, by Protestants. Even today, some traditional Catholics justify and express approval of the methods of the medieval church to force Christians and others to acknowledge the supremacy of the papacy as a religious and secular world authority.

Although the numbers suffering tortures and executions have probably been exaggerated, this is understandable given the horrors inflicted on the victims, and the fear it engendered in the communities. The facts are, at this time, in a state of flux, but the revisionists are considered by other historians to be underestimating the number of victims who were tortured and sent to the fire. The evidence suggests that the totals are in the thousands, not the hundreds, as some Catholic sources are presently claiming. Certainly, the methods of torture sanctioned by the popes, while yet claiming to be Jesus Christ's representative on earth, cannot be described as less than diabolical. It is no excuse to argue that it was justified on account it was a practice of the time in secular situations as those carrying out these barbaric practices were torturing and killing in the name of Christ who never condoned violence. People who conducted these practices could not claim to be part of the church founded by the Apostles as their actions would have been completely anathema to the first century church.

burned. This was the eve of the Reformation, and while the papacy was busy massacring European Christians, and respect for the church was dwindling in the wake of clerical corruption, increasing scholarship, the seed-bed for the revolution, was being stimulated and fostered by the Renaissance. Erasmus, and others, translated the Bible into several languages, thus making it available to the literate, and the printing press was invented that enabled the dissemination of ideas and literature across the continent.

Jan Hus

Amidst increasingly fierce opposition by the papacy, the move to restore a more biblically-based Christianity to Europe finally began at the turn of the sixteenth century.

In England, although it is true to say that the country was not ready for Protestantism by the first decades of the sixteenth century, and, apart from isolated pockets, did not want it, many were highly critical of the well-rehearsed history of the clerical corruption that was rife. Even prominent Catholics like Dean Colet favoured a reform of the church.

The anticlerical movement of the early sixteenth century was strong in the places that mattered and for good reason. Thus, while Catholic apologists rightly challenge the once-accepted story of a people highly dissatisfied with the old order in general and eager to replace it with another, they underplay the people's serious criticism of the shortcomings of a largely uneducated and often corrupt clergy. A significant number of these were career criminals who sought sanctuary in Holy Orders that provided them with the Benefit of Clergy, a clerical privilege that protected criminal clerics from the penalties of the law. The church was certainly in need of serious reform, and overseas visitors would note how the English people raged against their clergy. This phenomenon was epitomised by that

Tudor *cause célèbre*: the alleged murder of Richard Hunne[101], a London merchant tailor, by the bishop's chancellor, Dr William Horsey[102], for refusing to hand over his dead baby's christening gown as a mortuary fee to his priest. The groundswell of hostility towards the clergy that this famous case engendered in the capital ultimately powered the Reformation Parliament to rip the church to pieces when it was expedient for the King to permit them to do so.

The push towards reform during the first half of the sixteenth century arose simultaneously across much of Europe. When Luther accidentally triggered the Reformation, several crucial factors coalesced to drive the movement forward. The Renaissance had by now prepared the minds of the educated for the launch of new systems of thought and debate, scholars had translated the Bible into the vernacular, while the invention of the printing press ensured that the ideas challenging the status quo were circulated to the centres of learning.

The most crucial issue for debate at the time concerned the place of Scripture. The Protestants, like the Waldenses before them,

---

[101] 'Hunne's fascinating story has all the ingredients of good detective fiction: the dead body of a champion of the people who had challenged powerful vested interests; a staged scene of crime; a motley collection of rogues and suspects, including a corrupt jailer and part-time pimp; tales of intrigue, torture and false alibis; the ridiculous spectacle of the corpse propped up in a court of law to be prosecuted and found guilty in order that the evidence of murder could be legally obliterated by the fires of Smithfield; and, lastly, a chief suspect, a man of "great dignity, bearing and learning" who had murdered the popular local hero for being a chronic pain in the collective clerical neck. Ultimately, the circumstances and the ecclesiastical cover-up of the murder so seriously inflamed the anticlericalism that was rife in London that it gave rise to the Reformation Parliament that finally tore the Catholic Church to pieces.' (*The Tale of Dr William Horsey, Canon of Exeter Cathedral* by the author, at present in unfinished draft form.)

Importantly, Hunne's case also presented the King with the means of ejecting the popes from English soil when it was expedient for him to do so. The murky tale both highlights the undercurrents of corruption that epitomised the foundations of the old order and illustrates the belief system that sculptured the mental universe of the period. It makes it clear why reform was necessary and provides the background to the events that led to the march towards Protestantism.

[102] Unfortunately, he is a relative of the author.

maintained that Scripture alone was the final authority while Rome gave equal status to tradition, as is still the case. The crux of the argument to the Protestant was that Rome endorsed tradition even when, in their view, it contradicted Scripture or added to it, both of which the reformers understood the Scriptures condemned.

It is vitally important to comprehend the place and significance of the reformers rallying cry of *sola scriptura*. They held strongly to this Christian foundational belief as they recognised Christ's complete acceptance of the authority of the written Word as is evident in His words in Matt. 5v17, '*Think not that I came to destroy the law or the prophets: I am not come to destroy but to fulfil them. For verily, I say unto you, till heaven and earth pass, one jot or one tittle shall in no wise pass from the law till all be fulfilled.*' Elsewhere it is written in Psalm 38 v 2, '*Thou hast magnified thy Word above all thy name.*' The reformers, like the early disciples, bowed in submission to the ultimate authority of God's Word as the Apostle Paul had taught in these words: '*All scripture is given by inspiration of God, and is profitable for doctrine, for reproof, for correction, for instruction in righteousness: That the man of God may be perfect, thoroughly furnished unto all good works.*'

This raised a serious bone of contention between Catholics and Protestants which continues to this day.

The reformers, like the centuries of Christians before them, understood that God's written Word is the foundation of a Christian's conscience. Indeed, all the disciples of Christ acknowledge that there is an absolute standard by which a belief may be judged to be either true or false: and that is by measuring it by the yardstick of the Bible. It is not possible to claim to be a Christian and not recognise the rule of God's Word in life. As Ps. 119:140 says, '*Thy word is very pure; therefore, thy servant loveth it.*' It would be a contradiction for a person to claim to be a Christian and not immerse himself in the Scriptures for the marks of the Christian life are described in the Bible thus: '*Thy words were found, and I did eat them; and thy word was unto me the joy and rejoicing of mine heart.*' Jer. 15:16.

To the reformers, it was also important that Paul the Apostle constantly warned disciples not to go beyond what is written (see 1

Cor. 4:6)[103] while Moses was told, '*You shall not add to what I command you nor subtract from it.*' (see Deut. 4:2) In the same vein, Solomon reaffirmed this in Proverbs where it states, '*Every word of God is tested. Add nothing to his words, lest he reprove you, and you be exposed as a deceiver.*' (see Prov. 30:5-6) Protestants are also mindful of the words of John who closed the last words of the Bible with the same admonishment, stating, '*I warn everyone who hears the prophetic words in this book: if anyone adds to them, God will add to him the plagues described in this book, and if anyone takes away from the words in this prophetic book, God will take away his share in the tree of life...*' (see Rev. 22: 18-19)

Protestants objected to the Roman Catholic Church's addition of certain doctrines and traditions that, in their view, not only went beyond biblical teaching, but actually contradicted it, and this was, to them, a very serious matter. This appeal to the pre-eminence of the Bible, known as *sola scriptura*, was the cornerstone of the Reformation and, in the Protestant view, it could hardly have been stated more emphatically by Jesus Christ, the Apostles, and the early disciples. The Catholic Church, however, was not and is still not of the opinion that primary prominence must be given to the Scriptures, and adopts non-scriptural sources upon which to base some of its doctrines in addition to Scripture. Reformers argued that some of these non-biblical sources, which the Roman Church regarded as sacred traditions were un- or even anti-biblical and, therefore, undermined the gospel message. This resulted, according to the Reformers, in the Protestant and Catholic Churches providing a different gospel to the world: one emphasised the importance of *sola scriptura* and justification by faith alone, evidenced by works of faith, the indwelling of the Holy Spirit following conversion, and obedience to Christ, while the other placed its emphasis on non-biblical church traditions, in addition to Scripture, and salvation by the sacraments and good works. These were and remain, obviously, irreconcilable

---

[103] '*Do not go beyond what is written.*' New International Version.

and, historically, placed the two groups on a theological collision course[104].

Martin Luther's visit to Rome in 1517 impacted him deeply. He was so shocked by the anti-Christian character of the city and its Catholic hierarchy that he had witnessed in the heart of the Catholic church that his experience motivated him to declare, '*Unless I am convicted by Scripture and plain reason–I do not accept the authority of popes and councils for they have contradicted each other–my conscience is captive to the Word of God. I cannot and I will not recant anything, for to go against conscience is neither right nor safe. Here I stand, I cannot do otherwise, God help me. Amen.*' Luther simply discovered what had been the standard attested to by Jesus Christ and His Apostles, and to which the Church of Rome, before the papacy's evolution into a temporal power, had adhered.

At the same time that Luther underwent his conversion, other important individuals, nearly all highly schooled and influential academics were encountering a similar challenge and change of heart and there were many famous names amongst them: there was Melanchthon, who was with Luther at Wittenberg; Erasmus and Colet were based at Oxford; Bilney, Latimer, and Cartwright were at Cambridge, and Lefevre and Farel at Paris. Not all left the Catholic

---

[104] Catholics argue that they have scriptural support for regarding their traditions to be of the same authority as Scripture by quoting 2 Thess. 2 v 15: '*Therefore, brethren, stand fast, and hold the traditions which ye have been taught, whether by word, or our epistle.*' Alternatively, they quote 1 Cor.11 v 2. which states: '*I praise you for remembering me in everything and for holding to the traditions just as I passed them on to you.*' Protestants take issue with this interpretation by pointing out that Paul was referring to the teachings of the Apostles only and not to traditions created by men as were developed over a millennium by the papacy. They draw attention to Matt.15 v 6 to support their case. This warns: '*Thus, you nullify the word of God for the sake of your tradition,*' while *Mk 7 v 7* states a similar warning: '*Howbeit in vain do they worship me, teaching for doctrines the commandments of men.*' Every long-established organisation will inevitably develop traditions of their own; however, they must always, in a Christian setting, be in accordance with the teachings of Scripture which is the final authority, and rejected if found to be contrary to it. Here, Protestant and Catholic churches divide, and the issues at stake are crucial and irreconcilable.

church to become leaders of the Reformation, but, almost without exception, they were highly educated and academic men of their time who held offices of influence in academia and even in the royal courts. The flow and exchange of ideas and scholarship, with the pursuit of truth, become a characteristic of life, while friendship and the exchange of ideas occurred among the reformers as the movement spread across Europe and the British Isles. It was precisely because the reform began in Europe's Universities where academic churchmen demanded change that the Protestant Reformation was mostly successful. A web of social links was established as ideas were debated and exchanged, and this provided the necessary lines of communication for the reforming movement to spread rapidly across the continent. It was, indeed, astonishing that a revolution as vast as the Reformation that wrought such a change in peoples' thoughts and lives could be accomplished in a mere few years.

Some of these scholars understood Hebrew, Latin, and Greek, which was providential as it was the necessary requirement for studying the Scriptures. It was essential that they were translated into every European language so that the people would have access to them and, fortunately, the scholarship required for this was readily available in the universities. If, when the great reformers were preaching at Oxford and Cambridge, and other centres of learning and influence, Tyndale had not been busy smuggling copies of the New Testament in the vernacular into England from Europe so that every literate man could read the Scriptures for himself, there would have been little chance of the Reformation in England becoming so strongly rooted. A similar situation occurred in a number of other European countries, such as France and Germany. This coalition of factors created fertile ground for the biblical message of the early church to take root once again and escape its suppression by the medieval church, which had held it captive for centuries. Finally, the original teachings of Christ and his Apostles, which had become corrupted when the Church of Rome departed from its first-century roots in its mistaken attempt to fill the power vacuum left by the declining Roman Empire, was available to those who sought it.

The Reformation, therefore, as it swept across swathes of Europe, was, in the Protestant view, a movement which released millions from bondage to an apostate papacy and a superstitious belief system as they became re-acquainted with the New Testament gospel and the faith of the original Christians of the early Roman Church. Meanwhile, the rediscovery of the doctrine of justification by faith alone, evidenced by works of faith, led every sincere Christian into direct and personal contact with the God of revival. As the famous preacher Charles Spurgeon (1834-92) said, *'Think not that Luther was the only man that wrought the Reformation! There were hundreds who sighed and cried in secret, 'O God, how long?': in the cottages of the Black Forest, in the homes of Germany, on the hills of Switzerland, in the palaces of Spain, in the dungeons of the Inquisition and the green lanes of England.'* Luther may have ultimately lost his way and stumbled over the concept of works of faith as found in the epistle of James, leaving it to others to re-discover the complete message of the gospel, but he was certainly the catalyst for the burgeoning movement that ultimately released men's minds from the darkness of medieval superstitions.

Thus, the rapidity with which Roman Catholic totalitarianism was smashed was due to the reformers from their academic institutions working together, sharing ideas, and translators simultaneously making the Bible available to the ordinary person to study for himself. This provided him with the opportunity to test the validity of the teachings of Rome against those of the reformers. Of course, they made errors, some serious ones, and later refinements and corrections were necessary, although they were yet two hundred years in the future, but that such a near-complete revolution, albeit an imperfect one, was accomplished in such a short space of time remains one of the most astonishing achievements in history.

The nineteenth-century historian Jean-Henri Merle D'Aubigne, when commenting on the development of the medieval Church through the centuries, encapsulates the problems inherent in the manner in which the Roman Church evolved, in these words:

'...... Men accustomed to the ties and political forms of an earthly country transferred some of their views and customs to the spiritual

and eternal kingdom of Jesus Christ. The semblance of an identical and external organization was gradually substituted for the internal and spiritual unity which forms the essence of genuine religion. The precious perfume of faith was left out, and then men prostrated themselves before the empty vase which had contained it. The faith of the heart no longer uniting the members of the Church, another tie was sought, and they were united by means of bishops, archbishops, popes, mitres, ceremonies, and canons. The living Church having gradually retired into the hidden sanctuary of some solitary souls, the external Church was put in its place, and declared to be, with all its forms, of Divine institution.... As soon as the error as to the necessity of a visible unity of the Church was established, a new error was seen to arise—viz., that of the necessity of an external representative of this unity.'

The Reformation, which the Westcountry men sought to overturn, began the move to set the European population free from the oppressive and often barbarous totalitarian rule of papal Rome, thereby restoring, to quote D'Aubigne, *'the precious perfume of faith'* of Christ and that of the Apostles to the people once more.

Some Final Thoughts

From our twenty-first century perspective, we shudder at the cruelty inflicted on the men of the Westcountry and the massacres that occurred on Devon's fields. However, we need to remember that the brutality inflicted on the rebels, who could be construed as acting treasonably, did not compare with the six hundred years of atrocities that were perpetrated on European Protestants and their peaceful forerunners until the late seventeenth century by the papacy in its near-genocides of people who sought to live Christ-like lifestyles separate to the jurisdiction of Rome. This serves to grant us some perspective. These historic and, in 1549, future barbaric acts were inconsistent with the dawn of the modern age and the Westcountry rebels, although they were understandably fighting to protect their way of life and all that was precious to them, paid a terrible price for, in effect, attempting to hinder the movement that was both seeking to release Europe from the shackles of a totalitarian and repressive Rome while simultaneously pointing Christians back to the teachings of the Scriptures and restoring the Christianity of the early Roman Church. The 'rebels' were, indeed, although innocently, on the wrong side of history and the teachings of the early church.

It was certainly the barbarity inflicted on those who were the proto-type Protestants that gave further impetus to the movement which sought to curtail the power of Rome. The increase in the brutalities committed after the Reformation by the papacy inevitably impacted on the political status of ordinary Catholics who became disenfranchised in certain areas of life as governments sought to contain the actions of Rome as it fought to restore its jurisdiction over those who had rejected it.

Indeed, the accounts of the appalling tortures and massacres inflicted on the people of the continent makes England's Reformation appear comparatively bloodless after the Rising. This was because the country lacked a Catholic dynasty which would have been obliged to act in the same manner as the European royal families at the behest of the popes. At least Henry VIII's ejection of the papacy from England and, crucially, the early death of his daughter Mary spared the country bloodbaths on the scale experienced by countries ruled by Catholic monarchs[105].

The Westcountry men were naturally unaware of the might of the European revolutionary force which sought to overthrow many centuries of corruption, a force they desired to stop and reverse. They were only interested in how the revolution was impacting on their

---

[105] In very recent years, the papacy has commented that it regretted that such terrible cruelty was inflicted on the Protestants by Catholics but did not acknowledge that it was the popes themselves who bear the greatest moral burden for using such evil men to do their bidding. The ordinary Catholic often sympathised with their persecuted neighbours, and, no doubt, feared similar consequences, if they failed to obey the papal decrees. The accounts of the persecutions and genocide of the Waldenses makes it clear that Catholics often admired them and were reluctant to participate in their destruction. With the Vatican's failure to acknowledge and apologise for the predominant role it played in the instigation of the massacres of Protestants, the small population of Waldenses to whom it was addressed, rejected the papal apology.

lives, which was understandable and reasonable, while their natural conservatism, born of immobility, failed to provide fertile ground in which new ideas and learning could take root. The threat to all that was familiar, which would revolutionise every aspect of their existence, inevitably drove them to take desperate action to preserve the precarious foundations upon which their lives were structured. By the time they rose in revolt, the Reformation, although it had many checks over the next hundred years as the Counter-Reformation resulted in repeated severe bloody opposition and setbacks before it completely broke free of persecution by the end of the seventeenth century, was an unstoppable force as it captured the minds of large swathes of the population. With the benefit of hindsight, the curse of every historian, it is clear that the rebels did not possess the power to push back the European juggernaut of reform; however, the English Reformation, given the contemporary circumstances, was not so secure.

Tudor Rebellions under Henry were always doomed to failure, but with a divided Council ruling the country, and the Protector's initial leniency in dealing with the revolt, the outcome was not so certain. These men, who did not view themselves as rebels but as petitioners, were distinguished by the bravery born of desperation and, once they left the county, other discontents would swell their already substantial numbers as they marched to London to challenge a weak and unstable government. It is interesting to consider how the course and success of English Reformation history might have been altered if, instead of attempting to capture Exeter, the Westcountry men had bypassed the city and marched straight to the capital. With England riven by so many rebellions, mostly economic, surely large numbers would have joined the Westcountry men, thus greatly strengthening their force as they entered London? Could the Council and London have withstood such a large army? Would they have capitulated, and would Catholic Mary have become queen at this juncture? However, they chose an alternative plan, which may have been a major error that they compounded by not seeing it through to completion by diverting many of their force to attack Russell's army before further reinforcements joined his ranks. One major error made the consequences of the second inevitable.

Before the Battle of Fenny Bridges with Exeter on the verge of capitulation, the Westcountry men were certainly close to seizing power over the South West. The English Reformation, at this time, hung in the balance, and the Western rebels, had they seized Exeter and marched to London, gathering support on the way, possessed the potential to place the English Reformation at least on pause. If Mary had been brought to the throne at this juncture and Edward overthrown, or if she had not died prematurely, England would certainly once again have been brought under papal jurisdiction. If she had a child that had lived to become a Catholic monarch, England may never have struggled free of the papacy and may have remained Catholic to this day. The future success of the English Reformation at the time of the Prayer Book Rebellion was precarious, fragile, and uncertain. If the rebels had remained at the city for a few more days, ensuring her capitulation, or, more likely, if they had marched straight to London, the history of England may indeed have been very different. Given the potential consequences of the Rising on English history, the importance of the Prayer Book Rebellion, and its turning point, the Battle of Fenny Bridges, has clearly been seriously underestimated by centuries of historians, and it is time that its significance was given greater prominence.

A Modern-Day Catholic View of the Prayer Book Rebellion
by
Ruth Yendell ©

A Modern-Day Catholic view of
THE BATTLE OF FENNY BRIDGES
Prelude and Aftermath
by
Ruth Yendell

As a Catholic friend of the author, I read her book with admiration and appreciation. However, I did feel that a bit more information about the Catholic side of the story could be relevant, and she has kindly agreed to let me write an Appendix to this purpose.

There is little in print written from a Catholic viewpoint about these dramatic years because of the centuries of prejudice against Catholics which followed them. Thankfully, we are now at a place where we all want the divisions which resulted to be healed, and I hope that what I have to offer may help towards that aim.

History

One day back in the late 4th century after Christ, when St. Augustine of Hippo, after a turbulent youth, had finally found his way to Christianity, he was attending his mother, St. Monica, who was now near to death. He records her words at this time (Confessions Bk.9: 10-11): *'Son, for my own part I no longer find joy in anything in this world. What I am still to do here, and why I am here, I know not....One thing there was for which I desired to remain still a little longer in this life, that I should see you a Catholic Christian before I died. This, God has granted me in superabundance, in that I now see you his*

237

servant to the contempt of all worldly happiness. What then am I doing here?'

One of the important things about this beautiful *farewell to life* is that already, in 387 A.D., the word *Catholic* was used to describe the mainstream Christian Church, which had been held in unity from the time of St. Peter, the first Bishop of Rome, by his successors in that See. It was the same Catholic Christianity which came to our islands by way of Roman Britons like St. Patrick and St. Alban, by later Irish missionaries Ss. Aidan and Columba, and finally by another St. Augustine, of Canterbury, sent by Pope Gregory the Great in 596-7 A.D. to evangelise the Anglo-Saxons in Kent and the South of England.

The unity of the Catholic Church had not, however, come about without struggle. Particularly during the first four hundred years of Christianity, the Church had survived many attacks from heresy, promoted by self-appointed interpreters of scripture, who, while preaching a false and unfounded notion of Christianity, were often charismatic and drew a following, leading many people into error. The first instances of heresy are mentioned even in scripture itself, in St. Paul's writings and in the Book of Revelation. From those early times up to the Western Rising and, indeed, to the present day, one of the most important duties of the Roman Catholic Church, led by the Pope, has been to defend sound Christian doctrine against those who wanted to change it for their own purposes. When we come to the 16th century, the time of the Western Rising, such changes were being made by un-ordained persons on the orders of our (un-ordained) monarchs Henry VIII and Edward VI, and this was recognised by the Catholic majority as an attempt to deprive them, the ordinary people, of the true faith, and, therefore, of their hope for the salvation of their souls.

The importance of the Mass

The form of worship which had been brought to these islands was the worship handed down by the apostles and referred to by St. Paul. It is what Jesus told his disciples to do at the Last Supper, when, after they had eaten, He held up a piece of bread and said, '*This is my body, which will be given up for you*'; then He held up a chalice of wine and said '*This is my blood which will be shed for you and for many, for the forgiveness of sins*'. He then said '*Do this in remembrance of me.*' Clearly, this was a prophetic enactment of the sacrificial death which was very soon to come upon Him, and which was to pay the penalty for the sins of all humankind throughout all ages, past, present and future. In St. John's Gospel we are also told that Jesus had earlier said to His disciples and followers '*unless you eat my body and drink my blood you cannot have life in you*' (John ch.6). On both these occasions recorded in the Gospels, it is clear that Jesus meant His disciples to take literally the idea that He Himself, body and soul, humanity and divinity, becomes really present in the bread and wine offered thus on the altar. This is certainly what was understood by St. Paul and the very first Christians right through until the time of the Reformation. The re-enactment of the Last Supper by a priest commemorating Jesus' Passion, and the communion which the congregation then take, is God's way, Christ's way, of sharing His life with His people and raising them up to new life with Him. It is the very life-blood of any Catholic's spiritual life.

The Mass, therefore, is not merely a set of prayers and readings, it is an action, and a sacrifice to God, in which those who attend Mass participate. In order to preserve the authenticity of this action, from earliest times certain rules have surrounded it. A valid Mass can only be said by a priest validly ordained, that is to say, ordained by a bishop who can trace his own ordination, through other validly ordained bishops, back to the first apostles. Similarly, a set form of words said by the priest alone, representing Christ as he offers the bread and wine and repeating the words of Christ in the gospels, is necessary to make valid the transformation of the bread into the Body and Blood of Christ.

The Western Rising or Prayer Book Rebellion

From this I think it will be clear that in 1549, the imposition by Edward VI's representatives of a Protestant Prayer Book on a Catholic congregation to take the place of the holy Mass, with the deliberate intention of banishing the Catholic Mass from these islands, was hardly a minor matter.   Add to this, the belief first expressed in the Gospel of John, ch. 6, that our hope of eternal life is entirely bound up with receiving the true body and blood of Christ, and it becomes clear that Catholics at the time of the Western Rising knew all too well that the survival of their Church and the salvation of their souls was at stake. While Jenny Wilson is right to expose the other, more worldly, causes of resentment which added to the fury of the people, it is important to realise how deep was the insult to their religion and how seriously this would have been taken. When altar vessels and costly vestments were taken by the King's men, these things would have been valued by the parishioners not so much for their monetary value (although devout parishioners would probably have put generous offerings into the parish funds to purchase them in the first place) but because they were used in sacred worship. Snatching them from their churches was not merely theft, it was sacrilege.

Martyrdom

If I could refer again to the dying words of St. Monica, they also show us how important true doctrine was and still is to any faithful Catholic. Old and sick, she was still prepared to offer to God her suffering and prayers for as long as necessary in supplication for her son's conversion. Only when her prayers were answered could she die in peace. When Catholics of a later date saw what Edward VI, and, later, Elizabeth I, were doing to their Church they knew that this was not just a temporary 'blip' in running their beloved Church (and they did *love* their Church - who can look at our Cathedrals and pre-Reformation churches without realising that they were built out of love for God and His Church?). They, too, in great numbers were prepared to suffer and, if necessary, face martyrdom rather than conform.

However, to take up arms against one's king or his representatives as happened with the Prayer Book Rebellion or the Western Rising is not the same thing as accepting martyrdom which comes from means outside one's control. There is nothing in Christian teaching which condones throwing oneself deliberately into martyrdom, least of all in a way which injures others. Dying in battle, even for a good cause, worthy though this may be, has never been confused with martyrdom in Catholic tradition. Sometimes, however, the Christian conscience will demand that a course be followed which will probably lead to genuine martyrdom whether welcome or not. In that spirit, many brave men from Henry VIII's time onward, fled England to seek ordination abroad in Belgium or Rome, and then returned at clear risk of their lives to keep the Catholic faith alive in this country. They inevitably had to come in disguise, and many are the great houses in which a priest-hole can still be found, as a last hiding place if the officers of the law came to search the property. The number of those who hid them and the priests themselves runs into hundreds, and all faced a cruel martyrdom with great courage. Others, as in the Pilgrimage of Grace of 1536-7, did raise an army but tried to avoid violence, seeking parley with Henry VIII to persuade him to go back on his policy of dissolving the monasteries. The King promised them safety if they went home and then had about two hundred of them hanged for their pains. The peaceful method just didn't work. The people of Devon and Cornwall must have felt they had good grounds for taking up arms - not forgetting their other grievances.

Propaganda and Plots

Something must also be said about the fierce propaganda which Henry VIII initiated and Edward VI and Elizabeth I continued. Henry well knew that the people were not behind him in repudiating the Catholic faith and in particular in dissolving the monasteries, and as well as the horrific brutality which Jenny Wilson records so well, he also, and more subtly, used the weapon of propaganda to achieve his purpose. His agents did not live up to the standards of a true religious life, and while the Church was in need of reform in many areas, to make the accusation of corruption apply generally to all religious houses, and in the end to all Catholics, was pure propaganda.

The giving of Catholics a bad name persisted for centuries afterwards and can even today still be seen in a few isolated cases. Yet the tyrannical behaviour of the monarchs was hyped up as laudable (because it 'set England *free* from 'Rome') and their murderous Acts of Parliament were upheld right up until the 1791 Relief Act followed by the Catholic Emancipation Act in 1829. These measures at last permitted Catholics to worship freely, but there was still heavy discrimination against them in education, in the workplace and public employment, from which they were barred until well into the 20th century.

There was one other angle where propaganda played a large part. The slaughter of most of the 'rebels', i.e. the Catholic army, in the final battle of the Western Rising, meant that from then on, there were no further open rebellions. Catholics were forced to go underground, seeking to nourish their souls in secrecy wherever a clandestine Mass was being offered by one of the priests who had successfully returned to the country from the continent. The very secrecy of this, and indeed the success of the priests in preserving the Catholic faith by these means, meant that the paranoid monarchs and their governments were constantly suspecting a 'Catholic plot' or worse, 'a Jesuit plot'. The Jesuits were a newly founded order of missionary priests and featured greatly among the returning Catholic priests. As highly educated and cultured people, they were also the most able to refute the arguments of the Protestants, and were heroic in their defence of the Catholic faith, always expressed alongside a deep love for England and loyalty to the monarch in all matters, excepting only in things spiritual where they knew the monarch had no true authority.

At the same time, the forced secrecy and the heavy fines and confiscation of property led very many Catholics to flee abroad where they died in or of poverty, while others, when caught by the authorities were sent to gaol to languish there or die of gaol fever. It was, indeed, a sorry state of affairs for any Catholic. Here is the first verse of a poem written by one William Blundell fifty years after the Western Rising which must have expressed the feelings of all Catholics during those years:-

THE BATTLE OF FENNY BRIDGES 1549
PRELUDE AND AFTERMATH

We Catholics, tormented sore
With heresy's foul railing tongue,
With prisons, tortures, loss of goods,
Of land, yea, lives, even thieves among,
Do crave, with heart surcharged with grief,
Of thee, sweet Jesus, some relief.

It is not surprising, in those circumstances, that a few more hot-headed and politically minded Catholics did get involved in plots of one kind or another. Of these, the best known are (1) the collusion with Catholic Spain to invade England and bring back a Catholic monarchy; (2) the Babington Plot which was possibly contrived by the Elizabethan spymasters in order to justify the execution of Mary Queen of Scots, but, if genuine, was an attempt to replace Elizabeth with Mary Stuart who was Catholic, but who also had strong ties with France; and (3) the Gunpowder Plot, born of sheer frustration when James I, before his accession, promised release to all Catholics from their fines which had been allowed to fall into arrears during the interregnum. But, on his accession, he not only reinstated the fines, finding he had not enough money to keep his Scottish courtiers happy, but also demanded back payments for the time when they had not been enforced.

It does appear, however, that patriotism was as powerful an influence as religion among Catholics at that time. The first of the above plots resulted in making Catholic Spain an enemy whereas she had been a friend and ally until Henry VIII's time. Yet the English Catholics, even during Elizabeth's reign which was so harsh to them, appear to have been quite clear that they would fight for England against Spain if the need arose. Similarly, although Mary Queen of Scots was Catholic, if she had succeeded Elizabeth, England would have almost certainly become a vassal of France. Catholics longed for a tolerant monarch, but they would not countenance the indignity of becoming part of France! So, the greater proportion of Catholics again chose to suffer in silence. As for the Gunpowder Plot in 1605, all sensible Catholics lamented it because they knew it would only bring further trouble. It's worth observing, however, that 'gunpowder plots' were not unusual at that time, and were used by Protestants as well as Catholics, but because of the usual prejudice, Guy Fawkes' attempt is remembered where others are not. The fear of 'Catholic plots' endured right through to 1678 when Titus Oates stirred up fear and rage in London by spreading a rumour of a plot which was totally fabricated for his own criminal purposes. It was not exposed as a fabrication until many Catholics had been thrown into prison, and others judiciously murdered. The power of propaganda should not be under-estimated!

Thus, the Western Rising was for Catholics only the beginning of a much longer period of fear, deprivation and persecution. In our present times, we can at last see that many of the problems arose from the actions of monarchs who were insecure on their thrones, and desperate to preserve their position for themselves and their heirs; and from collective greed by those who could profit from the plunder of the church properties; and from a disregard for the freedom of the individual conscience in matters of religion. Hopefully, if we can see the facts from a balanced point of view, much can now be healed.

I hope this gives just a small idea of what was behind the religious side of the Western Rising.

*

THE ORIGINAL FLYER DATED 1913 FOR FRANCES ROSE-TROUP'S BOOK 'THE WESTERN REBELLION OF 1549'.

With Illustrations.
Demy 8vo.
14/= net.

The Western Rebellion of 1549.

An Account of the Insurrections in Devonshire and Cornwall against religious innovations in the reign of Edward VI.

By FRANCES ROSE-TROUP, F.R. Hist. S.

** This is a history of the commotions in the West Country when the use of the first Book of Common Prayer was enforced, as it were, at the point of the bayonet. Exeter was besieged for six weeks and many conflicts occurred in the vicinity. These almost forgotten encounters had an important influence on the course of the Reformation. The causes of the rising are fully discussed and fresh light is thrown on the subject by material gleaned from unpublished documents. The story, graphically told, is full of exciting incidents which will hold the attention of the reader.

Date of Publication : 16th October.

Messrs. SMITH, ELDER & Co. will be obliged if the Editor will kindly send them an intimation in the event of a review of the accompanying volume appearing in his Journal.

15, WATERLOO PLACE, LONDON. S.W.
16th October, 1913.

245

The Articles of vs the Commoners of Deuonshyre and Cornewall in diuers Campes by East and West of Excettor

1. Fyrst we wyll haue the general counsell and holy decrees of our forefathers observed, kept and performed, and who so euer shal agayne saye them, we hold them as Heretikes.

2. Item we will haue the Lawes of our Soverayne Lord Kyng Henry the viii, concernynge the syxe articles, to be in vse again, as in hys tyme they were.

3. Item we will haue the masse in Latten, as was before, and celebrated by the Pryest wythoute any man or woman communycatyng wyth hym.

4. Item we will have the Sacrament hange over the hyeyghe aulter, and there to be worshypped as it was wount to be, and they whiche will not therto consent, we wyl have them dye lyke heretykes agaynst the holy Catholyque fayth.

5. Item we wyll have the Sacramet of the aulter but at Easter delyuered to the lay people, and then but in one kynde.

6. Item we wil that our Curattes shal minister the Sacramet of Baptisme at all tymes aswel in the weke daye as on the holy daye.

7. Item we wyl haue holy bread and holy water made euery sondaye, Palmes and asshes at the tymes accustomed, Images to be set vp again in every church, and all other auncient olde Ceremonyes vsed heretofore, by our mother the holy Church.

8. Item we wil not receyue the newe seruye because it is but lyke a Christmas game, but we wyll haue oure olde service of Mattens, masse, Evensong and procession in Latten as it was before. And so we the Cornyshe men (whereof certen of vs vnderstande no Englysh) vtterly refuse thys newe Englysh.

9. Item we wyll haue euerye preacher in his sermon, and every Pryest at hys masse, praye specially by name for the soules in purgatory, as oure forefathers dyd.

10. Item we wyll have the whole Byble and al bokes of scripture in Englysh to be called in agayn, fol we be enformed that otherwise the Clergye, shal not of log time confound the heretykes.

11. Item we wyll haue Doctor Moreman and Doctor Crispin which holde our opinions to be sauely sent vnto vs and to them we requyre the Kinges maiesty, to geue some certain liuinges, to preach amonges vs our Catholycke fayth.

12. Item we thinke it very mete because the lord Cardinal Pole is of the kynges bloode, should not only haue hys free pardon, but also sent for to Rome and promoted to be of the kinges cousayl.

13. Item we wyll that no Gentylman shall haue anye mo servantes then one to wayte ypo hym excepte he maye dispende one hundreth marke land and for euery hundreth marke we thynke it reasonable, he should have a man.

14. Item we wyll that the halfe parte of the Abbey landes and Chauntrye landes, in euerye mans possessyons, how so euer he cam by them, be geuen again to two places, where two of the chief Abbeis was with in euery Countye, where suche half part shalbe taken out, and there to be establyshed a place for devout persons, whych shall pray for the Kyng and the common wealth, and to the same we wyll have al the almes of the Churche box geven for these seven yeres.

15. Item for the particular grieffes of our Countrye. We wyll haue them so ordered, as Humfreye Arundell, and Henry Braye the Kynges Maior of Bodma, shall enforme the Kynges Maiestye, yf they maye haue saluecoduct vnder the Kynges great Seale, to passe and repasse, with an Heroalde of Armes.

16. Item for the performance of these articles we will haue iiii Lordes viii Knightes xii Esquyers xx Yome, pledges with us vntill the Kynges Maiestie haue grounted al these by Parliament.

248

The articles were signed by the five 'chiefe captaynes' and 'the foure Governours of the Campes'.

*

The governors were Henry Bray, Mayor of Bodmin, Henry Lee, Mayor of Torrington, Roger Barrett (Priest) and John Thompson (Priest). The dominant influence of the priests is clear in the framing of the demands.

The chief captain signatories were Humphrey Arundell, John Bury, John Sloeman, Thomas Underhill, and William Segar. Bury of Silverton was second in command to Arundell, making him leader of the Devon force. Underhill and Segar were ring-leaders of the Sampford Courtenay uprising and the revolt was often referred to as 'Underhill's Rebellion'.

The confidence expressed in the wording and the strident tone, in comparison to the first set of articles, reflects the confidence instilled into the Devonshire men by the arrival of the Cornish at Exeter in the second week of July.

The Council gave the demands due consideration and drafted three responses, but were not prepared to compromise on any of the religious articles.

Bibliography

Primary Sources

The Description of the Citie of Excester : John Hooker alias Vowell
*Spanish Chronicle: Chronicle of King Henry VIII of England, Being
a Contemporary Record of Some of The Principal Events of The
Reigns of Henry VIII and Edward VI. (translated by Martin A. Sharp
Hume 1889)*
The Life and Raigne of King Edward the Sixth: John Hayward
Letters of the Privy Council
Chronicles of England, Scotland and Ireland 1578: Hollingshead
Survey of Cornwall 1602: Carew, *(1769 edition)*
Itinerary 1542: J. Leyland
The Feniton Parish Records held at Honiton Museum

Secondary Sources

A Devonshire Village in the Olden Days: Rev. A. W. Watson, Rector
of Feniton 1929
*Catholics: The Church and its People in Britain and Ireland, from
the Reformation to the Present Day:* Roy Hattersley *(Vintage)*
*Fullye Bente to Fighte Oute the Matter: Reconsidering Cornwall's
Role in the Western Rising 1549: English Historical Review no 538
Professor* Mark Stoyle. *(2014)*
Henry VIII: J.J. Scarisbrick *(Chaucer Press, 1968)*
*'Kill all the gentlemen?' (Mis)representing the western rebels of
1549:* Professor Mark Stoyle *(Institute of Historical Research, vol.97,
no.255 February 2019)*
*Pre-Reformation London Summoners and the Murder of Richard
Hunne:* Richard Wunderli *(Journal of Ecclesiastical History Vol:33,
No 2)*
Revolt in the West: John Sturt *(Devon Books, 1987)*
Richard Hunne: W.R. Cooper

Saints and Sinners: A History of the Popes: Eamon Duffy *(Yale University Press, 1997)*

The Affairs of Richard Hunne and Friar Standish: J. Duncan M. Derrell

The Constitutional History of England: F.W. Maitland *(Cambridge, 1968)*

The Decline and Fall of the Roman Church: Malachi Martin *1981*

The Devon Gentleman: A Life of Sir Peter Carew: John Wagner *(University of Hull Press 1998)*

The Earlier Tudors 1485-1558: J.D. Mackie *(Clarendon, 1951)*

The English Reformation: A.G. Dickens *(B.T. Batford, Ltd, 1964)*

The English Reformations: Religion, Politics and Society under the Tudors: Christopher Haigh *(Clarendon, 1993)*

The History of Protestantism by J. A. Wylie, *1870*

The History of the Waldenses by J.A. Wylie, *1889*

The Infallibility of the Church by George Salmon, *1914*

The Pope and his Council by Ignaz von Dollinger, *1870*

The Stripping of the Altars: Eamon Duffy *(Yale University Press 2005)*

The Tragedy of the Lollard's Tower: Arthur Ogle, *(1949)*

Troubles Connected with the Prayer Book, 1549: Nicholas Pocock, *(1884)*

The Western Rebellion of 1549: Frances Rose-Troup, *(1913)*

Tudor Cornwall: A.L. Rowse *(1941)*

Tudor Constitutional Documents 1485-1603: J.R. Tanner *(Cambridge University Press, 1951)*

The Blind Devotion of the People: Popular Religion and the English Reformation: Robert Whiting, *(Cambridge, 1989)*

The South-Western Rebellion of 1549: Prof. Joyce Youings *(1979)*

Index

A

B

C

H

I

J

K

L

258